Shipwrecks of the Forth and Tay

Bob Baird

Whittles Publishing

Published by
Whittles Publishing,
Dunbeath,
Caithness KW6 6EY,
Scotland, UK
www.whittlespublishing.com

© 2009 Bob Baird

ISBN 978-1904445-74-6

Title page image: *Diving the* Exmouth *(Courtesy of Shane Wasik)*

Printed in Latvia by InPrint

Contents

Acknowledgements

I should like to record my thanks to all who have helped me enormously in various ways in the preparation of this book, and would especially like to express my gratitude to Dr Andrew Jeffrey, Kevin Heath, Martin Sinclair, Gavin Barnett, Clark Ross, Ron Young, Pamela Armstrong, John Stevenson and Ian Whittaker.

Over the years that I have been gathering information, I have also collected a large number of photographs. Some photographs were taken by myself, or obtained directly from copyright holders, while others were found in the public domain in a variety of publications and websites, or sent to me by numerous individuals. Many of these sources did not include information about the copyright owners.

A considerable effort has been made to trace and acknowledge copyright holders, and to obtain permission to use photographs, but it has not been possible to trace them all. Due to the age of many of these photographs, however, in most cases the copyright periods have long expired. I apologise for any apparent negligence.

Editor's Note

Empty wreck data categories (e.g. depth, draught and length) signify that no current information was available at the time of publication. Values and their respective units (whether metric or imperial) have been presented according to, and consistent with, usage and context.

Preface

For as long as I can remember I have been fascinated by ships, wrecks and marine salvage, and over the years, have read many books and articles, and gathered diverse pieces of information on this subject. Since taking up diving as a hobby nearly 30 years ago, my interest has been further developed and focused mainly on wrecks in Scottish waters.

Transferring the information I had collected over the years to a computer database, enabled snippets of information from various sources to be compared and assessed, and an orderly picture began to emerge. I very quickly realised I had the basic details for a book on the subject, but in order to make it more than merely a list, much more research was required to add meat to the bones, both for the sheer enjoyment of extending my own personal knowledge, and also to make it a more useful and enjoyable source of information to others with a similar interest.

My first book, *Shipwrecks of the Forth* was published in 1993. During my quest for further information on wrecks in the Forth, I kept stumbling on references to wrecks in other areas, and with the discovery of each new piece of information, the area covered by my database gradually expanded to include the entire east coast of Scotland, the North coast, and the west coast from Cape Wrath down to Sanda Island off the Mull of Kintyre.

This extended knowledge led me to write two more books – *Shipwrecks of the West of Scotland*, published in 1995, and *Shipwrecks of the North of Scotland*, published in 2003.

Shipwrecks are not just undersea scrap yards. They are living maritime museums, and if you know something of their stories, diving on the wrecks is that much more enjoyable. Most divers are keen to dive on wrecks and to learn something about them, although there is some reluctance amongst divers to divulge jealously guarded wreck information to other divers, who often tend to be regarded as potential competitors. I have found from personal experience, however, that being willing to share my knowledge with others generally brings its own rewards in the form of reciprocal information and friendships with fellow enthusiasts, and vastly improved the quality of my own diving.

In the introduction to *Shipwrecks of the Forth*, I said that research for a book of this nature could never be wholly complete, but that one has to stop at *some* point to produce the first edition. Many readers of that book kindly supplied more information, (often correcting mistakes I had made!), and some even provided photographs.

The time has now come to produce a revised, updated edition, incorporating the vast amount I have learned in the 15 years since I wrote the first *Shipwrecks of the Forth*. I am conscious, though, that there is still a great deal I do not know, and would always welcome further information.

GPS Positions

It seems appropriate here to say something about the wreck positions given in this book. Prior to the introduction of the WGS84 datum, all the Admiralty charts, and wreck positions, were in the previous OSGB 36 datum. All positions in my research material were also in OSGB 36, and therefore this was the basis of the positions I gave in my first three books.

The OSGB 36 charts include a note regarding satellite-derived positions, and the adjustments that should be made to each chart when using WGS84-standard GPS positions. (Note that these adjustments vary from one chart to another).

At a late stage during the writing of my third book, *Shipwrecks of the North of Scotland*, the Admiralty Hydrographic Department announced that they would be revising and reprinting the Admiralty charts from the OSGB 36 datum to a new standard datum – WGS84.

The charts themselves remain unaltered, but the lines of latitude have been moved to the south, and the lines of longitude to the east. This means that the latitude and longitude of a fixed position (e.g. a wreck), has changed. Latitude has increased in all areas of the UK, while longitude has increased west of the Greenwich meridian, and decreased east of the Greenwich meridian. A complication is that the amount of the change is not constant – it varies by about 175 metres in the south of the UK to about 110 metres in the north. A change of this magnitude may not seem very significant in the middle of an ocean. Close to shore, however, or when seeking to avoid hazards such as reefs near the surface, it does require care to be taken in ensuring that your GPS is set to the datum of the chart you are using.

When searching for a wreck, the GPS should be set to the datum of the position given for the wreck. All of the positions given in my previous books were in OSGB36 datum, but for this book, I have updated positions to WGS84 datum. I have been aware of quite a number of people who failed to understand the difference between OSGB36 and WGS84. When GPS sets were introduced only a few short years ago, they were set by the manufacturers to the WGS84 datum, and electronic charts for use in computers are in WGS84 datum. A number of people entered OSGB36 positions into their new GPS sets, without realising the difference between OSGB36 and WGS84, and wondered why their new GPS sets didn't take them to the wreck they expected to find. Then these people criticised me for giving wrong positions.

I have done my best to select what I consider to be perhaps the most accurate of the sometimes vague and conflicting information available. When an exact position is not known, I have endeavoured to provide as close an estimate as the information currently available to me will permit, and this is indicated in the text. I should be delighted to receive corrected positions from anyone who finds any errors in the positions I have given. By far the clearest explanation that I have found, of the navigation problems associated with the change from OSGB 36 to WGS84 is given in the following paper written by Lt. Cdr. N. McEachan, Royal Navy Wrecks' Officer, Admiralty Hydrographic Department:

"Locating wrecks with GPS" by Lt. Cdr. N. McEachan
"There are many problems associated with locating wrecks using a GPS receiver. A few thoughts from the Wrecks' Officer on our records and GPS might be in order to dispel confusion (or create more). Firstly let us consider the way that our records are structured.

From 1 January 1999 the listed position for the wreck or obstruction is given in degrees, minutes and decimals of a minute. From that date too, for new information, the positions listed in the 'Surveying Details' text field is given in the same format. Prior to that the positions given in Wrecks' section printouts have been given in degrees, minutes and seconds both in the listed positions and in the 'Surveying Details'. Entries in the 'Surveying Details' prior to January 1999 will remain in this format. A note is inserted in the records to indicate from where the change of format applies. In an ideal world all entries in the 'Surveying Details' text would all be amended, however with some 58000 records to consider this is, realistically, not going to happen. Considerable effort is being put into to editing the text of each record to take out all of the irrelevant material and make the remainder easier to read. Completing this task will take a number of years.

Many navigation receivers will give positions in degrees, minutes and decimals of a minute or as degrees, minutes and seconds. My own Garmin hand held will do this. Take care which you use! It is easy to convert seconds to decimal minutes – simply divide the seconds by 60. If we supply data a table giving the decimal equivalents of seconds is included. In older descriptive text we run the degrees, minutes and seconds together without spaces. Thus 51° 45' 24"N becomes 514524N. In current and future text 51° 45.40'N will be written as 5145.40N. Why? Simply to avoid typing all the spaces!

In passing it is worth considering what both 0.01 of a minute and a second (approx 0.017 minutes) represent on the Earth's surface. One hundredth of a minute is some 18.5 metres in latitude and about 12 metres in longitude in the South of England or some 9 metres in longitude in the North of Scotland. A second is 1/60 of a nautical mile and thus it is about 30 metres in latitude and some 20 metres in longitude in the South of England or some 15 metres in longitude in the North of Scotland. OK so far? It might be time for tea before considering the joys of datums.

The idea of a datum arises because the dry part of the world is lumpy. When surveyors use a theodolite to take measurements of angles and various instruments to measure distances, they have to have some way of calculating the results. For small areas (for instance when setting out a supermarket building) it is fine to assume that the earth is flat. We have all done some trigonometry at school and the formulae are relatively simple. (Does anyone remember the sine and cosine rules)? Now on a bigger scale, say over the United Kingdom, things get a bit more complicated. Clearly the lumpy surface of the real world is too complicated to use for calculation and the Earth is not flat so another shaped surface has to be used. Take a sphere, roughly the size of the earth. Squash it along the

North/South direction and wiggle it a bit to get the best fit over the UK. Bravo! Keeping it simple, you have now Ordnance Survey 1936 datum (we call it OGB in our listings). Calculations on this curved surface are complicated but possible. (The squashed sphere is known as Airey's Spheroid – he was the Astronomer Royal in the latter part of the last century). Over the greater part of Europe another spheroid is used, the International Spheroid, and the best fit over the whole of Europe from the West of Ireland to the Ural Mountains is known as European Datum.

OK so far? Put the tea aside and try something a little stronger. Charts of our coastal area have always been on Ordnance datum as this was convenient and prior to the advent of satellite navigation systems it did not matter. However GPS is a global system and the squashed sphere that is a good fit in the UK is not the best fit to the real, lumpy surface over the whole world. So a revised, squashed sphere was invented. It is known as the World Geodetic System 1984, or WGS84 for short (we call it WGD in our listings). Logical to call it WGS when it fits the world. The trouble is that this squashed sphere does not match up with the Ordnance Survey one in the UK, so there is a difference in apparent position for the same point on the Earth's surface when you go from one to the other. This has caused some problems to those not familiar with the idea of applying shifts to the position displayed on the GPS receiver. Consequently UK coastal charts are being reissued referred to WGS84, thus no correction to position will be necessary prior to plotting. In the fullness of time all the charts from all nations in Northern European waters will doubtless be so amended. Around the UK our data will generally give both the OGB position for the object and the WGD position. You will see that there are simply two positions for the same item at the same point on the Earth's surface! Where the surveyed position for the object has been established on WGD the position will be the accurate, surveyed position. Where this is not the case the WGD position will be calculated from the OGB position by mathematical means or, where this is not possible, by the use of the shifts shown in the title block of the chart. The method of establishing the WGD position will be shown in the listing. Modern GPS receivers can generally be set to show either position. You simply set the receiver datum to Ordnance Survey and use the OGB position or set the receiver to WGS84 and use the WGD position and Bob's your uncle. Ideally you can find the wreck. Note that charts that have been amended and reissued as noted above will state that they are referred to a WGS84 compatible datum, while some wreck records will state that they are now referred to ETRS89 (European Terrestrial Reference System). This is an academic difference and for all practical purposes the WGS84 and ETRS89 positions are identical.

So you think that you are going to find the wreck? Ah, it is not yet that simple. Remember that there are errors in the GPS system. Some small ones are inherent with cheaper units but for a long period the accuracy of the system was deliberately degraded by the USA. The quoted accuracy of the system was then 100 metres for 95% of the time. So for over an hour a day it could well have been be outside 100 metres. Recently the degradation was removed and raw GPS positions are certainly good to better than

15 metres. Differential GPS allows virtually all errors to be removed, both for the older degraded positions and for the current undegraded system. Positions should be good to a few metres. Do remember that this position is for the receiving antenna, not for the echo sounder transducers!

Still not found the wreck? In addition the wreck had to be positioned too, usually by the survey vessel sounding over the top. However the survey ship had positioning errors as well and the size of these errors, despite the best efforts of the survey team and always assuming that no gross mistake was made, will depend on the navigation system employed. For modern work the wreck position will be good to probably a dozen metres, but for old work it could be dozens of metres. If Decca was used many years ago (remember it was the latest thing in the early 1950s) possibly tens of dozens of metres are possible. Many records are based on positions reported by the sinking vessel, members of the public, fishermen etc. Often there is no way of knowing how accurate the report is (or was) and they have to be accepted at face value. Perhaps you have found the wreck now?

Reach for the smelling salts, for the wreck may not be there at all! Vast, and steadily increasing, torrents of data flow into the Hydrographic Office and an increasing amount of this data causes chart corrections (the well known Notices to Mariners weekly booklet) to be issued. Clearly not all amendments to the chart carry the same urgency or importance and due to the sheer volume of potential corrections many amendments are held over to the next New Edition of the chart. A wreck could have been disproved or lifted, or the depth over it may have been amended, but the chart (even if corrected to date) will not show this. The latest data is available from the Wrecks' Section. Best of luck with the wreck searching! We are always interested in new information. In many areas the survey information is scarce or incomplete. Even an accurate GPS position for a wreck previously only positioned by Decca is immensely valuable. Details of a new wreck could save the loss of a net or a nasty accident. We will keep information in confidence for a period of 5 years if requested, but we must chart the hazard if it is significant to navigation."

1

Introduction

The compass
Modern compasses have a scale marked in degrees, with 0 at North round clockwise to 360 again at North. In days gone by, the compass rose was marked in Points and Quarter Points. Some compass cards are marked with degrees and points, the degrees being on the outside. There are 32 compass points in a circle of 360 degrees. One point, therefore, equals 11.25 degrees, and a quarter point, which is the smallest division shown on a card marked in that way, equals marginally less than 3 degrees (2.8125 degrees). The illustration shows the compass and the names of the points and quarter points and the table below gives their equivalents in degrees. Note that none of the by-points or quarter points takes its name from a three-letter point: For example, N by E is correct, not NNE by N, and NE by N ¾N is correct, not NNE¼E.

The present metric series of Admiralty charts have compass roses marked in degrees true, on the outside of the rose, and degrees magnetic, on the inside, the difference between them being the local magnetic variation. The amount and direction of the annual change is also given within the compass rose.

If information concerning the position of a wreck includes a compass bearing, it is important to note the date from which the bearing originates, and to take account of the local magnetic variation in the area over the years which have elapsed since the date of the information.

Sweeping of wrecks
Charted wrecks that have been swept are indicated on the chart by a bar with upright vertical projections at either end, immediately below the wreck symbol, which contains a figure representing the depth.

The word *swept*, as applied to wrecks, is commonly misunderstood, and often erroneously presumed to mean that a sweep wire has literally swept, or removed, the superstructure off a sunken vessel for the purpose of increasing the safe clearance depth.

This is complete nonsense. It would require a wire of infinite breaking strain to be towed by a ship of infinite power and propeller efficiency, and could only apply to wrecks which were sitting upright on the bottom.

Swept wreck symbol

Points and Quarter-Points of the Compass

Point	Heading°	Point	Heading°	Point	Heading°	Point	Heading°
NORTH	0	EAST	90	SOUTH	180	WEST	270
N ¼ E	2.8125	E ¼ S	92.8125	S ¼ W	182.8125	W ¼ N	272.8125
N ½ E	5.625	E ½ S	95.625	S ½ W	185.625	W ½ N	275.625
N ¾ E	8.4375	E ¾ S	98.4375	S ¾ W	188.4375	W ¾ N	278.4375
N by E	11.25	E by S	101.25	S by W	191.25	W by N	281.25
N by E ¼ E	14.0625	E by S ¼ S	104.0625	S by W ¼ W	194.0625	W by N ¼ N	284.0625
N by E ½ E	16.875	E by S ½ S	106.875	S by W ½ W	196.875	W by N ½ N	286.875
N by E ¾ E	19.6875	E by S ¾ S	109.6875	S by W ¾ W	199.6875	W by N ¾ N	289.6875
NNE	22.5	ESE	112.5	SSW	202.5	WNW	292.5
NE by N ¾ N	25.3125	SE by E ¾ E	115.3125	SW by W ¾ S	205.3125	NW by W ¾ S	295.3125
NE by N ½ N	28.125	SE by E ½ E	118.125	SW by W ½ S	208.125	NW by W ½ S	298.125
NE by N ¼ N	30.9375	SE by E ¼ E	120.9375	SW by W ¼ S	210.9375	NW by W ¼ S	300.9375
NE by N	33.75	SE by E	123.75	SW by W	213.75	NW by W	303.75
NE ¾ N	36.5625	SE ¾ E	126.5625	SW ¾ W	216.5625	NW ¾ W	306.5625
NE ½ N	39.375	SE ½ E	129.375	SW ½ W	219.375	NW ½ W	309.375
NE ¼ N	42.1875	SE ¼ E	132.1875	SW ¼ W	222.1875	NW ¼ W	312.1875
NORTH EAST	45	SOUTH EAST	135	SOUTH WEST	225	NORTH WEST	315
NE ¼ E	47.8125	SE ¼ S	137.8125	SW ¼ W	227.8125	NW ¼ N	317.8125
NE ½ E	50.625	SE ½ S	140.625	SW ½ W	230.625	NW ½ N	320.625
NE ¾ E	53.4375	SE ¾ S	143.4375	SW ¾ W	233.4375	NW ¾ N	323.4375
NE by E	56.25	SE by S	146.25	SW by W	236.25	NW by N	326.25
NE by E ¼ E	59.0625	SE by S ¼ S	149.0625	SW by W ¼ W	239.0625	NW by N ¼ W	329.0625
NE by E ½ E	61.875	SE by S ½ S	151.875	SW by W ½ W	241.875	NW by N ½ W	331.875
NE by E ¾ E	64.6875	SE by S ¾ S	154.6875	SW by W ¾ W	244.6875	NW by N ¾ W	334.6875
ENE	67.5	SSE	157.5	WSW	247.5	NNW	337.5
E by N ¾ E	70.3125	S by E ¾ E	160.3125	W by S ¾ S	250.3125	N by W ¾ N	340.3125
E by N ½ E	73.125	S by E ½ E	163.125	W by S ½ S	253.125	N by W ½ N	252.125
E by N ¼ E	75.9375	S by E ¼ E	165.9375	W by S ¼ S	255.9375	N by W ¼ N	345.9375
E by N	78.75	S by E	168.75	W by S	258.75	N by W	348.75
E ¾ N	81.5625	S ¾ E	171.5625	W ¾ S	261.5625	N ¾ W	351.5625
E ½ N	84.375	S ½ E	174.375	W ½ S	264.375	N ½ W	354.375
E ¼ N	87.1875	S ¼ E	177.1875	W ¼ S	267.1875	N ¼ W	357.1875

When a wreck is said to have been swept, this simply means that its minimum clearance depth has been determined by the use of one of the following two methods:

Oropesa sweep

The Oropesa sweep used by minesweepers was named after the ship in which it was first tried out in 1918.

A heavy torpedo-shaped float took the sweep wire out on to the minesweeper's quarter, about 500 yards astern. An *otter* attached to the sweep wire below this float, and a *kite* attached to the wire immediately astern of the trawler, controlled the depth of the wire, working on the principle of air kites. The kite held the inboard end of the sweep wire down in the water, while the otter at the other end kept the sweep wire curving out about 250 yards on the minesweeper's quarter.

The mine sweeper following behind steamed just inside the other's curving sweep, and in larger groups, every following did the same, so that only the lead ship was at risk from mines as she nosed into unswept waters.

Cutters on the sweep wire severed the mooring cables of the mines, which were exploded or sunk by gunfire as they bobbed to the surface.

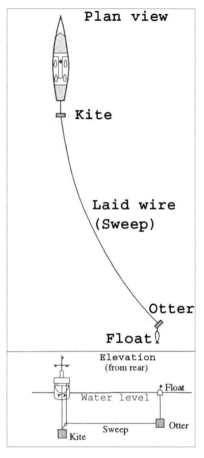

Oropesa sweep

Bar or drift sweep

In this alternative, more accurate, method of measuring the minimum depth of a wreck, a rigid iron bar is suspended horizontally below a ship drifting over the wreck. The bar is hung over the side on three measured lines – one at each end, and one in the middle to avoid any bending effect on the bar. The depth of the bar is adjusted until the bar just avoids fouling the wreck as the ship drifts over it.

By computing the time of the measurement against tidal prediction tables, the depth is converted to chart datum.

Very often a heavy wire is used instead of a rigid bar. Note that the gear is put over the up-tide side of the vessel so that she will drift away with the tide from any snags.

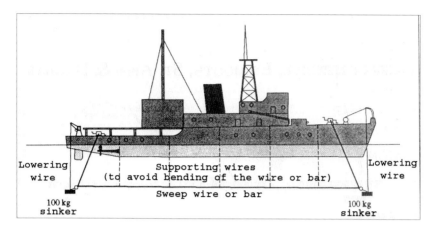

Bar (drift) sweep

Tonnage

Gross tonnage: is a measure of space, not of weight, and indicates the total permanently enclosed space of a ship – i.e. her internal volume – and is calculated on the basis of 100 cubic feet = 1 ton.

Net tonnage: is the Gross Tonnage less the space occupied by engines, boilers, bunkers, crew's quarters and all other space, which, although essential for the working of the ship, is "non-earning". The Net Tonnage, therefore, indicates how much revenue-earning space there is in the ship.

Tons displacement: is the actual weight of the ship in long tons (2240 lbs Avoirdupoids), as determined by the equivalent weight of water displaced by the ship when afloat.

Tons deadweight: is the total weight of cargo, fuel, stores, crew and all other items which are not actually a part of the ship, but which the ship can carry when she is floating down to her load marks.

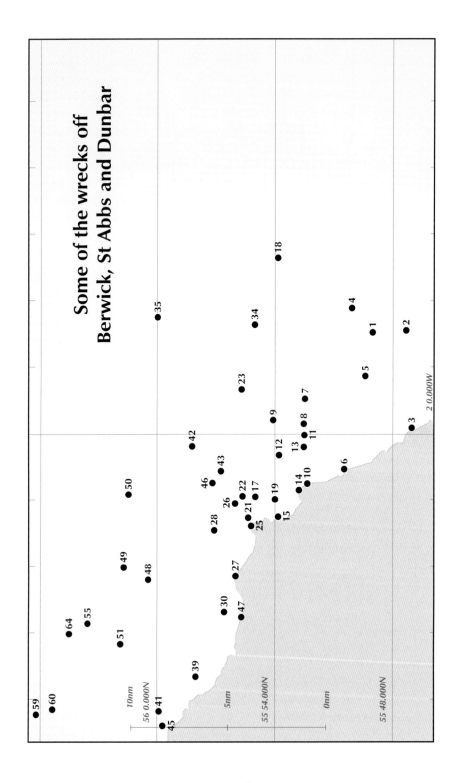

Some of the wrecks off
Berwick, St Abbs and Dunbar

2

Berwick, St Abbs and Dunbar

The Norwegian steamship Venus *(Courtesy of Geir Jørgensen)*

VENUS

Wreck No: 1			Date Sunk: 14 April 1917
Latitude: 55 49 02 N			Longitude: 01 50 47 W
GPS Lat: 5549.036 N	**WGS 84**		GPS Long: 0150.789 W
Location: 5 miles E of Berwick			Area: Berwick
Type: Steamship			Tonnage: 715 grt
Length: 211.2 ft	Beam: 29.7 ft		Draught: 13.6 ft
How Sunk: Mined			Depth:

The Norwegian steamship *Venus* (ex-*Jern*, ex-*Serantes*, ex-*Sif*) sank after striking a mine five miles off Berwick on 14 April 1917. The mine had been laid by the *UC-50* on 15 March. The *Venus* was en route from Blyth to Drammen with a cargo of coal. Fourteen men were killed. The wreck lies 5.6 miles, 56° from Berwick.

RING

Wreck No: 2		Date Sunk: 3 March 1917
Latitude: 55 47 20 N PA		Longitude: 01 50 30 W PA
GPS Lat: 5547.300 N	**WGS 84**	GPS Long: 0150.500 W
Location: 4 miles E by N of Berwick		Area: Berwick
Type: Steamship		Tonnage: 998 grt
Length: 230.5 ft	Beam: 32.8 ft	Draught: 14.5 ft
How Sunk: by *UC-41*		Depth: 35 metres

The Norwegian steamship *Ring* was built by Nylands of Christiania in 1897. She was sunk by the German submarine *UC-41* four miles E by N of Berwick on 3 March 1917. She had been en route from Skein to Tonnay Charente, France, with a cargo of ammonium nitrate fertiliser.

CAMEO

Wreck No: 3		Date Sunk: 6 February 1907
Latitude: 55 47 01 N		Longitude: 01 59 26 W
GPS Latitude: 5547.015 N	**WGS 84**	GPS Long: 0159.440 W
Location: Seal Carr, Sharper Head		Area: Berwick
Type: Steamship		Tonnage: 117 grt
Length: 89.1 ft	Beam: 16.5 ft	Draught:
How Sunk: Ran aground		Depth: 12 metres

The Leith steamship *Cameo* was wrecked on Seal Carr Rock, Sharper Head, Berwick on 6 February 1907. She had a cargo of coal. The wreck is said to be well scattered amongst rock and kelp. Her bell and whistle are in Eyemouth SAC's club house.

H-11

Wreck No: 4		Date Sunk: 17 December 1921
Latitude: 55 50 06 N		Longitude: 01 48 36 W
GPS Lat: 5550.107 N	**WGS 84**	GPS Long: 0148.601 W
Location: 7.38 miles NE of Berwick		Area: Berwick
Type: Submarine		Tonnage: 364/434 tons
Length: 150.3 ft	Beam: 15.8 ft	Draught: 12.3 ft
How Sunk: Foundered		Depth: 67–72 metres

An article in *The Scotsman* newspaper on Wednesday, 19 July 2006 announcing that South Queensferry divers had discovered a First World War submarine, brought forth information that had been a closely-guarded secret for four years.

The South Queensferry divers were members of a group who had been taken out by Marine Quest Boat Charter of Eyemouth to dive on a wreck that they had expected to be a

H23, *an H-class submarine, similar to* H11 *(Courtesy of David Page, Navyphotos)*

trawler. Instead, they said that they found an apparently intact submarine, which the divers estimated to be around 5 metres high and 45 metres long, lying on its port side with the bows clear of the seabed. The submarine showed little sign of damage, with the conning tower, periscopes and hatches in good condition.

Marine Quest Boat Charter is run by Iain and Jim Easingwood, who operate their dive boat *North Star* out of Eyemouth. Fishing is a family tradition, and the Easingwoods, who have known the local fishermen's marks all their lives, are keen to take divers out to investigate previously undived wrecks. They estimate that there are at least another 20 wrecks in the area that have still to be explored by divers. Although they had known about the existence of this wreck for many years, they had always assumed it to be a trawler. It was something of a revelation to be told that it was a submarine. The Easingwoods and the divers were naturally interested to know more about the wreck – not least its identity.

H34 *(Courtesy of David Page, Navyphotos)*

The newspaper article brought a response from former professional diver Ron Young, who is a well-known wreck researcher and author. He was able to say that this submarine was found and dived four years previously by Bishop Auckland divers Andy Anderson and Ian Wright. On their behalf, Ron had carried out a lot of research, and had discovered that the boat was almost certainly the First World War British submarine *H11*. He went on to give an enormous amout of technical and historical information about that submarine, including its exact position, and the fact that the wreck was upright and fully intact at a depth of over 70 metres (67 metres lowest astronomical depth). The *H11* wreck is 7.38 nm (nautical miles) NE of Berwick, and 9.55 nm, 185° (E by S ½S) of Eyemouth.

Neither the South Queensferry divers nor the Easingwoods had given the position of their submarine, but suspicions became aroused that there must be two submarines off Eyemouth, because the submarine found by the South Queensferry divers was apparently at only 57 metres at low water – 60 metres at high tide, and lying on its port side! They said that their submarine has a crane on the foredeck in front of the bridge (but note the torpedo crane on all the H-boat pictures), and some damage beyond the bridge. The fin-shaped hydroplane on the port side is in the down position. There is no gun to be seen, and apparently no torpedo tubes either, as would be expected in an H-class submarine (or, indeed, any other submarine).

Ron Young explained: "The H-class had four 18-inch bow torpedo tubes, arranged in pairs, one above the other, however they were not covered by the more or less standard tube covers, 'H' boats had two half circular covers as part of the bow, that open to the front and the shape of the bow was very different from other submarines, with an identification of its own." Furthermore, the H-class had no gun.

H11 was built by the Fore River Shipbuilding Co., Quincy, Massachusetts, USA in 1915. Later H-boats were built by Canadian Vickers Ltd. at Montreal.

H11 was sold at Chatham to James Kelly of Arbroath on 29 November 1921. She was removed from the Medway on 12 December 1921 and towed slowly towards the River Tay, but sank off the coast of Northumberland on 17 December 1921.

In April 2007 Marine Quest's boat *North Star* took a different party of divers to *their* submarine, which is nearly six and a half miles from the position of the *H11* given above. It was immediately obvious to these divers that this was, in fact, the wreck of a Type VIIC U-boat – *U-714*, depth-charged and sunk on 14 March 1945 (see Wreck No. 8).

The wreck is lying with a list to *starboard* (not port), and the "crane" identified by the South Queensferry divers, is in fact the U-boat's snorkel. The same group of divers visited the *H11* the following day, in 72 metres, and confirmed its identity.

The rotating bow has begun to split along the prow seam. The hydroplanes are folded on the sides. A breach in the pressure hull has left a four metre square hole between the bow and conning tower. The torpedo loading hatch and the forward hatch are closed. A crane (a real one! – see photos on previous page) with brass fittings is lying a couple of metres forward of the conning tower. The conning tower shroud, made of copper or brass or bronze, is lying on the port side of the tower, and a net and trawl boards are on top of the conning tower. All that is visible inside the conning tower are rectangular brass mountings, with no fittings attached, and a copper, or brass, pipe from which the end fitting is missing. A conduit of piping, in various stages of decay, leads aft towards the stern, where there are two small propellers about a metre in diameter. The rudder is all but gone, apart from a metal post and edging band.

EGHOLM

Wreck No: 5		Date Sunk: 25 February 1945
Latitude: 55 49 24 N		Longitude: 01 54 46 W
GPS Lat: 5549.408 N	**WGS 84**	GPS Long: 0154.766 W
Location: 5 miles NE of Berwick		Area: Berwick
Type: Steamship		Tonnage: 1317 grt
Length: 254.6 ft	Beam: 37.2 ft	Draught: 16 ft
How Sunk: Torpedoed by *U-2322*		Depth: 52–58 metres

The Danish steamship *Egholm* was built by Frederikshavn Værft & Flydedok A/S, Copenhagen (Yard No. 167) for DFDS in 1924. She arrived in Lisbon on 11 April 1940 (two days after the Germans invaded Denmark), and was laid up there for the next three years and seven months until she left on 16 November 1943. The next day she was requisitioned by

The Danish steamship Egholm *(Courtesy of Kim Neilsen)*

the Ministry of War Transport in London, and placed under the management of Ellerman's Wilson Line.

On 25 February 1945, while en route from Leith to London, she was torpedoed by *U-2322* (Heckel) off Berwick, at about 555000N, 015200W. Two of her crew and three gunners were lost out of 23 crew and three gunners. Twenty-one survivors were landed on the Tyne.

The position has also been described as 8 miles south-east of St Abbs Head. The Hydrographic Department also notes that a wreck at approximately 554920N, 015000W gave off oil shortly after the *Egholm* was sunk on 25 February 1945.

A wreck 150 feet long by 35 feet beam, oriented 045/225°, was reported at about 5547N, 0144W on 7 April 1945. The depth here is 73 metres. A wreck was also reported at about 5548N, 0146W on 29 April 1945. These reports would all seem to be estimates of the position of the wreck of the *Egholm*.

BARON STJERNBLAD

Wreck No: 6		Date Sunk: 23 April 1917
Latitude: 55 50 29 N		Longitude: 02 03 10 W
GPS Latitude: 5550.484 N	**WGS 84**	GPS Longitude: 0203.171 W
Location: 400 yd S of Gull Rock, Burnmouth		Area: Berwick
Type: Steamship		Tonnage: 991 grt
Length: 203.9 ft	Beam: 31.3 ft	Draught: 15.8 ft
How Sunk: Torpedoed & gunned by *UC-44*		Depth: 16–18 metres

The Danish steamship Baron Stjernblad *(Courtesy of Kim Neilsen)*

The Danish steamship *Baron Stjernblad* was built in 1890 by Motala M.V. of Gothenburg. She was captured by the German submarine *UC-44* on 23 April 1917. When a torpedo failed to sink her, she was shelled until she did start to go down.

The wreck was reported to lie in 23 metres of water close to the shore, south-east of Ross Point near Berwick, at 555000N, 020400W PA.

The scattered remains of a steamship has been found amongst the rocks 400 yards south of Gull Rock, which is off the cliffs north of Burnmouth harbour, and south of Fancove Head. There is lots of broken and partially-buried non-ferrous metal and two very old Admiralty pattern anchors lying nearby.

Peter Collings suggests this is a vessel named *Congo*, but that is the name by which Dunbar fishermen know the *Halland*. This wreck is probably the remains of the *Baron Stjernblad*.

MAGNE

Wreck No: 7		Date Sunk: 14 March 1945
Latitude: 55 52 28 N		Longitude: 01 56 51 W
GPS Lat: 5552.469 N	**WGS 84**	GPS Long: 0156.850 W
Location: off Eyemouth		Area: Eyemouth
Type: Steamship		Tonnage: 1226 grt
Length: 246.9 ft	Beam: 37.1 ft	Draught: 14 ft
How Sunk: Torpedoed by *U-714*		Depth: 64 metres

The Swedish steamship Magne *(Courtesy of Donald McPhie)*

On 14 March 1945 the Swedish steamship *Magne* was in convoy FS 1756 from Liverpool via Methil to London with a cargo of zinc ingots, potatoes and hemp. At 1400 hours she was sunk off Eyemouth by a torpedo fired by the *U-714* (KL Hans-Joachim Schwebke). Ten of her crew of 21 were lost. The wreck lies largely intact on an even keel. The fo'c'sle deck has rotted away, allowing access below, but the bow, which is of the old-fashioned vertical design, is otherwise intact with both anchors still in the hawseholes. Just aft of the fo'c'sle, a mast with a net draped over it, rises up five metres. The forward hold has collapsed. Winches and hull plates lie on the seabed. The wreck is then flat to the single boiler, which is four metres high, with no superstructure above it. Behind the boiler is the triple expansion steam engine, with the condenser sitting vertically on the starboard side. A spare steel propeller lies just behind the engine. Heading aft, the deck is in a state of collapse with winches tilting to port. The aft hold is flattened, then the stern rises up. The poop deck has totally rotted away, leaving the steering gear exposed. The stern is of a rounded design with the rudder and four bladed propeller still in position.

HMS *Wivern*, one of the escorting destroyers, turned towards the sinking *Magne* and put a doctor and a Leading Seaman in a carley float to assist, before setting off to search for the U-boat.

She was joined by HMSAS *Natal*, which by chance was in the area. Unlike *Wivern* she was new and had some of the latest anti-submarine (A/S) equipment, including the Squid A/S mortar. *Natal* was informed by *Wivern* of the likely location of the U-boat, and she made asdic contact almost immediately. Her squids were fired off and the explosions brought up a quantity of light diesel oil and pieces of wreckage. After a second attack, in which more oil and a metal tank surfaced, HMSAS *Natal* suddenly lost asdic contact. *Natal*'s CO, Lt. Cdr. D.A. 'Stoker' Hall, DSC, firmly believed the U-boat had been sunk, and left to continue his journey to Scapa Flow in the Orkneys.

Wivern was now on her own. She was an old boat with outdated equipment. She would be alone for some hours as it would take time for support to arrive from Rosyth. Her Captain, C.C. Anderson, decided that it was important to be sure the U-boat was destroyed and, after many hours searching, in the late evening, and ten miles from the position of *Natal*'s attack, oil was sighted.

The position was depth-charged until all charges were expended and again there was no wreckage or bodies to be seen, but the oil was now thick and black. (This seems like a description of furnace oil, which U-boats do not run on – *Wivern* may have depth-charged an old steamship wreck.) Captain Anderson was fairly certain by this time that the U-boat would not surface again. Support ships were now arriving over the horizon and having reported the position in which he had dropped depth charges (which he assumed to be the position of the U-boat), *Wivern* left to catch up with the convoy, which had continued its journey. The support ships were also old with poor equipment, and they failed to find anything.

Type VIIC U-boat (Courtesy of Fine Art Models)

U-714

Wreck No: 8		Date Sunk: 14 March 1945
Latitude: 55 52 32 N		Longitude: 01 59 04 W
GPS Lat: 5552.533 N	**WGS 84**	GPS Long: 0159.065 W
Location: 3½ miles E of Eyemouth		Area: Eyemouth
Type: Submarine		Tonnage: 761 grt
Length: 221 ft	Beam: 20.5 ft	Draught: 15.8 ft
How Sunk: Depth-charged by HMSAS *Natal*		Depth: 57–60 metres

Type VIIC U-boat conning tower detail (Courtesy of Fine Art Models)

Type V11C U-boat, 761 tons displacement surfaced, 865 tons submerged. Fitted with 5 torpedo tubes, 4 bow and 1 stern, 1 × 88 mm and 1 × 20 mm guns. Powered by two diesel engines and two electric motors, and with a maximum diving depth of 309 feet, the *U-714* (KL Hans-Joachim Schwebke) was depth-charged by the South African Navy frigate *Natal*, 10 miles NE of Berwick on 14 March 1945.

HMSAS *Natal* was built by Blyth S.B. & D.D. Co. She was launched in 1944 as the 1435-ton frigate HMS *Loch Cree*. However, on 1 March 1945, just before completion, she was transferred to the South African Navy and renamed HMSAS *Natal*. The ship was completed on 8 March 1945, and after completing trials, the *Natal* was granted a two-day postponement of her scheduled sailing date. Her commanding officer, Lt. Cdr. D.A. 'Stoker' Hall, DSC, had asked for this on the grounds that his crew needed more time to familiarise themselves with this class of vessel. Most crewmembers – all volunteers – had not served in purpose-built warships before. They had come off tiny whalecatchers and trawlers, converted in South African ports to serve as A/S vessels or minesweepers.

At about 0900 hours on 14 March 1945 HMSAS *Natal* sailed from the Tyne, bound for Scapa Flow and then for the Western Approaches Escort Group antisubmarine training base at Tobermory on the Isle of Mull. Four hours later, with the crew still shaking-down and finding their way around their new ship, a southbound vessel, *Sheaf Crown*, signalled urgently that a merchantman had just been torpedoed and sunk in her vicinity. This was off the east coast of Scotland, and the position given by *Sheaf Crown* showed that the sinking had occurred just five miles to the north of HMSAS *Natal*, off the fishing harbour of St Abbs. The frigate arrived there to find survivors of the sunken ship – later identified as the Danish cargo vessel *Magne* – bobbing about in a lifeboat and several liferafts. A veteran Royal Navy V & W class destroyer, HMS *Wivern*, was on the scene, and while Lt. Cdr. Hall was offering the assistance of his newly-commissioned vessel, the frigate made a positive submarine contact off the port beam, using her new-type 147B 'Sword' asdic scanning equipment which allowed for a vertical as well as a lateral fix to be made. Loch-class frigates had also been fitted with 'Squid' – at that time a top secret ahead-firing weapon using depth-charge mortars – and this was now used with devastating effect, with the firing of two salvos of six mortars each. These brought a quantity of light diesel oil and pieces of wreckage to the surface. HMSAS *Natal* suddenly lost asdic contact.

HMS *Wivern* claimed a share in the kill, on the basis of a depth-charge 'attack' she made later that day on an oil-slick ten miles south of *Natal*'s encounter with *U-714*. But naval authorities discounted this claim. It was later learned that the destroyer, with her outdated equipment, had at no stage been able to make asdic contact with the submerged U-boat and that her depth-charge 'attack' on an oil slick later in the day had produced no wreckage. All the recognised authorities have credited HMSAS *Natal* solely with this successful attack. After the second attack – in which more oil and a metal tank surfaced – it was assumed the U-boat had gone straight to the bottom. This was later confirmed on 18 March when a hunter-killer group, sent from the Tyne and led by HMS *Ascension* of Escort Group

17 carried out a "tin opener" on the spot by depth-charging the seabed at the position of the attack and brought a considerable quantity of U-boat flotsam to the surface. This included wooden gratings, locker doors, a Baedeker guide to Paris, a sack of condoms with instructions in German, an ornamental submarine badge – a hand-carved shield depicting a diving U-boat – a memento that was sent to *Natal* by C.-in-C. Rosyth who, with a Board of Admiralty headed by Admiral of the Fleet Sir Andrew Cunningham, sent signals to the frigate congratulating her on her early "kill". HMSAS *Natal*'s feat so soon after commissioning was described at the time as "unique in the annals of the Royal Navy."

The asdic team on *Natal* had only worked together as a team for four days and that was in a land-trainer, so it was quite an achievement. The Official Historian paid tribute to *Natal*'s crew by describing the sinking as: "Sent her to the bottom with a promptitude, which would have done credit to a much more experienced crew."

The ship received an RN battle honour ('North Sea 1945'), and a number of individual decorations were awarded, including a Bar to Lt. Cdr. Hall's DSC, won for gallantry in the Mediterranean.

ACCOUNT OF THE INCIDENT BY LT. CDR. D. HALL, COMMANDING OFFICER, HMSAS *NATAL* 14 MARCH 1945:

"I was proceeding independently from Newcastle to Methil at speed 12k with twin foxers streamed. This was the ship's first voyage since commissioning on 12th March. At 1325 the southbound SS *Sheaf Crown* reported a merchant ship sunk (SS *Magne* of FS 56) just astern of her and about five miles ahead of me. I immediately ordered 'defence stations' to be piped. HMS *Wivern* steaming in the vicinity reported that she was carrying out a search and picking up survivors and requested me to assist by carrying out a square search of four miles using the rafts datum point: 5552N, 0153W. The search was commenced at 1350. When two miles from the datum point a good echo was reported. This was confirmed by the A/S CO. Use was made of the STU which gave a short sharp echo with a straight trace [STU is a short transmission unit – a device which sends out asdic beams much closer to the host vessel than conventional units do – the implications being that the target is very close to the hunting ship] the plot indicated that the submarine was approaching at slow speed. During the last stages of the attack (6 squids set for 120 feet at 1421 hours) the submarine seemed to take avoiding action by turning to starboard, which was not confirmed by the recorder trace. As it was this rating's first attempt at recording, I think he was unable to keep up with the information supplied by the A/S cabinet.

After the first attack a large amount of oil came to the surface. Officers and engine room personnel said it smelled of diesel oil. In addition, a heavy cylindrical tank came to the surface and was later recovered. It appeared to be made of pre-fabricated steel of sturdy structure. When opened, a pair of leather bellows was visible inside and these commenced to start pumping. It was of course a dinghy container. The ship's doctor applied his stethoscope and as no ticking was heard, it was presumed safe to keep it.

Contact was regained at extreme range and classified as 'submarine'.

During the run in on the second attack (6 squids set for 120 feet at 1438 hours) the submarine appeared to be zigzagging at slow speed towards us. The second attack brought up much oil and a much smaller metal tank, which later sank.

During the third run HMS *Wivern* came up in support but was unable to gain contact. After the fourth run when I lost contact, HMS *Wivern* dropped a marker in the position of the second attack while I recovered the wreckage which had been brought to the surface during my first attack."

Local fishermen, who have snagged their nets on it, know this wreck as the *Tom Bains*, and it was assumed to be a trawler. In 2007, however, the wreck was dived in 57 metres depth of water, and found to be a substantially intact submarine lying with a list to starboard. The wreck rises to 51 metres at the bow, which is clear of the seabed.

The conning tower is still in place. The periscopes are still there, but the "winter garden" has become detached, and has fallen to the seabed off the starboard side of the boat. The AA gun is also lying there. The snorkel is in the down position. Its hinge is about one metre forward of the port side of the conning tower. The wooden decking is still in place, but the recess in the deck, into which the snorkel retracted, has corroded away, leaving the snorkel lying proud of the hull. The head of the snorkel has become detached, and is lying close by.

A life raft container is apparently attached to the winter garden, rather than recessed into the hull. (Note, another life raft container came to the surface when *U-714* was depthcharged). The hull is broken towards the stern, and there are large tanks lying on the seabed. Many pipes and fittings were observed, and it was considered that they may have been blown off.

The twin screws and rudders are still there, and one stern torpedo tube. The stern casing is holed above the port propeller. The hole is about two metres square and the stern tube and hydroplane control rods are visible. A crack around the join between the stern tube and the pressure hull is also evident. The damage to the stern of the boat appears to have been the result of *Natal*'s squid attack.

RINGHOLM

Wreck No: 9		Date Sunk: 20 April 1917
Latitude: 55 54 04 N		Longitude: 01 58 46 W
GPS Lat: 5554.073 N	**WGS 84**	GPS Long: 0158.769 W
Location: 5.4 miles E by S of St Abbs Head		Area: Eyemouth
Type: Steamship		Tonnage: 710 grt
Length: 181 ft	Beam: 29.7 ft	Draught: 13.7 ft
How Sunk: By *UC-41*		Depth: 52–63 metres

The Norwegian steamship *Ringholm* (ex-*Rigg*, ex-*Gokstad*) was built in Porsgrunn, Norway in 1910. She was a three-island steamship with one deck, and her triple expansion steam engine was located amidships. On 20 April 1917 she was sunk by the *UC-41* (KL Kurt Bernis). According to *Lloyd's War Losses*, she was en route from North Shields to Skein with a cargo of coal. At the time of attack St Abbs Head was bearing WNW ½W, distant 5 miles. This suggests the position of attack was about 5553N, 0200W.

An intact, upright three-island vessel with bows pointing NW was found within one mile of that position in 2001. The wreck was estimated to be about 58 metres long (191 ft) by 9 metres (29.7 ft) beam, closely matching the dimensions of the *Ringholm*. The wreck has a least depth of 52 metres in a total depth of 60 metres and lies 123/303° with the bows 303°. The position of this wreck is 5.4 nm, 100° from St Abbs Head, or 3.8 nm ENE of Eyemouth.

Divers who have dived from the Marine Quest charter boat *North Star* out of Eyemouth say that the wreck is intact, listing about 45° to starboard on a hard seabed at 64 metres depth. There are two holds containing coal. The wooden decking is breaking up, and the bow and stern areas are open and accessible. There are gangways running aft to a metal deck over the steering gear area. There is one boiler, and a four-bladed steel propeller.

A dinner plate bearing the Ringholm's *original name* Gokstad, *and the crest of her first owners, Grefstad & Herlofson of Arendal, was recovered from the wreck in November 2007 (Courtesy of Jim Macleod)*

The steamship President *(Author's collection)*

PRESIDENT

Wreck No: 10		Date Sunk: 28 April 1928
Latitude: 55 52 05 N		Longitude: 02 04 15 W
GPS Lat: 5552.350 N	**WGS84**	GPS Long: 0204.250 W
Location: Whaltness, S of Eyemouth		Area: Eyemouth
Type: Steamship		Tonnage: 1945 grt
Length: 280 ft	Beam: 40.5 ft	Draught: 18.2 ft
How Sunk: Ran aground		Depth: 10 metres

The President *aground just north of Scout Point, Eyemouth (Author's collection)*

The President *(Author's collection)*

The steamship *President* was built in 1907 by S.P. Austin & Son of Sunderland. While en route from Hamburg to Methil she ran ashore in a channel between rocks under the cliffs 150 metres north of Scout Point, just south of Eyemouth. The crew were able to scramble ashore using a ladder.

The wreck is broken up in shallow water close inshore in a gully off Agate Point, near the South corner of the golf course. The vessel was completely destroyed. Only the boilers remain, upright in the sandy gully, with broken steel wreckage scattered around.

CRAMOND ISLAND

Wreck No: 11		Date Sunk: 2 April 1941
Latitude: 55 52 30 N PA		Longitude: 02 01 00 W PA
GPS Lat: 5552.500 N	**WGS 84**	GPS Long: 0201.000 W
Location: 120°, 5 miles off St Abbs Head		Area: St Abbs
Type: Trawler		Tonnage: 180 grt
Length: 112.3 ft	Beam: 21.9 ft	Draught: 11.3 ft
How Sunk: By aircraft		Depth: 67 metres

The Leith-registered steel steam trawler *Cramond Island* was built in 1910 by Mackie & Thomson of Glasgow, engine by W.V.V. Ligerwood of Glasgow.

The *Cramond Island* had been hired by the Admiralty for naval purposes during the First World War, and was hired again in November 1939 for use as a boom gate vessel.

On 2 April 1941 she was on her first patrol trip off St Abbs Head with a scratch crew drawn from other trawlers in Granton. Davie Laing of Broughty Ferry had just joined her. He was at the wheel and the Skipper, who was beside him, said that an approaching aircraft was "one of ours". Then there was one big bang and *Cramond Island* sank very quickly. There was a moderate southeasterly wind and a rough, confused sea. *Cramond Island* suffered at least one direct hit. Eleven of her crew got away in a boat and two on a raft. Two were lost, one from a direct hit by a bomb, the other drowned.

A message about the *Cramond Island* reached Eyemouth Lifeboat Station at 1420 hours on 2 April, and the *Frank and William Oates* (ON 795) was launched at 1435 hours. The attack had been seen by fishermen at St Abbs, including the Lifeboat Coxswain, so the *Annie, Ronald and Isabella Forrest* (ON792) launched from there at 1440 hours. St Abbs lifeboat reached the boat at 1510 hours and picked up the eleven men, two of whom were found to be badly burned. When one of the survivors was climbing aboard the lifeboat he inadvertently released the breeches buoy. This was not immediately noticed by the lifeboat crew and it became tangled in the propeller as the lifeboat made for the raft. The lifeboat crew made sail, rigged sweeps and hoisted a red flag. Five shore boats had put out from St Abbs, as had three fishing boats from Eyemouth. The FV *Spes Bona* towed the lifeboat into Eyemouth. The men on the raft were rescued by another fishing boat, the *Milky Way*.

Due to her skipper's misidentification of the aircraft, *Cramond Island* was reported sunk in error by British aircraft 120°, 5 miles off St Abbs Head. Thirteen Group Fighter Command Operational Record Book for 1941 states that the attack was in fact carried out by a lone Ju-88, which was plotted by the Observer Corps three miles east of St Abbs Head at 1359 hours. It says that the attack took place 3–5 miles east of St Abbs Head and Naval records show the attack took place five minutes later, at 1404 hours.

RNLI records give the position as approximately three miles east of Eyemouth, and the wreck charted at 5552.510N, 0201.110W PA fits that description very well.

The raider was intercepted three miles south of Alnmouth by Flight Lieutenant J.R.C. Young of 317 Squadron – claimed as damaged but not shot down. The wreck is upright and apparently intact. The wheelhouse seems to be undamaged, and there are still two radio sets in it. A gun on a tripod has fallen on the bow, which is well clear of the seabed. The hull of the vessel slopes down to the stern, which blends into the seabed at 67 metres.

FORTUNA

Wreck No: 12		Date Sunk: 2 April 1941
Latitude: 55 53 46 N		Longitude: 02 01 53 W
GPS Lat: 5553.766 N	**WGS84**	GPS Long: 0201.875 W
Location: 2¼ miles NE of Eyemouth		Area: St Abbs
Type: Trawler		Tonnage: 259 grt
Length: 128.4 ft	Beam: 22 ft	Draught: 11.8 ft
How Sunk: By aircraft		Depth: 56 metres

The Grimsby steam trawler *Fortuna* was built in 1906 by Cook, Welton & Gemmell of Beverley and was hired as an Auxiliary Patrol trawler in June 1940. She was asked to assist the *Cramond Island* when that vessel was attacked by an aircraft, but nothing more was heard of the *Fortuna*, though the bodies of two of her crew were washed ashore at Berwick on 5 April. It was obviously assumed that the *Fortuna* must have met the same fate as the

Cramond Island, as she was also reported sunk in error by British aircraft 120° off St Abbs Head on 2 April 1941. Perhaps *Fortuna* was sunk by the same German aircraft that sank the *Cramond Island*, but the weather at the time was bad, with a gale and rough seas. It is therefore possible that the *Fortuna* might have been overwhelmed by the rough seas.

The *Fortuna* was tentatively thought to lie at 555230N, 020000W PA.

In 2001 a wreck was discovered at 5553.766N, 00201.875W (WGS84), 2.13 nm, 055° from Eyemouth. The wreck appears to be upright and intact, approximately 102 feet long by 20 feet beam, and standing up 7 metres, although some of this apparent height is thought to be entangled nets, suspended by floats. The wreck is oriented 055/235°, with the bows pointing 235°, towards Eyemouth.

When dived in 2006 it was found to be a steam trawler with a gun on it. The bell has been recovered. It reads: FORTUNA 1906 GRIMSBY.

AURIAC

Wreck No: 13		Date Sunk: 23 April 1917
Latitude: 55 52 31 N		Longitude: 02 01 08 W
GPS Lat: 5552.518 N	**WGS 84**	GPS Long: 0201.139 W
Location: 5 miles ESE from St Abbs Head		Area: St Abbs
Type: Steamship		Tonnage: 871 grt
Length: 200 ft	Beam: 29.3 ft	Draught: 15.2 ft
How sunk: By submarine *UC-44* – gunfire		Depth: 60 metres

The Leith steamship *Auriac* was built by Osbourne, Graham & Co., Sunderland in 1890. At 0720 hours on 23 April 1917, while en route from Rouen to Leith with a cargo of empty oil drums, the *Auriac* was attacked by gunfire from the *UC-44*, which appeared on the surface about a quarter of a mile from the ship. The first shot struck the ship and the second shot wounded the man at the wheel. The master stopped the engines as the third shell burst near the bridge. As shells were bursting all around the ship, the men took cover, but after about seven minutes of the firing, a shell killed the bosun. Soon after, a boat was lowered and 14 of the crew got away from the ship. Two other crewmen jumped overboard and were picked up by the boat. *UC-44* cruised around the *Auriac*, firing at her as the crew pulled for the shore. They were picked up by two motor fishing boats and landed at St Abbs. The *Auriac* sank at 1027 hours, a few minutes after the crew landed ashore.

According to *Lloyd's Losses: the First World War* she was sunk by a submarine 10 miles east of Eyemouth on 23 April 1917 while en route from Rouen to Leith with a cargo of empty oil drums. *British Vessels Lost at Sea 1914–1918* gives the position of attack as 5 miles ESE from St Abbs Head, which would give a position of about 555300N, 020000W PA.

An unknown wreck charted at 5552.518N, 0201.139W, 4.6 miles SE by E from St Abbs Head might very well be the *Auriac*.

The steam trawler Maritana *ran aground in fog on Buss Craig Rock, Hurcars, Eyemouth on 19 March 1927 (Author's collection)*

MARITANA

Wreck No: 14
Latitude: 55 52 44 N
GPS Lat: 5552.730 N
Location: Hurcar Rock, Eyemouth Harbour
Type: Trawler
Length: 86 ft   Beam: 18.1 ft
How Sunk: Ran aground

Date Sunk: 19 March 1927
Longitude: 02 05 00 W
GPS Long: 0205.000 W
Area: Eyemouth
Tonnage: 97 grt
Draught: 8.4 ft
Depth: 18 metres

The steel steam drifter *Maritana* was built by G. Brown of Greenock in 1907. She had an 18-inch compound engine by White & Hemphill of Greenock. She fished out of Port

Maritana *high and dry (Author's collection)*

Gordon, Banffshire until 1915, when she was requisitioned for war service as a submarine net vessel/minesweeper, and fitted with a six-pounder anti-aircraft gun. In 1920 she was returned to Portgordon for fishing, and was sold to new owners in Buckie in 1922.

On 19 March 1927 she was wrecked on the Hurker Rocks when attempting to enter Eyemouth in fog.

ALFRED ERLANDSEN

Wreck No: 15		Date Sunk: 17 October 1907
Latitude: 55 53 42 N		Longitude: 02 07 14 W
GPS Lat: 5553.831 N	**WGS84**	GPS Long: 0207.494 W
Location: Ebb Carrs Rock, St Abbs		Area: St Abbs
Type: Steamship		Tonnage: 954 grt
Length: 208 ft	Beam: 31 ft	Draught: 14.1 ft
How Sunk: Ran aground		Depth: 15 metres

In dense fog on the night of Thursday, 17 October 1907 the Danish steamship, *Alfred Erlandsen*, en route to Grangemouth from Libau in Denmark with a cargo of pit props, ran aground on Ebb Carrs rocks off St Abbs. The ship's whistle alerted the villagers to the plight of the vessel, but in the darkness and thick fog, nothing could be seen of the ship. At that time St Abbs had no lifeboat or other rescue apparatus. The Eyemouth lifeboat, two miles to the south, was called out, as was the Skateraw lifeboat some 12 miles to the north-west. Rocket apparatus was also sent by horse-drawn cart from Eyemouth, but by the time it arrived, the ship's whistle had been silenced by the inrushing water flooding the furnaces. Although numerous attempts were made to fire a line to the distressed vessel, the rockets did not have sufficient range, and all fell short. The lifeboats had no engines and had to be rowed through the heavy easterly swell, the Skateraw boat taking four hours to reach the scene.

By that time the *Alfred Erlandsen* and her crew of 16 had disappeared beneath the surface, and all that remained were the pit props and other floating debris being hurtled around like battering rams by the waves, to the great danger of the lifeboats. As there were no survivors left to save, the lifeboats headed home. By the time the Skateraw lifeboat returned to her base, she had been at sea for ten hours. In the morning, however, one survivor, a Great Dane dog was found wandering the clifftops, having made it ashore through the surf. The dog lived for many years thereafter, and helped to raise money for the Red Cross during the First World War, as the incredible tale of his survival was related over and over again.

As a direct result of the *Alfred Erlandsen* disaster, a lifeboat station was established at St Abbs in 1911, funded mainly by the Usher Brewery family who lived in the village.

The wreck is now completely broken up.

VIGILANT

Wreck No: 16	Date Sunk: 29 September 1976
Latitude: 55 53 42 N	Longitude: 02 07 12 W
GPS Lat: 5553.700 N	GPS Long: 0207.200 W
Location: Ebb Carrs Rock, St Abbs	Area: St Abbs
Type: Trawler	Tonnage:
Length: Beam:	Draught:
How Sunk: Ran aground in fog	Depth: 18 metres

On 29 September 1976 the trawler *Vigilant*, which was less than a month old, struck Ebb Carrs Rock in fog. Her skipper and three of the five crew were asleep in their bunks at the time. After striking the rocks the *Vigilant* sank so quickly they all had to jump into the sea. Two men in a local boat in Eyemouth harbour saw the wreck and put to sea to save them. Although *Vigilant*'s hull was wooden, her wheelhouse was steel and it remains reasonably intact on the seabed.

CAMPANIA II ?

Wreck No: 17	Date Sunk: 5 March 1917
Latitude: 55 54 59 N PA	Longitude: 02 05 44 W PA
GPS Lat: 5554.978 N	GPS Long: 0205.738 W
Location: off St Abbs Head	Area: St Abbs
Type: Drifter	Tonnage: 90 grt
Length: 89.6 ft Beam: 19.2 ft	Draught: 8.7 ft
How Sunk: Foundered in a gale	Depth: 42 metres

The wooden steam drifter *Campania II* was built in 1907 by J. & G. Forbes of Sandhaven, and was powered by a 16-inch compound engine by Cooper & Greig of Dundee. She was hired by the Admiralty in 1915 and employed as a net drifter armed with a three-pounder gun. Her crew of 12 were all lost when she disappeared in a gale off St Abbs Head on 5 March 1917. The unknown wreck charted at 5554.978N, 0205.738W PA might be the *Campania II*.

TILLIECORTHIE

Wreck No: 18	Date Sunk: 1 March 1917
Latitude: 55 53 50 N PA	Longitude: 01 44 00 W PA
GPS Lat: 5553.830 N	GPS Long: 0144.000 W
Location: 13 miles E of St Abbs	Area: St Abbs
Type: Steamship	Tonnage: 382 grt
Length: 138.6 ft Beam: 26.4 ft	Draught: 9.9 ft
How Sunk: By *UC-41*-gunfire	Depth: 68 metres

The steamship *Tilliecorthie* was transporting coal from Seaham to Peterhead when she was captured off the Farne Islands by the German submarine *UC-41* (KL Kurt Bernis) and sunk by gunfire on 1 March 1917. Her Master was taken prisoner.

Lloyd's World War One Losses gives the position of attack as five miles east of Longstone Light, but *British Vessels Lost At Sea 1939–45* gives the position as 16 miles N ½ E from Longstone, and she is charted as Wk PA at 555350N, 014400W, 13 miles E of St Abbs Head.

BEN SCREEL

Wreck No: 19		Date Sunk: 25 December 1942
Latitude: 55 54 00 N		Longitude: 02 05 56 W
GPS Lat: 5554.010 N	**WGS84**	GPS Long: 0205.927 W
Location: 2 miles NE of Eyemouth		Area: St Abbs
Type: Trawler		Tonnage: 195 grt
Length: 115.3 ft	Beam: 22.1 ft	Draught: 11.9 ft
How Sunk: Mined		Depth: 56–64 metres

The steam trawler *Ben Screel* (ex-*Gertrude Cappleman*) was built in 1915 by Hall Russell of Aberdeen (Yard No. 562). She left Methil with a crew of nine on 18 December 1942, and was last seen on Christmas Day. *British Vessels Lost At Sea 1939–45* merely states "presumed mined off St Abbs Head about 25th December 1942." Her wreck was thought to possibly lie about 1½ miles E of St Abbs at approximately 5554N, 0205W.

The *Ben Screel* had been attacked twice before – the first time on 2 June 1941 when she was bombed at 5530N, 0130W, and the second time on 12 November 1941 when she was bombed 14 miles NE by N off St Abbs Head.

ODENSE

Wreck No: 20		Date Sunk: 5 May 1917
Latitude: 55 54 44 N		Longitude: 02 09 12 W
GPS Lat: 5554.730 N	**WGS84**	GPS Long: 0209.200 W
Location: Pettico Wick, St Abbs Head		Area: St Abbs
Type: Steamship		Tonnage: 1756 grt
Length: 261 ft	Beam: 36 ft	Draught: 16.7 ft
How Sunk: U-boat gunfire (*UC-77*)		Depth: 10 metres

On 5 May 1917 the Danish steamship *Odense* (ex-*Fredericia*, ex-*Nord*) was captured one mile ENE of St Abbs Head by the *UC-77*. *Lloyd's World War One Losses* gives the position of attack as 555600N, 021230W, 1½ miles ENE of St Abbs Head. The U-boat fired a torpedo at the *Odense*, but missed and so shelled her, killing two of the crew. The other members of the crew abandoned ship. The attack was broken off with the arrival of British aircraft.

Location of the *Odense*

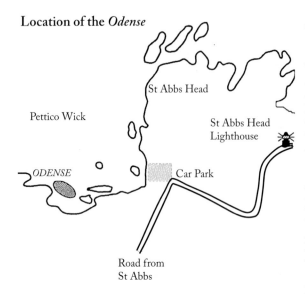

St Abbs Head

Pettico Wick

St Abbs Head
Lighthouse

ODENSE

Car Park

Road from
St Abbs

The damaged vessel did not sink, but drifted ashore in Pettico Wick, the bay to the west of St Abbs Head, where repair work was carried out over a period of several months. It had been hoped to finally refloat her on the high spring tide on 3 October 1917, but a storm blew up the day before, and she was lost.

The *Odense* was carrying a cargo of peanuts, hence she is known locally as "The Peanut Boat". The wreck is completely broken up, with ribs and scattered plates covered in kelp. Her boiler stands vertically in 12 metres of water. More wreckage lies at 555456N, 020915W.

BEAR

Wreck No: 21		Date Sunk: 11 January 1891
Latitude: 55 55 22 N		Longitude: 02 07 36 W
GPS Lat: 5555.360 N	**WGS84**	GPS Long: 0207.596 W
Location: 1.25 miles E of St Abbs Head		Area: St Abbs
Type: Steamship		Tonnage: 596 grt
Length: 174.4 ft	Beam: 25.6 ft	Draught: 14.3 ft
How sunk: Collision with *Britannia*		Depth: 63 metres

The steamship *Bear* was built in 1877 by R. Dixon & Co. of Middlesbrough. On 11 January 1891, while en route from Middlesbrough to Grangemouth with a cargo of pig iron, she was sunk in collision with the steamship *Britannia* off St Abbs Head. Twelve of her crew were lost. The wreck is upright and fairly intact, oriented 131/313°, with the bows pointing 313°. She stands up 6 metres from the seabed in a general depth of 69 metres.

The *Britannia*, belonging to James Currie & Co. of Leith, left that port on the evening of Saturday, 10 January, bound for Newcastle with 45 passengers and a general cargo. The *Bear*, owned by J. Watson and Co. of Glasgow, was on its way from Middlesbrough to Grangemouth, with a cargo of pig iron. At approximately 3.30 a.m. they collided off St Abbs Head. It was very dark at the time, the weather being described as "dark but clear". The wind was WSW force 5. From the accounts of the survivors, it seems that both vessels lights were quite visible to the watches on each while they were a considerable distance apart. According to the description given by David Wilson, the first mate of the *Britannia*, the helm of the *Bear* was starboarded to cross the bow of the Leith steamer, but the two survivors of the *Bear* state that by blowing the whistle they gave the *Britannia* warning that they were starboarded, finding it impossible, from the position the vessels were then in, to port. The collision seems to have been the outcome of a misunderstanding by those on board both vessels. On their sighting each other, it appears that a single blast of the whistle was given from the Leith steamer to warn the *Bear* to port, and two blasts were given from the latter vessel indicating a desire for the *Britannia* to starboard. Whatever interpretation was made of these signals, it is certain that both vessels maintained their courses, and consequently ran into each other.

The bows of the *Britannia*, whose engines had been reversed, struck the *Bear* amidships on the starboard side, and cut a huge hole in her. The sea poured in, and in less than half a minute the *Bear* foundered, carrying with her the captain and thirteen of the crew, only two of whom were saved. The *Britannia's* passengers were wakened by the collision, and were naturally very agitated and concerned for their safety. Their fears were somewhat allayed on being told that although the bows were burst open, allowing water to enter into the collision compartment and the fore cabin, the vessel would be able to float for a good while. The *Britannia* at once lowered a boat to rescue any of the crew of the *Bear* who might be floating about on the water. With the aid of a light they managed to pick up the second mate, A. J. Anderson, and the lamp trimmer, A. Ireland, who were in an exhausted state from their efforts to keep above water.

Although a prolonged search of the area was carried out no one else from the foundered steamer could be seen, and the boat returned to the *Britannia*. The condition of this steamer was becoming serious because of the ingress of water, and the passengers were obviously greatly alarmed. Rockets were fired, but two steamers passed without taking the slightest notice of these signals. Carron Company's steamer *Thames*, which was on its way from Grangemouth to London, hove in sight fully an hour after the collision, and on discovering that there was something wrong with the *Britannia*, it stood by. The 45 passengers were at once transferred to the *Thames*, but none of their effects were sent after them. A hawser was then passed between both steamers, and the *Britannia* was towed stern foremost slowly up the Firth. All the crew had remained on board.

The towing proceeded with utmost care, because of the state of the vessel, and it was three o'clock in the afternoon when they were two miles to the westward of Fidra Island. At this point it was seen that the water had gained so much in the vessel that she could not remain afloat for much longer. This was made known to the *Thames*, and the signal had hardly been given to beach the *Britannia* when the cables between the vessels broke, and the unfortunate steamer foundered immediately afterwards, throwing Captain Robinson and the eight crewmen into the water. Fortunately, the Alloa tug *Yorkshire Lass* arrived on the scene at this time and rendered valuable assistance in saving the lives of the men struggling in the water. With the exception of Captain Robinson, all the immersed men had life belts on, and by means of ropes, those on the tug succeeded in rescuing seven, including the captain. Of the other two crewmen, the first mate, David Wilson, swam to the side of the *Thames*, and was taken safely on board, while unhappily the engineer, David Ettershanks, was drowned. The vessel had gone down with all the passengers' effects. The *Thames* returned to Leith Roads, accompanied by the *Yorkshire Lass*. The passengers were transferred from the *Thames* to the tug, and the *Yorkshire Lass*, with the two survivors of the *Bear*, and the 45 passengers, Captain Robinson, and the crew of the *Britannia*, steamed for Leith harbour. Arriving there shortly after 7.00 p.m., they were all taken to the Sailors' Home.

The two survivors of the *Bear* were questioned regarding the collision. A. J. Anderson, the second mate, stated that Captain Howrie was on watch at the time, while he himself was in bed. He was wakened suddenly by the shock of a terrible crash, and on getting out of his berth and looking forward, he could see nothing but steam issuing from the stoke hold. He rushed out of his cabin, but had not gone far when the vessel went down, half a minute after colliding. He was dragged under water, but succeeded in getting to the surface, and saw something floating a short distance away. Swimming to it, he discovered it to be a fisherman's basket, to which he clung until he caught hold of a tank, which had come out of the starboard boat. He took a long time to get to this support because the swell on the water kept floating it beyond his reach. He next got hold of a hatch, and used it to keep himself afloat until he was picked up by the *Britannia*'s boat. In addition to the captain, there were three other crewmembers on watch – Ireland, Estle and Watkins, but apart from Ireland, the trimmer, he expressed the belief that not one of the others in the vessel ever came to the surface. Ireland's voice was the only one he heard.

Britannia was later salvaged and returned to service. She was eventually wrecked off the Farne Islands on 25 September 1915.

SEA HUNTER & FOUR SEASONS

Wreck No: 22		Date Sunk: 30 October 1985
Latitude: 55 55 38 N		Longitude: 02 07 46 W
GPS Lat: 5555.631 N	**WGS84**	GPS Long: 0205.759 W
Location: 1.7 miles, 69° from St Abbs Head		Area: St Abbs
Type: MFV		Tonnage: 31 grt
Length: 51.2 ft	Beam:	Draught:
How Sunk: Snagged nets and foundered		Depth: 74 metres

Two wrecks are charted very close together here. The motor fishing vessel *Sea Hunter* took in water and sank when her fishing gear caught fast on a wreck about one and a half miles east of St Abbs Head on 30 October 1985. The *Sea Hunter* was a very small vessel of only 31 grt, and 51 ft long. She protrudes 6 metres up from the seabed.

The wreck on which she snagged her net is the MFV *Four Seasons*, which sank on 19 August 1975. She is also quite small – apparently only 33 ft long by 24 ft wide, and standing 4 metres high at 5555.613N, 0205.679W. She lies 110/290°.

ROSSO

Wreck No: 23		Date sunk: 7 March 1952	
Latitude: 55 55 40 N		Longitude: 01 55 59 W	
GPS Lat: 5555.659 N	**WGS84**	GPS Long: 0155.978 W	
Location: 6 miles NE by E ¼E from Eyemouth		Area: St Abbs	
Type: Ssteamship		Tonnage: 1253 grt	
Length: 232 ft	Beam: 37.2 ft	Draught: 15 ft ft	
How Sunk: Foundered		Depth: 65–72 metres	

The Swedish steamship *Rosso* was built by A/B Oresundsvarvet in 1919. She sprang a leak six and a half miles north-east-by-east of Eyemouth, while en route from Methil to Oaxen, Sweden, with a cargo of coal on 7 March 1952. The position description plots at 555600N, 015500W PA. Her SOS sparked off a search of the area, but no trace was found of the ship or her crew of 22 men.

The wreck was dived on 3 September 2006. It was found to be an intact centre island steamship, sitting with a slight list, in a scour 72 metres deep. The deck is at 65 metres, with winches and mast and supports still in position. One of the holds contains crates of blue glass medicine bottles with plastic tops.

The above position has been given for the *Rosso*, but another position three miles NNE looks very promising. A wreck at 5558.446N, 0154.052W is 70 metres long – matching the length of the *Rosso*.

STRATHRANNOCH

Wreck No: 24		Date Sunk: 6 April 1917	
Latitude: 55 55 00 N		Longitude: 02 07 00 W	
GPS Lat: 5554.876 N	**WGS84**	GPS Long: 0206.746 W	
Location: ¾ miles E of St Abbs Head		Area: St Abbs	
Type: Trawler		Tonnage: 215 grt	
Length: 117.7 ft	Beam: 22.1 ft	Draught: 12.2 ft	
How Sunk: Mined		Depth: 57 metres	

The steel steam trawler *Strathrannoch* was built in 1917 by Hall Russell of Aberdeen. She was requisitioned for use as a minesweeper during the First World War, and was mined and sunk off St Abbs Head on 6 April 1917 with the loss of all 13 members of her crew. A huge explosion was witnessed by members of the Coastguard, who were watching the minesweeper proceeding ½–¾ mile offshore. HMS *Ratapiko*, an accompanying minesweeping trawler, was on the scene within ten minutes. Several other small vessels, and St Abbs lifeboat arrived very shortly afterwards, but all that could be found was the *Strathrannoch*'s small boat, floating undamaged. A Court of Enquiry was of the opinion that the mine explosion caused a secondary explosion of the *Strathrannoch*'s gun shell magazine.

Depth to the seabed is 60 metres, and the very smashed up wreck rises to 57 metres. Entangled nets may rise to 47 metres. It is pitch-black down there with underwater visibility of only 2–3 metres, so it is not the easiest wreck to explore. The wreck is broken into two sections. The bow section, which is upright, is about 12 metres long, and lies 38 metres west of the stern section. The stern section is about 18 metres long, and sticks up 7 metres at a very steep angle. The propeller is almost the highest point of the wreck.

Divers who thought they were on the bow section found brass letters that spelled out "STRATHRANNOCH", thereby making a positive identification of the wreck. Because of the very poor underwater visibility, these divers were unable to see the stern section of the wreck.

The bow section is at 5554.875N, 0206.773W, and the stern section is at 5554.881N, 0206.742W (WGS84).

GLANMIRE

Wreck No: 25		Date Sunk: 25 July 1912
Latitude: 55 55 14 N		Longitude: 02 08 14 W
GPS Lat: 5555.228 N	**WGS84**	GPS Long: 0208.242 W
Location: 300 metres off St Abbs Head		Area: St Abbs
Type: Steamship		Tonnage: 1141 grt
Length: 242.2 ft	Beam: 33.2 ft	Draught: 15.3 ft
How Sunk: Ran aground		Depth: 30 metres

The steamship *Glanmire* was built in 1888 by W. B. Thompson of Dundee. While en route from Amsterdam to Grangemouth in thick fog, she struck Black Carrs Rock at about 6.20 a.m. on 25 July 1912, then drifted off to sink half an hour later in 30 metres, about 300

Glanmire *at Bristol in 1912 (Courtesy of G.E. Langmuir Collection)*

metres north of St Abbs Head Lighthouse. Her 15 passengers and 22 crew reached shore safely in two boats.

The *Glanmire* is the most accessible wreck in the St Abbs area and can often be dived even when conditions inshore are too rough. It lies on a flat gravel bottom only a few minutes from the harbour in approximately 30 metres of water. A lot of wreckage remains but after more than 90 years on the seabed most of it is now flattened, although some parts rise about 5 metres from the bottom. The boilers stand upright, as does the steel propeller, but the rest of the wreck is broken up and covered in white and orange soft corals. The *Glanmire* resembles the colourful reefs for which this stretch of coast is renowned, and one of the main attractions of this wreck is the fish life. Some of them are also very colourful, such as red/orange/green lumpsuckers, big blue wolf fish, and the occasional black–grey conger eel. A considerable current runs over the wreck, making it imperative to dive only in the half hour of slack water.

TRANSIT A: Line up LH edge of red tank at lighthouse with centre of gable end of small building attached to large building.

TRANSIT B: To the north-east, line up notch on skyline with RH edge of rock pinnacle.

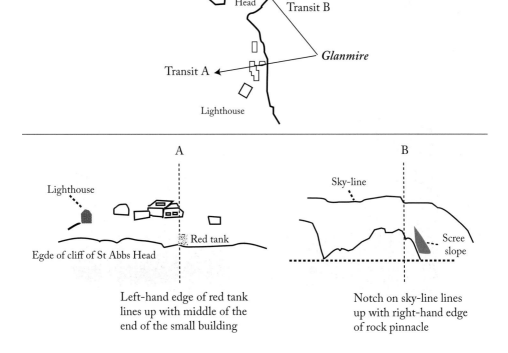

Transits for the *Glanmire*

Transit B

Transit A

Glanmire

St Abbs Head

Lighthouse

A

B

Lighthouse

Sky-line

Red tank

Egde of cliff of St Abbs Head

Scree slope

Left-hand edge of red tank lines up with middle of the end of the small building

Notch on sky-line lines up with right-hand edge of rock pinnacle

ADAM

Wreck No: 26		Date Sunk: 4 December 1940	
Latitude: 55 56 24 N		Longitude: 02 06 54 W	
GPS Lat: 5555.997 N	**WGS84**	GPS Long: 0206.283 W	
Location: 1.6 miles NE of St Abbs Head		Area: St Abbs	
Type: Barge		Tonnage:	
Length:	Beam:	Draught:	
How Sunk: Foundered		Depth: 64–70 metres	

The British oil barge *Adam* foundered while under tow off Coldingham on 4 December 1940. The C.-in-C. Rosyth gave the approximate position as 90°, 3–4 miles from Eyemouth at about 555230N, 015900W, and although a wreck is charted PA in that position, it is not the *Adam*. On 9 December 1940 C.-in-C. Rosyth reported that the refuelling barge was no longer a danger to navigation. This suggests it must have finally sunk, after drifting for a time. It has been speculated locally that the *Adam* drifted ashore somewhere in the St Abbs Head – Eyemouth area – but a further position was described as one mile south-east of No. 21 light buoy, at about 555624N, 020654W, and a wreck is charted extremely close to that position at 5555.997N, 0206.283W, 1.6 nm, 052° from St Abbs Head Lighthouse.

NYON

Wreck No: 27		Date Sunk: 17 November 1958	
Latitude: 55 55 54 N		Longitude: 02 12 48 W	
GPS Lat: 5555.900 N	**WGS84**	GPS Long: 0212.800 W	
Location: Between Souter and Fast Castle		Area: St Abbs	
Type: Motor Vessel		Tonnage: 5058 grt	
Length: 420 ft	Beam: 57 ft	Draught: 28 ft	
How Sunk : Ran aground		Depth: 18 metres	

The Swiss MV *Nyon* was outward bound from the Forth in thick fog when she ran aground about three miles north-west of St Abbs Head on the evening of Saturday, 17 November 1958. Despite being a fairly new vessel, *Nyon* was not equipped with radar, which could have enabled the captain to navigate his ship safely through the fog, and avoid running ashore. She stuck fast with her bow impaled on the rocks near the Souter or Standing Man, at the foot of the cliffs below Dowlaw farm. When the fog cleared later that night the ship could clearly be seen with her lights ablaze in calm water.

St Abbs lifeboat *W. Ross Macarthur of Glasgow* went alongside to take off the crew, but *Nyon*'s captain refused to abandon ship. In the prevailing calm conditions, he was hopeful that it might be possible to get his ship off the rocks and save it. He asked for concrete to plug the hole in the bows, and despite the fact that it was by then Sunday morning, concrete was eventually obtained from Berwick-on-Tweed, and delivered by farm tractors to the top of the cliffs above the *Nyon*. By this time the coastguards had

The bow section of the Nyon *still on the rocks after the stern section was removed (Author's collection)*

The Swiss MV Nyon *aground below Fast Castle (Author's collection)*

rigged a line with a pulley, and this was used to lower the concrete to the stranded vessel. Despite the attempt to plug the holes in her hull with the concrete, the ship remained firmly aground by the bow. Unfortunately, she had been in ballast at the time of grounding, and was, therefore, already riding high in the water. With no cargo to jettison, it was impossible to lighten the ship further to allow her to float off the rocks. The combined efforts of three tugs was unable to pull the *Nyon* off the rocks. Even after the failure of these attempts, the captain was still unwilling to leave his ship until the Swiss owners could arrange their own salvage. Dutch salvage experts were engaged, and during the month they continued to work, trying to free the ship from the grip of the rocks, St Abbs lifeboat and fishing boats from Eyemouth attended the scene on numerous occasions during 18–27 November.

Eventually, St Abbs lifeboat took off 30 crewmen from the *Nyon*, when it was finally decided to cut the ship in two, leaving the bows impaled on the rocks, but freeing the stern section. This was towed to Rotterdam, where a new bow was built on.

The rebuilt vessel finally sank at 503803N, 001224E in the English Channel, after a collision with the Indian motorship *Jalazad* off Beachy Head, Sussex, on 15 June 1962. The bow section to aft of the bridge remained stuck on the rocks below the cliffs near Fast Castle, where it broke up and now lies scattered on the seabed amongst the rocks at the foot of the cliffs. Almost 50 years later, it may still be possible to see the remains of the lifting tackle installed at the top of the cliff during the salvage attempts.

GASRAY

Wreck No: 28		Date Sunk: 5 April 1945
Latitude: 55 57 04 N		Longitude: 02 08 38 W
GPS Lat: 5557.064 N	**WGS84**	GPS Long: 0208.627 W
Location: 2 miles N¾ E St Abbs Head		Area: St Abbs
Type: Steamship		Tonnage: 1406 grt
Length: 234.3 ft	Beam: 36.3 ft	Draught: 16 ft
How Sunk: Torpedoed by *U-2321*		Depth: 60 metres

The British steamship *Gasray* was originally intended to be named *War Char*, but she was completed in 1919 by her builders, W. Harkess & Son Ltd., Middlesborough, as the *Whitworth*. In 1936 she was renamed *Uhti*, and, in 1939, renamed *Springfal*, finally being renamed *Gasray* in 1940.

At 1859 hours on 5 April 1945, she was torpedoed 2 miles N¾E from St Abbs Head, while en route, in ballast, from Grangemouth to Blyth. It was originally believed that she had been torpedoed by *U-978* (Pulst), but Pulst's attack was on an unidentified steamship estimated to be at least 6000 tons, in AN1520, which equates to about 5903N, 0304W, in the vicinity of Sule Skerry, off the west of Orkney.

Further examination of U-boat records has since revealed that the *Gasray* was in fact torpedoed by *U-2321* (Hans-Heinrich Barschkis) two miles north of St Abbs Head at

1859 hours on 5 April 1945 in AN5146, which equates to about 5557N, 0205W. Other positions have been given as 555500N, 020600W and 555500N, 020400W.

Of her 18 crew and four gunners, six crewmembers were lost. The master, eleven crewmembers and four gunners were rescued – six by the St Abbs Lifeboat *Annie Ronald and Isabella Forrest* and ten by the British coaster *Clova*. The lifeboat landed them all at St Abbs.

The wreck is broken into at least two parts. One part about 35 metres long lies 100/280° and stands up approximately 8 metres from the bottom at 5557.064N, 0208.627W (56 metres in 64 metres). Another part measuring 20 metres in length oriented 050/230° and stands up 3 metres from the seabed at 5557.093N, 0208.697W (63 metres in 66 metres).

MAGICIENNE

Wreck No: 29		Date Sunk: 4 May 1940
Latitude: 55 56 06 N		Longitude: 02 19 45 W
GPS Lat: 5556.100 N	**WGS84**	GPS Long: 0219.750 W
Location: North end of Pease Bay		Area: St Abbs
Type: Schooner		Tonnage: 250 grt
Length: 116.3 ft	Beam: 27.2 ft	Draught: 12.8 ft
How Sunk: Ran aground		Depth: 2 metres

The Swedish 250-ton, three-masted wooden schooner *Magicienne* was built at St Malo in 1912. She had an auxiliary two-cylinder oil engine. She ran aground on 4 May 1940, en route from the Faroes to Blyth with a cargo of salt. The hull was finally blown up by the army, but part of the wreck is visible at low tide close to the rocks at the north end of the sandy beach at Pease Bay.

DOVE

Wreck No: 30		Date Sunk: pre-1919
Latitude: 55 56 30 N PA		Longitude: 02 16 00 W PA
GPS Lat: 5556.500 N		GPS Long: 0216.000 W
Location: 1½ miles NW of Fast Castle		Area: St Abbs
Type: Trawler		Tonnage: 168 grt
Length: 118 ft	Beam: 20.7 ft	Draught: 10.9 ft
How Sunk:		Depth: 28 metres

The wreck charted PA, 1½ miles NW of Fast Castle was reported in 1919, and is said to be a vessel named *Dove*. When the wreck is found, it may be possible to recover parts such as the bell, or the engine-makers plate, which should establish her true identity.

The Hull trawler *Dove* (H1033) was built in 1877 by Edwards Bros. in North Shields, the engine by N. E. Marine of Sunderland. She sank in the North Sea during a hurricane on 6 March 1883, but whether this is the part of the North Sea where that *Dove* sank is not certain. The wreck near here might well be a different *Dove*.

A wreck in 41 metres of water, approximately half a mile off Fast Castle, was dived in 2007. The position was estimated to be about 5556.390N, 0212.763W. This must be a fairly old wreck, as the hull is wooden with iron cladding. It is estimated to be 30–40 metres long. There is one boiler, and a triple expansion steam engine. The wreck is deeply embedded in the silty seabed, making it impossible to examine the propeller under the stern, but a spare four-bladed propeller is lying on the stern. An Admiralty pattern anchor is on the bow, with a further two smaller anchors on the stern. There is great amount of coal on and around the wreck. The identity of this wreck has not been established.

NYMPH

Wreck No: 31		Date Sunk: 18 December 1810
Latitude: 55 58 30 N PA		Longitude: 02 25 00 W PA
GPS Lat: 5558.500 N		GPS Long: 0225.000 W
Location: Torness		Area: Dunbar
Type: 5th rate man o' war		Tonnage: 937 bm
Length: 141.8 ft	Beam: 38.2 ft	Draught:
How Sunk: Ran aground		Depth:

PALLAS

Wreck No: 32		Date Sunk: 18 December 1810
Latitude: 55 59 30 N PA		Longitude: 02 27 00 W PA
GPS Lat: 5559.500 N		GPS Long: 0227.000 W
Location: Torness		Area: Dunbar
Type: 5th rate man of war		Tonnage: 667 bm
Length:	Beam:	Draught:
How sunk: Ran aground		Depth:

In December 1810 two Royal Navy frigates, the *Pallas* and the *Nymph*, were returning to Leith after a month's cruise off Norway. At about 9.00 a.m. on 17 December, as the *Pallas* approached the mainland, the weather came down and visibility dropped. She approached some fishing boats and was told that they were off Stonehaven. Sailing on southwesterly they saw a light, and thought it was the Arbroath Harbour light. Next they expected to see the floating light at the Bell Rock, south of Arbroath.

Captain George Moncke then recalculated his sailing times and speeds, and reckoned that they had in fact seen the Bell Rock light, and set course for the May Island, in the Firth of Forth – the next light on the route.

The captain had himself been on watch for five hours, so he went below at about 10 p.m. for a break, and to figure out again where they should be. After just a few minutes, the first officer reported that they had sighted the light on the May. As the captain made his way back to the deck, they ran aground. They found themselves driven repeatedly against rocks on a falling tide, and realised eventually that they were not on the Bell Rock, or the May Isle, but against the mainland, possibly in St Andrew's Bay.

In the morning light they discovered their true position, on the Lothian shore near Dunbar. The light they had thought was the May, was, in fact the light of a fire at a limekiln on the mainland. Strong swimmers amongst the crew tried to swim ashore, but several died. Small boats were used to lift the men off, but some capsized and men drowned.

That same night the *Nymph* also ran ashore nearby, Captain Edward Clay apparently also misled by irregularities in the lights at Bell Rock and the May. Two weeks earlier a French vessel, the *Aimable*, had run ashore at the same place, for the same reasons.

Presumably, the coal brazier light on the May had not been maintained – anyway, it was not seen. In 1810 the light at the Bell Rock was a floating light. There was also a floating bell, which tolled due to the action of the waves, and this is how Inchcape Rock came to be known as the Bell Rock.

The very next year, in 1811, Robert Stevenson, grandfather of the author Robert Louis Stevenson, completed the present 115-feet-high lighthouse on the Bell Rock. The first lighthouse in Scotland was constructed on the Isle of May in 1636. It was known as the Beacon, and its coal fire in a large iron basket on the flat roof, consumed from one ton of coal per night in the summer, to three tons per night during the longer winter nights. During the construction of the lighthouse, the architect was drowned in one of the sudden, unpredictable storms for which the Forth is notorious, and Eppie Laing, an Anstruther woman, was burned at the stake, having been accused of causing the storm by witchcraft!

The cost of operating that light was offset by taxes on vessels using the Forth ports. Foreign ships paid a tax twice the amount imposed on Scottish ships. Despite the Union of the Crowns in 1603, English ships were classed as foreign. (Scotland and England were separate countries until the Act of Union in 1707.) The present lighthouse, the Tower, was built in 1816. It shines out from 240 feet above sea level, and is visible for some 26 miles, emphasising the danger of the May to shipping. Many vessels have been lost both on its shoreline and in its vicinity. Wreckage from both wartime and peacetime shipping casualties is strewn around the island, especially among the shallows of the east coast, and some of the wreckage is visible on the shore.

Looking through old newspaper accounts of shipping casualties, storms feature repetitively as the major cause of shipwreckings. Apart from the wind, darkness and fog have been a fearsome combination. The May Island lighthouse keepers' reports frequently mention vessels running on to the May in fog and darkness, and that the light was not seen, and the foghorn was heard only once, or maybe twice, before the vessel struck.

For much of the maritime history of the Forth, there were no lighthouses, and furthermore, vessels were at the mercy of the wind, until the latter part of the 19th century, when sail started to give way to steam. More than 50% of the several hundred vessels lost in the Forth area during the past 150 years or so have been lost due to running aground. This has been by far the commonest cause of shipwrecks. (Some 500 were lost between the years 1850 and 1900 alone!)

The Beacon on the May Island

Earlier records are incomplete and elusive, but the very fact that the first lighthouse in Scotland was constructed on the May Island in 1636 suggests that even by then there must have been a sufficiently large number of losses to justify the establishment of that light.

The remains of this old lighthouse are still visible (Author's collection)

TEMPO ?

Wreck No: 33		Date Sunk: 3 December 1940
Latitude: 55 57 30 N PA		Longitude: 01 41 00 W PA
GPS Lat: 5557.500 N		GPS Long: 0141.000 W
Location: 15 miles E of St Abbs Head		Area: St Abbs
Type: Steamship		Tonnage: 629 grt
Length: 178.7 ft	Beam: 29.5 ft	Draught: 12.2 ft
How Sunk: By aircraft		Depth: 60 metres

The Norwegian steamship *Tempo* (ex-*Ingvar*, ex-*Tempo*, ex-*Borgvold*) was built in 1903 by P. Larsson of Thorskog, and registered in Oslo. She was en route from Gothenburg to Hull with a cargo of paper, when she was attacked by German aircraft on 3 February 1940, while on the Methil to Hull leg of the journey. *Lloyd's* give the position of attack as 555900N, 013500W. Five of her crew were lost. The survivors claimed that the German aircraft fired at the lifeboats.

Tempo's Captain Albert Knudsen said the attack by three large bombers occurred close to Longstone light, approximately 7–8 miles from the coast, while he was having his meal at around 10 o'clock that morning. He had initially planned to go to bed as he had been up all night, but had changed his mind, and this appears to have saved his life, because the bomb that sank *Tempo* went straight through his cabin. (The second mate and a helmsman were on the bridge at the time.) Hearing the sound of machine-gun fire, he ran out on deck, and when the aircraft returned, he and the others present, had to seek shelter in the chart house. During this second attack bombs were also dropped, one of which hit the aft end of the ship. As it was clear she would sink very quickly, both lifeboats were launched, the captain and eight men in one, the first mate and five men in the other.

The aircraft returned a third time. The captain believed at least four bombs were dropped altogether. He says the bombers came back twice after they had got in the lifeboats, one of them firing at them with machine guns from 200–300 meters above them, with the bullets hitting the water just a metre from the boats. When asked whether he thought it possible the Germans were unaware of the nationality of the ship (Norway was still neutral at that time), he said *Tempo* had clear nationality markings on her sides, in addition to the Norwegian flag flying aft, and the visibility was good. After circling them for about 20 minutes the bombers flew off and the lifeboats headed for land.

A boat containing the captain and some of the crew landed safely at Eyemouth, but another boat containing six crewmembers drifted further south and unfortunately ended up on the wrong side of the pier at Berwick-upon-Tweed. It hit the rocks and capsized before coming ashore. Four of the six were dead and a fifth died later in the Harbour Master's house. The only survivor from this boat was Able Seaman Olav Lillenes, who somehow managed to get to shore.

The wreck charted at 555730N, 014100W PA, 15 miles east of St Abbs Head, might be the *Tempo*.

UTOPIA

Wreck No: 34		Date Sunk: 10 August 1915
Latitude: 56 00 00 N PA		Longitude: 01 49 30 W PA
GPS Lat: 5600.000 N	**WGS84**	GPS Long: 0149.500 W
Location: 12 miles E of St Abbs Head		Area: St Abbs
Type: Steamship		Tonnage: 155 grt
Length: 100.6 ft	Beam: 19.8 ft	Draught: 10 ft
How Sunk: By submarine *U-17* – gunfire		Depth: 49 metres

The iron steamship *Utopia* was built by Mackie & Thomson, Glasgow in 1891. She was captured by a U-boat 12 miles east of St Abbs Head on 10 August 1915, and sunk by gunfire after *Utopia*'s crew were in their lifeboat.

Thirteen shells were fired at the *Utopia*, but the survivors did not see her sink due to a heavy rain storm and haze which obscured her from view. When they heard a heavy explosion in her direction at about 6.00 p.m., they were in no doubt that their vessel had sunk. After five hours in the lifeboat, the survivors were picked up by the Danish steamship, *Rodfare*, and taken to Leith.

The Hydrographic Department has recorded the *Utopia* at 555500N, 014700W PA, but no wreck is charted there. The nearest charted wreck is at 5555.017N, 0150.116W in about 73 metres depth.

SCOT

Wreck No: 35		Date Sunk: 23 April 1917
Latitude: 56 00 00 N PA		Longitude: 01 49 30 W PA
GPS Latitude: 5600.000 N	**WGS84**	GPS Longitude: 0149.500 W
Location: 12 miles E by N of St Abbs Head		Area: St Abbs
Type: Steamship		Tonnage: 1564 grt
Length: 252.1 ft	Beam: 36.4 ft	Draught: 18.3 ft
How Sunk: By submarine *UC-44* – gunfire		Depth: 49 metres

The Danish steamship *Scot* (ex-*Bangarth*) was built by Palmers Co. of Newcastle in 1895. En route from Copenhagen to Burntisland in ballast on 23 April 1917, she was captured by the *UC-44* about 12 miles E by N of St Abbs Head. Her crew were ordered to leave their ship, then the U-boat opened fire on the *Scot* with its deck gun, but the vessel did not sink. A party of Germans went across to the *Scot* in one of the Danish lifeboats and placed scuttling charges. When they were fired, the *Scot* sank.

Twelve miles E by N of St Abbs Head plots in 560000N, 014930W PA, and this is the charted position for the *Scot*. A wreck estimated at 70 metres long (231 feet) has been found at 5558.446N, 0154.052W. Could this be the *Scot*?

The Danish steamship Scot *(Courtesy of Kim Neilsen)*

ABERAVON

Wreck No: 36	Date Sunk: 5 February 1878
Latitude: 55 57 45 N PA	Longitude: 02 23 00 W PA
GPS Lat: 5557.750 N **WGS84**	GPS Long: 0223.000 W
Location: Thorntonloch, 2½ miles E of Dunbar	Area: Dunbar
Type: Steamship	Tonnage: 382 grt
Length: 197.5 ft Beam: 25.6 ft	Draught: 14.2 ft
How Sunk: Ran aground	Depth:

The iron steamship *Aberavon*, was en route from Middlesbrough to Grangemouth with a cargo of pig iron, when she ran aground at Thorntonloch, two and a half miles east of Dunbar on 5 February 1878, and became a total loss.

ANDROMEDA

Wreck No: 37	Date Sunk: 05 01 1911
Latitude: 55 57 45 N PA	Longitude: 02 23 00 W PA
GPS Lat: 5557.750 N **WGS84**	GPS Long: 0223.000 W
Location: Stranded at Longcraig	Area: Dunbar
Type: Schooner	Tonnage: 223 grt
Length: 109.3 ft Beam: 27.2 ft	Draught: 12 ft
How sunk: Ran aground	Depth:

The Russian three-masted wooden schooner *Andromeda* stranded at Longcraig on 5 January 1911 while en route from London to Bo'ness with a cargo of scrap iron. She was built at Riga in 1900.

KING JAJA

Wreck No: 38		Date Sunk: 13 October 1905
Latitude: 55 57 45 N PA		Longitude: 02 23 00 W PA
GPS Lat: 5557.750 N	**WGS84**	GPS Long: 0223.000 W
Location: Stranded at Longcraig		Area: Dunbar
Type: Steamship		Tonnage: 201 grt
Length: 125.3 ft	Beam: 19.8 ft	Draught: 9.3 ft
How sunk: Ran aground		Depth: 5 metres

On 14 October 1905 the Methil steamship *King Jaja*, bound from Newcastle to Methil with a cargo of steel rails, got into difficulties near Dunbar in a violent northerly gale, and was driven ashore. Dunbar lifeboat went to her assistance, but the *King Jaja* got off under her own steam. Later, however, she was driven ashore again, and the lifeboat put out a second time. This time, the *King Jaja*'s position was critical, and she could not be refloated. *King Jaja* was built in 1870 by J. & R. Swan of Glasgow.

PROSUM

Wreck No: 39		Date Sunk: 24 October 1908
Latitude: 55 57 45 N PA		Longitude: 02 23 00 W PA
GPS Lat: 5557.750 N	**WGS84**	GPS Long: 0223.000 W
Location: Longcraig Rocks, Thorntonloch		Area: Dunbar
Type: Steamship		Tonnage: 684 grt
Length: 200 ft	Beam:	Draught:
How Sunk: Ran aground		Depth: 5 metres

The steamship Prosum *aground (Courtesy of Dunbar Historical Society)*

The Prosum *broken in two (Courtesy of Dunbar Historical Society)*

The Norwegian iron steamship *Prosum* ran ashore at Longcraig, Thorntonloch, near Dunbar on 24 October 1908. She had been en route from London to Grangemouth, and broke in two after running on to the Bathe Reef.

It has been reported that only a winch assembly remains, but perhaps the diver who reported this merely failed to find other wreckage, of which there must be a substantial amount in the area, as quite a number of vessels have been lost here over the years.

A wreck charted at 555800N, 022200W PA, 0.8 miles off Thorntonloch, in about 11 metres depth might be remains of the *Prosum*.

LIVLIG

Wreck No: 40		Date Sunk: 6 March 1917
Latitude: 55 54 00 N PA		Longitude: 02 06 30 W PA
GPS Lat: 5554.000 N	**WGS84**	GPS Long: 0206.500 W
Location: ½ mile off St Abbs Head		Area: Dunbar
Type: Schooner		Tonnage: 277 grt
Length: 118.8 ft	Beam: 26.4 ft	Draught: 13.2 ft
How sunk: Foundered		Depth: 55 metres

The Norwegian wooden schooner *Livlig* (ex-*India*, ex-*Dos Hermanos*, ex-*India*) was built in 1872. She foundered in a gale "abreast St Abbs head, ½ mile offshore" on 6 March 1917, while en route from Langesund to Hartlepool with a cargo of pit props. One member of her crew was lost, but Eyemouth Lifeboat Coxswain William Miller was awarded the RNLI Bronze Medal for saving the rest of the crew of the *Livlig*, which was totally wrecked off St Abbs.

RIVER GARRY

Wreck No: 41		Date Sunk: 18 November 1893
Latitude: 55 59 51 N		Longitude: 02 24 57 W
GPS Lat: 5559.852 N	**WGS84**	GPS Long: 0224.955 W
Location: 1 mile N of Torness Power Station		Area: Dunbar
Type: Steamship		Tonnage: 1294 grt
Length: 240 ft	Beam: 33.2 ft	Draught: 18.2 ft
How Sunk: Foundered in hurricane		Depth: 30 metres

The steamship *River Garry* was built in 1883 by Workman Clark of Belfast. Her crew of 19 were all lost when she foundered in a force 12 NNE hurricane off Goatness Point, near Dunbar, on 18 November 1893 while en route from Leith to London with a cargo of coal. Her broken-up remains lie on a rock and shingle bottom at 26–30 metres. Her boilers stand up 6 metres, and at the bow the anchor winches can be seen, with the anchor chains running out over the seabed. The transits are the chimney on the left of Torness power station in line with a prominent house on the hillside behind, and Barns Ness lighthouse just touching the left of the tall building at the cement works. The wreck is sometimes buoyed.

DUNSCORE ?

Wreck No: 42		Date Sunk: 5 December 1934
Latitude: 55 58 12 N		Longitude: 02 01 06 W
GPS Lat: 5558.200 N	**WGS84**	GPS Long: 0201.100 W
Location: 5 miles ENE of St Abbs Head		Area: St Abbs
Type: Steamship		Tonnage: 176 grt
Length: 100 ft	Beam: 20.1 ft	Draught: 8.3 ft
How Sunk:		Depth: 74 metres

A wreck is charted in this position 5 miles ENE of St Abbs Head, and may be the *Dunscore*, a 176-grt iron-hulled steel-screw steamship built in 1898 by J. McArthur & Co., Paisley, engine by Bow, McLachlan & Co., Paisley. She foundered off St Abbs Head on 5 December 1934 while en route from Seaham to Fraserburgh with a cargo of coal. St Abbs Lifeboat rescued the crew of six men.

UNKNOWN

Wreck No: 43		Date Sunk:
Latitude: 55 56 43 N		Longitude: 02 03 21 W
GPS Lat: 5556.723 N	**WGS84**	GPS Long: 0203.349 W
Location: 4 ¼ miles N by E of Eyemouth		Area: St Abbs
Type:		Tonnage:
Length:	Beam:	Draught:
How Sunk:		Depth: 57–64 metres

An apparently intact and upright wreck has been found in the above position. It lies 000/180°, and is about 40 metres (132 feet) long by 15 metres (49.5 feet) beam, standing up 5 metres from the seabed. That beam dimension seems far too large for the length of the wreck, which is upright and apparently intact.

ECCLEFECHAN

Wreck No: 44		Date Sunk: 23 February 1900	
Latitude: 55 58 45 N PA		Longitude: 02 25 30 W PA	
GPS Lat: 5558.750 N	**WGS84**	GPS Long: 0225.500 W	
Location: Near Skateraw Rocks		Area: Dunbar	
Type: Barque		Tonnage: 2105 grt	
Length: 290.7 ft	Beam: 42.2 ft	Draught: 23.8 ft	
How Sunk: Ran aground		Depth: 8 metres	

The Glasgow-registered iron barque *Ecclefechan* was built by R. Duncan of Port Glasgow in 1882. She was lost near Skateraw Rocks on 23 February 1900 while en route from Chittagong to Dundee with a cargo of 3050 tons of jute. She ran aground while sailing under all sails. Captain G.E. Hind had probably neglected to take into account the setting of the tide, and had not established his position by sounding.

Ecclefechan breaking up (Author's collection)

MALABAR

Wreck No: 45		Date Sunk: 7 April 1920	
Latitude: 55 59 42 N PA		Longitude: 02 26 10 W PA	
GPS Lat: 5559.700 N	**WGS84**	GPS Long: 0226.170 W	
Location: ½ mile NE of Barns Ness		Area: Dunbar	
Type: Steamship		Tonnage: 1896 grt	
Length: 287.7 ft	Beam: 34.8 ft	Draught: 22.5 ft	
How Sunk: Ran aground		Depth:	

SS Malabar *aground off Barns Ness (Courtesy of Dunbar Historical Society)*

The iron steamship *Malabar* was built in 1877 by R. Dixon & Co. of Middlesbrough for the Zapata Steamship Co. of Newcastle. En route from Almeria to Leith with a cargo of esparto grass and silver lead on 7 April 1920, she reportedly struck a sunken wreck about six miles off Goatness. Leaking badly, she steered for the shore and ran aground on Goatness Point near Barns Ness Lighthouse, five miles east of Dunbar, at 11.00 p.m.

Skateraw lifeboat was launched and took off Captain G.W. Robinson and his 23 crew. The rescued men were landed at Dunbar, as sea conditions were too bad for the lifeboat to return to Skateraw. The stranded *Malabar* lay broadside to the shore, two cables out from the lighthouse. The tidal range here is 15 feet, and 2 feet of water covered her deck at high tide.

She broke amidships, her port fore bulwark was washed away and her tween deck bulkhead was badly crumpled. Some of her deck cargo was washed away. About 200 tons of silver lead was accessible at low water, but the rest would have to be recovered by divers. On 10 April 176 bars of lead were recovered, but during the night of 13 April the vessel collapsed and the after end broke up. Nevertheless, it was hoped that the recovery of the remaining lead cargo could resume later that day. Several reports were given in various editions of the *Haddingtonshire Courier*. The editions of 25 June 1920 and 27 August 1920 describe the position of loss as Goatness reef, off Barns Ness.

Ian Whittaker gives the position as 5559.250N, 0226.500W, ½ mile N of Barns Ness.

In 1959 HMS *Egeria* reported a wreck about two cables south-east of the Ruddystone, half a mile north-east of Barns Ness, and it is charted as WK PA. There is a considerable compass anomaly in this area, probably caused by the presence of a great amount of iron.

One transit given for this wreck is Barns Ness lighthouse in line with a conspicuous repeater tower on the hillside inland of the lighthouse. This must refer to the pylons on Blackcastle Hill. If that transit is correct, the wreck must lie slightly further west, at about 5559.700N, 0226.600W.

Boat-shaped lead ingots recovered from this wreck, strongly suggest that this is the *Malabar*.

GWENDOLINE

Wreck No: 46		Date Sunk: 17 November 1893
Latitude: 55 57 08 N		Longitude: 02 04 25 W
GPS Lat: 5557.129 N	**WGS84**	GPS Long: 0204.422 W
Location: 3 miles NE of St Abbs Head		Area: St Abbs
Type: Steamship		Tonnage: 525 grt
Length: 165 ft	Beam: 23.1 ft	Draught:
How Sunk: Foundered		Depth: 63–69 metres

The wreck at 555708N, 020425W was discovered in 2003. It is apparently an intact and upright vessel, oriented 120/300°, with the bows pointing towards the WSW. Least depth is 63 metres in a total depth of 69 metres. The dimensions of the wreck were estimated as 65 metres (214 feet) long by 30 metres (100 feet) wide. This is a very strange ratio of beam to length for a ship, which makes me wonder how reliable these dimensions are. A beam dimension of 30 metres is at least twice, or even three times, the width of any vessel known to have sunk in the area. Perhaps the width dimension includes a debris field or a net, or has simply been incorrectly recorded.

The Middlesbrough-registered iron steamship *Gwendoline* was built by Raylton Dixon of Middlesbrough in 1876 (Yard No. 129) for Swan & Co. She left Bo'ness on 17 November 1893, bound for Hull with a cargo of coal. She was never heard from again and was notionally presumed to have been lost off Bamburgh on 20 November.

In 2006 divers recovered the bell from the wreck three miles north-east of St Abbs Head, thereby enabling the wreck to be positively identified. *Gwendoline* was 50 metres long by 7 metres beam. A china plate bearing the company crest was also recovered. (Note the flag in the crest has an image of a swan.)

Plate recovered from the Gwendoline
(Courtesy of Dave Ward)

Close-up detail of plate from Gwendoline
(Courtesy of Dave Ward)

Verbormilia *on Hirst Rocks, 6 February 1940 (Courtesy of Dunbar Historical Society)*

VERBORMILIA

Wreck No: 47		Date Sunk: 6 February 1940
Latitude: 55 55 42 N PA		Longitude: 02 16 30 W PA
GPS Lat: 5555.700 N	**WGS84**	GPS Long: 0216.500 W
Location: Hirst Rocks, Redheugh		Area: St Abbs
Type: Steamship		Tonnage: 3275 grt
Length: 331.0 ft	Beam: 48.3 ft	Draught: 22.0 ft
How Sunk: Ran aground		Depth: 4–8 metres

The steamship *Verbormilia* ran aground in bad weather and was wrecked on Hirst Rocks, Redheugh, west of Fast Castle on 6 February 1940.

Eyemouth Lifeboat *Frank and William Oates* (ON795) was launched at 2330 hours into a southeasterly wind and choppy sea. There was dense fog, and the LSA team could not reach the stranded ship owing to snowdrifts. The *Verbormilia* had a crew of 31, and 25, including the Boatswain's wife, were taken off by the lifeboat. Six officers were taken off later in the morning, but Captain Humphries refused to leave. By the early afternoon on the seventh, seas were breaking over the wreck. Meanwhile, the lifeboat had landed the survivors and returned to the scene with two Admiralty Salvage Officers. Captain Humphries was finally persuaded to leave his ship, and the lifeboat returned to station at 1730 hours.

Verbormilia (ex-*Danubio*), built in 1907 by W. Gray & Co., Hartlepool, was the only ship owned by the *Verbormilia* Steamship Co. of London. The ship was gradually demolished by the Dunglass Salvage Co. of Dunbar, using their drifter *Jacob George*.

Tom Dykes of Redheugh farm, whose land borders the shore, saw the *Verbormilia* gradually diminishing as the salvage work progressed, and is of the opinion that there can be very little of the ship left, but divers have reported that there are still fairly substantial sections remaining in 4–8 metres of water.

UNKNOWN

Wreck No: 48		Date sunk:
Latitude: 56 00 30 N PA		Longitude: 02 13 00 W PA
GPS Lat: 5600.500 N	**WGS84**	GPS Long: 0213.000 W
Location: 6 miles N of St Abbs Head		Area: Dunbar
Type:		Tonnage:
Length:	Beam:	Draught:
How Sunk:		Depth: 60 metres

Charted as Wk PA in 60 metres. A small wreck about 25 metres long by 12 metres beam and 5 metres high, oriented 160/340° has since been found one and a half miles away at 5558.926N, 0212.640W. Is this and the next wreck one and the same?

UNKNOWN

Wreck No: 49		Date sunk: WWII?
Latitude: 56 01 42 N		Longitude: 02 12 00 W
GPS Lat: 5601.700 N	**WGS84**	GPS Long: 0212.000 W
Location: 7 miles NW of St Abbs Head		Area: Dunbar
Type:		Tonnage:
Length:	Beam:	Draught:
How sunk:		Depth: 62 metres

The wreck charted in 62 metres at 560200N, 021200W PA, seven miles north-west of St Abbs Head, was reported on 1 April 1945. It is thought to be an unknown Second World War loss.

In 1960 the position was established, apparently more accurately, as 560142N, 021200W, but the charted position has not been altered.

Interestingly, what seems to be a large wreck has been found not far away from the above two wrecks, at 5600.896N, 0214.577W. This wreck is apparently 100 metres long by 40 metres wide (330 feet by 132 feet) and is thought to be broken in two pieces. Dimensions obtained using side-scan sonar are notoriously unreliable. While the length dimension is credible, it may not be accurate, but the width dimension seems way too large.

CAPTAIN

Wreck No: 50		Date Sunk: 7 February 1933
Latitude: 56 02 46 N		Longitude: 02 07 02 W
GPS Lat: 5602.767 N	**WGS84**	GPS Long: 0207.027 W
Location: 7.8 miles N. of St Abbs Head		Area: Dunbar
Type: Steam trawler		Tonnage: 143 grt
Length: 100.3 ft	Beam: 20.1 ft	Draught: 11.3 ft
How Sunk: Foundered		Depth: 68–72 metres

The wreck in this position was reported to be 60 metres long by 5 metres wide and 3.5 metres high. Assuming these dimensions were accurate, they suggested the possibility that this might be a submarine.

The bell of the SS Captain *(Courtesy of Jim Macleod)*

When dived in October 2007, however, this was found to be the wreck of the Granton steam trawler *Captain*, which foundered on 7 February 1933. The wreck is upright and intact with a slight list to starboard, and lying 145/325°. It is 68 metres to the deck and 72 metres to the steel propeller. The steel trawler *Captain* was built by Hall Russell, Aberdeen in 1898 (Yard No. 308) for T.L. Devlin of Granton. She had a two-cylinder steam engine. She was requisitioned as a fishery reserve vessel in 1917, and was returned to Devlins in 1919. Devlins sold the *Captain* to another Granton owner, G.F. Liston, in 1926. On 7 February 1933 the *Captain* sprang a leak and foundered off St Abbs Head. Skipper Philip Liston and his eight crew took to the small boat. The crew rowed for six hours before being picked up by a local fishing yawl. The wreck was identified by the bell.

The reported length of 60 metres is twice the true length of this wreck – reinforcing my scepticism about dimensions estimated by side-scan sonar.

HALLAND

Wreck No: 51		Date Sunk: 15 September 1940
Latitude: 56 01 52 N		Longitude: 02 18 56 W
GPS Lat: 5601.864 N	**WGS84**	GPS Long: 0218.927 W
Location: 70°, 8 miles from Dunbar		Area: Dunbar
Type: Steamship		Tonnage: 1264 grt
Length: 238 ft	Beam: 37.2 ft	Draught: 13.7 ft
How Sunk: Bombed		Depth: 63 metres

The steamship *Halland* was built in 1923 by Howaldt, at Keil and registered in Copenhagen. After the German invasion of Denmark, the Halland was requisitioned by the Ministry of Transport for the duration of the hostilities and was attacked by aircraft eight miles off Dunbar while en route from London to Dundee with 1900 tons of cement. The vessel was badly hit and sank quickly. Seventeen of her crew of 22 were lost. The trawler *Sparta* took surviving crewmembers to Methil. Dunbar fishermen refer to this wreck as the *Congo*.

The Danish steamship Halland *(Courtesy of Kim Neilsen)*

The wreck was found in 1993, sitting upright and intact on the bottom. Least depth to the deck is 63 metres. The bridge plating had fallen away, and portholes were strewn around that area. The compass, crockery, and assorted bottles have been found, and the hold is full of cement. The emergency steering wheel still stood at the stern, and the stern and bridge area are very picturesque.

TRANSITS:

A The northern edge of Torness power station in line with the conspicuous radio mast on Cocklaw hill to the South West of Torness.

B Line up Barns Ness Lighthouse in line with the cement works chimney.

C Left-hand edge of the cement works in line with the chimney.

U-74

Wreck No: 52		Date Sunk: 16 May 1916
Latitude: 56 03 43 N		Longitude: 02 29 38 W
GPS Lat: 5603.731 N	**WGS84**	GPS Long: 0229.746 W
Location: 3½ miles, 200° to Dunbar		Area: Dunbar
Type: submarine		Tonnage: 755 grt
Length: 187.4 ft	Beam: 19.5 ft	Draught: 16.2 ft
How sunk:		Depth: 43 metres

The wreck charted at 560943W, 022938W, 3½ miles, 200° to Dunbar, was for many years thought to be the dredger *Cyclops*, which sank in 1924. The wreck was dived in

1990 by Gordon Wadsworth, who found that it was in fact a submarine. By a process of elimination, he concluded that it must be the First World War German U-boat *U-77*. He kept his discovery secret, and it was not until 1993 that local divers, thinking they were descending on the *Cyclops*, also found it to be the wreck of a submarine.

UE1-class minelaying U-boats, nicknamed *Children of Sorrow*, displaced 755 tons surfaced, 832 tons submerged. Only two torpedo tubes were fitted – one above the surfaced water line in the bow, offset to the port side, and one in the stern, offset to the starboard side, sited in the aft casing, also above the surfaced water line. These boats originally had an 88-mm deck gun but they were upgunned to the 105 mm. This gun was fitted on the deck aft of the conning tower.

Saddle tanks with fuel bunkers were fitted on each side, to give a range of 7880 miles at 7 knots. Two hinged masts were fitted to carry the radio aerial, which was strung between them in the raised position. The masts were both mounted offset to the port side, one mid-way between the conning tower and the bow, the other mid-way between the conning tower and the stern.

These boats had two propellers, each powered by a 450-hp Körting diesel engine and a 400-hp electric motor. The 34 mines were stored in a dry compartment inside the hull, near the stern, and were expelled by cog drive through two tubes one metre in diameter, located below the water line at the stern. As the mine storage compartment occupied the space where the engine room would normally have been located, the engines were moved forward to the centre of the boat.

The shape of the bows is similar to UE1-class U-boats. There is no net cutter, which is a feature shown on a drawing of the *U-75*, but not on others of the same class. The hydroplanes are rounded in shape – this is a feature peculiar to UE1-class U-boats – and there is only one torpedo tube built into the port side of the hull near the bow. There is no gun forward of the conning tower, but there is a gun on the aftercasing, behind the conning tower. There is no anchor in the traditional position on the bows. This is undoubtedly a UE1-class minelaying U-boat. Depth to the bottom at low water slack is 41.5 metres.

The wreck is sitting upright, settled into the mud with a slightly bow up attitude. The bows stick up about 3 metres from the bottom. The forward hydroplanes are clear of the seabed, and the central anchor position below the bows is just visible above the mud. The port side of the hull is intact, but the plating on the starboard side has gone. A torpedo is embedded in the mud just off the port side of the bow. The nose of the torpedo, with the detonator visible, protrudes from the mud. The conning tower area is a jumble of wreckage and pipes, and not recognisable as what may be expected of a "normal" conning tower. Two periscopes project up from the conning tower area, covered in dead mens fingers and anemones, like the rest of the wreck. Looking through the small viewing ports in the sides of the conning tower, the inside appears to still be dry.

A brass plate with German writing has been recovered from the remains of a wooden slatted walkway on the deck. I personally have not seen that plate, but I am told that the

U-75 *was another UE1–Class U-boat [note the net cutter] (Author's collection)*

writing translates as "Torpedo loading hatch." The forward escape hatch is closed, and the foremast lies on the seabed off the port side of the wreck. The winch for raising and lowering it is still on the forward casing, behind the torpedo tube. The tube is exposed with very little plating still remaining.

The deck gun is still in place behind the conning tower, but just aft of the gun, the hull of the U-boat disappears into the mud of the seabed. Although the outer hull cladding has rusted away leaving the pressure hull visible, the main section of the U-boat, from the bow to just behind the gun is visible and gives the impression of being intact as it goes into the soft mud. Whatever may be left of the hull seems to be completely buried just aft of the gun.

U-75 differed slightly from other UE-class boats in the shape of the bow, which was fitted with a net cutter, as shown in a sillhouette drawing of the *U-75* in Eberhard Rossler's book, *The U-Boat*, and also in the photograph above.

Four UE1-class U-boats were lost in the North Sea during the First World War:

U-74 (KL Erwin Weisbach) was thought to have been sunk by four trawlers off Aberdeenshire at 1255 hours on 27 May 1916, 25 miles south-east of Peterhead. This would suggest at about 571500N, 010900W, but the Hydrographic Deptartment gives the position as 5710N, 0120E. All 34 of her crew were lost.

The original log for the attack by the British auxiliary patrol vessels has not survived, neither has the war diary of the patrol section to which *Sea Ranger, Rodino Oku* and *Kimberley* were attached. This is not unusual. What has survived, however, is a report which was prepared for release to British newspapers. It is vague and not altogether convincing. It would appear to originate from an interview with the C.O. of the group on board the trawler *Sea Ranger:*

U-BOATS SUNK

Lieutn. Henry James Bray, D.S.O., R.N.R., described the fate of U 74 with 39 on board – on May 27, 1916, off the Aberdeenshire coast. He was in charge of H.M. trawler Sea Ranger, *having with him H.M. trawlers* Rodino, Oku *and* Kimberley. *The* Oku *closed with the submarine and fired at two and a-half miles range, the rest following. The fire of all four took effect. She replied with three shots.* Sea Ranger *and* Oku *attempted to ram her, but she sank and was destroyed. There were no survivors.*
Prize bounty of £195 awarded.

The attack began at 1230 GMT. A British auxiliary patrol group operating "one hundred miles seaward of Peterhead was alerted by smoke issuing from a submarine under sail'. One of *Sea Ranger's* shells struck the submarine, which returned fire. Numerous British shells apparently hit the submarine (which was described as having one gun forward and one aft). The auxiliary patrol was noted more for its enthusiasm than its skill. The crew were part time fishermen who trained only spasmodically. They were equipped with 6- or 12-pounder guns that could neither be trained nor elevated. However despite the submarine being (apparently) armed with 4.1-inch and 22-pounder guns, the trawlers were able to close sufficiently to pour in fire at point blank range.

The submarine attempted to dive to safety "only to rise to the surface with a heavy list and on an erratic course like some drunken thing." It dived for the last time at 1330 hours leaving only a trail of oil but no debris. Experience suggests that it is wise to be cautious, if not downright sceptical, about many of the sinking claims of the auxiliary patrol.

It does not take two weeks to carry out the mission she was assigned – *U-74* sailed on 13 May 1916. Nor was she required to sail as far north as 57°10'N or 57°15'N. Note also that published accounts of the action describe the submarine engaged by the trawlers as having two deck guns (one forward, one aft). *U-74* did not have a forward gun. It is therefore not hard to conclude that the attack by the trawlers was not against *U-74*, as the press release stated. The trawlers probably engaged some other submarine which was not sunk.

The attack seems to have taken place in the patrol area of *U-47*, which did have two guns, but Johannes Feldkirchner, her commander at that time, did not mention this attack in his patrol report.

U-75 (Fritz Schmolling) was mined in the North Sea, off Terschelling at 2225 hours on 14 December 1917 while departing on patrol. Schmolling and seven men were rescued by the German steamer *Nordstern*. The remaining 23 of her 31 crew were lost. The Hydrographic Department gives the position as 5359N, 0524E.

U-77 (Erich Gunzel) was lost in the North Sea on 7 July 1916. She left Heligoland on 5 July to lay mines off Kinnaird Head, near Fraserburgh, and mines, which could only have come from the *U-77*, were found and recovered in that area two days later. After setting out on her mission neither she nor any of her 33 crew was ever heard from again.

Her orders also clearly stated: "Kein Handelskrieg" – no warfare against merchant shipping. This must have referred to attacks on merchant ships with torpedoes or gunfire, and was probably to avoid disclosing her presence, and therefore the possible location of her mines. But the mines she laid would not be able to differentiate between naval and merchant ships.

U-77 was thought to have been sunk on 7 July 1916 when rammed by a trawler, but no British trawler was reported sunk, or even damaged that day! She was also said to have been sunk by gunfire from HM trawlers on 7 July 1916 at 5800N, 0300W PA, which is in the Moray Firth. All 33 aboard were lost. Another suggestion is that she was possibly sunk by the trawler *Albatross*, or her own mines.

As *U-77* left Heligoland on 5 July 1916 to lay mines off Kinnaird Head, she cannot have been the U-boat claimed to have been sunk by trawlers in that area on 27 May.

Reliable sources indicate that at least some mines were swept up near Kinnaird Head. At this point, she should be regarded as missing. It is possible she was lost in a mine-handling accident like *U-74* and may be found near Kinnaird Head. It is also possible that she was lost in a diving accident or through some other operational cause, or that she hit a mine near the German coast.

U-78 (Johann Vollbrecht) was torpedoed by HM submarine *G2* (Lt. H.N. Lake) in the Skagerrak at 0230 hours on 28 October 1918. The crew of 40 were all lost. The Admiralty Hydrographic Department gives the position as either 5225N, 0225E or 5602N, 0508E.

One individual claimed to have found the stern section of *U-74*, but no other diver has found the stern section, either by accident, or by making a deliberate search for it, although several have tried. He said, in 1999, that he had dived the U-boat many times during the previous five years, and had found the stern section by accident when looking for *U-77* (as he thought at the time) in 1998. He suspected it could be the wreck mentioned in *Dive Scotland Volume III*, Wreck No. 1567, recorded at 560342N, 022936W, which is approximately where he said he found it.

After locating it with a magnetometer, he said he hooked into it using a grappling hook. Once down on the muddy seabed, he says he found the exploded, or imploded, remains of the stern section, which was roughly about the size of a large coach, with two large propellers and the rudder attached. Immediately by the cut off point of the wreckage is what appeared to be parts of an exploded mine – a heavy chain secured to the seabed and fragments of metal dissimilar to that of the U-boat. The remains allegedly stand about one metre clear of the seabed, with no identification markings. He described it as a large section of the hull, with the shattered remains of a diesel engine inside.

He said the stern section is lying south-west of the bow and is in the same sort of condition as the bow section. He tried to reach the stern section from the bow section by reeling off a line from the conning tower, but although his line was more than 60 metres long, he still had no sight of the stern section.

This diver claimed that "the extreme stern of this submarine's wreck lies a distance from the rest of the boat, the starboard mine-chute is open. There is the possibility that one of her mines fouled a propeller, because a chain is wrapped around one of them and the mine may have struck the boat and exploded."

He went on to say: " … the location must obviously be known to locals, as there are many articles of fishing tackle snagged on this part, as on the bow. [Note there is no fishing gear on the bow!] The forward part of the wreckage itself is given as position 5603.66N, 0229.95W very close to the wreck of the dredger *Cyclops* at 5603.44N, 0232.35W. [Note these positions are actually 1.43 nm apart!] It is sitting upright though it is slowly sinking into the mud over the last few years. The bow is still clear of the seabed and the torpedo tubes are closed, as was the escape hatch. There is a gun on the deck, still loaded with live shells, and also there may be mines on board as this was a mine-laying submarine. [Note there is no shell in the gun, and any mines would be in the stern section.] A brass compass together with other navigational aids and a few small portholes adorned the conning tower. They may still be there because people treat it as a war grave. I have not found any markings on the hydroplane grease points, propellers or shafts, to confirm that this is in fact U-77."

According to this diver, "… the forward part of the wreckage lies at GPS 5603.660N, 0229.950W. The stern section, which appears to have been blown off, probably in an explosion with her own mines, apparently lies about 100 yards SW of the forward section at about 560340N, 022903W – GPS 5603.633N, 0229.133W"

The position he gave for the forward section is slightly out. It actually lies at 560343N, 022943W. The exact position over the conning tower is 5603.731N, 00229.746W (WGS84). The approximate position he gave for the stern section is not 100 yards SW of the forward section, as described above, but is actually 0.356 nm, 105° (True), or 721 yards E by S ¼ S from the forward section.

After breaking in two, neither section of the U-boat would be capable of propelling or manoeuvring itself. In all probability the entire crew would be killed instantly. Buoyancy would immediately be lost, and both parts would sink to the seabed. Logically, therefore, both parts must be very close to each other.

The wreck is frequently visited by many divers, and I find it hard to believe that after many years of trying, no-one else would find this alleged stern section – if it existed. Many echo-sounder searches have been made, carefully "mowing the lawn" around the bow section, but with no trace of any other wreckage in the vicinity for quite a distance in all directions. Side-scan sonar searches show that there is nothing but flat mud for a wide area around the bow section of the wreck, and magnetometer searches also fail to detect any other nearby wreckage. Those who have searched are confident that if it existed, they would have found it, and are left with the belief that the stern section must simply be buried, still attached to the forward section. This opinion is supported by a magnetometer reading which suggests the entire submarine is there, and shining a torch obliquely across the seabed aft of the gun reveals an indentation pattern in the mud where the after section of the submarine has sunk into it.

The wreck was believed to be that of the Imperial U-boat *U-77*, until details of her patrol were ascertained in 2004. Although nothing has been recovered from the wreck to enable a positive identification to date (November 2008), it now seems certain that this is the remains of Erwin Weisbach's boat, *U-74*. Kplt. Erwin Weisbach took command on 24 November 1915, and *U-74* was formally allocated to the Germany-based 1 U-Flottille at Brunsbüttel on 18 March 1916. There were numerous failures and delays before her first operational patrol, but *U-74* finally sailed from Germany on 25 March 1916 and laid mines in the Firth of Forth area, then returned to Heligoland on 4 April 1916.

The steamship *Sabbia* detonated one of the mines and sank off the May Island on 20 April 1916 when she was en route from Burntisland to London with a cargo of coal. On 13 May *U-74* left Heligoland on a second mission to lay more mines off the Forth.

The evidence is overwhelming that the UEI-class wreck off Dunbar is undoubtedly that of *U-74*, not *U-77*. The German naval archives survived the Second World War and were captured by the Allies. Many files, including those on *U-74* and *U-77*, were micro-filmed. Copies of these microfilms are available from the U.S. National Archives and Records Administration. The files contain the Kriegstagebücher (KTBs) – war diaries, or what would commonly be called "logs" – of both boats before their final missions, along with copies of the orders the two submarines received for their last patrols. (The KTB for *U-74*'s first patrol of 25 March–4 April 1916 to the Firth of Forth is in there. *U-74* was lost on her second patrol. *U-77* was lost on her first patrol.)

U-74 was to lay mines in the Firth of Forth. *U-77* was to lay mines off Kinnaird Head. In both cases, these respective locations were the only place authorized for minelaying. Just as significantly, both boats were ordered to return home after laying their mines. Neither was authorized to engage in "Handelskrieg", i.e. to operate against merchant shipping, which would have given them wider latitude as to where they could operate after dropping their mines. *U-74* was also lost well before 27 May 1916 – probably about the 16th.

While some unknown mechanical or drill failure may have contributed to the loss of *U-74*, the immediate cause of loss is assumed to be the explosion of one of her own mines. Another possible cause for her loss was that an internal explosion of her own mines took place, as the crew prepared them for release.

There is evidence that *U-77* was sent to the Kinnaird Head area, but there is no evidence that she was ever sent to the Forth area. Similarly, there is evidence that *U-74* was sent to the Forth (twice), but no evidence that she was ever sent to the Kinnaird Head area. According to Paul Kemp in *U-boats Destroyed*, *U-74* had been ordered to lay a minefield off Rosyth as part of German plans for preliminary moves for a sortie by the High Seas Fleet (which would culminate in the battle of Jutland), and the UEI wreck off Dunbar is within *U-74*'s assigned minelaying area.

Diving the wreck should only be attempted at slack water, and a good look-out kept for shipping traffic. The transits for this wreck are the left edge of the centre tower of Tantallon Castle in line with the stone cross of St.Baldred's Boat, and a small wood its own width to the left of the cement works chimney near Dunbar.

LETTIE

Wreck No: 53		Date Sunk: 9 November 1941	
Latitude: 55 55 00 N PA		Longitude: 02 00 00 W PA	
GPS Lat: 5555.000 N		GPS Long: 0200.000 W	
Location: Off St Abbs Head		Area: St Abbs	
Type: Tug		Tonnage: 89 grt	
Length:	Beam:	Draught:	
How Sunk:		Depth:	

British Vessels Lost at Sea 1939–45 states HM tug Lettie was sunk, cause unknown, off St Abbs Head on 9 November 1941. She has also been described as an auxiliary patrol vessel.

OCEAN GLEANER

Wreck No: 54		Date Sunk: 12 November 1976	
Latitude: 56 00 24 N		Longitude: 02 30 30 W	
GPS Lat: 5600.400 N		GPS Long: 0230.500 W	
Location: 3 cables E of Dunbar harbour		Area: Dunbar	
Type: MFV		Tonnage:	
Length:	Beam:	Draught:	
How Sunk: Ran aground		Depth: 12 metres	

The wreck of the steel MFV Ocean Gleaner lies in about 40 feet of water, 3 cables east of the old entrance to Dunbar harbour, 2° off north of the flagstaff at Dunbar East golf clubhouse.

The wreck lies in a gully between rocks, which might make it a difficult echo sounder target. The bows of the vessel are apparently missing, but perhaps they are lying in another gully nearby.

SABBIA

Wreck No: 55		Date Sunk: 20 April 1916	
Latitude: 56 03 34 N		Longitude: 02 17 05 W	
GPS Lat: 5603.560 N	WGS84	GPS Long: 0217.090 W	
Location: 10 miles SE of May Island		Area: Dunbar	
Type: Steamship		Tonnage: 2807 grt	
Length: 314.6 ft	Beam: 46.8 ft	Draught: 13.7 ft	
How Sunk: Mined		Depth: 55 metres	

The steel steamship *Sabbia* was built in 1908 by Clyde SB, Port Glasgow (Yard No. 280) for Nav Libera-Triestina SA, Trieste, which was at that time part of Austria-Hungary. Trieste became part of Italy in 1918. In August 1914 the *Sabbia* was at Newcastle-upon-Tyne, and was one of 34 enemy steamers detained in United Kingdom ports on the outbreak of the First World War. The Admiralty intended to use these ships in the east coast coal trade to relieve a shortage of tonnage available to supply coal to London. Some of the gas companies had supplies for only 10 days, and additional steamers were badly needed. *Sabbia* was therefore requisitioned by the Admiralty for use as a collier. On 20 April 1916, while en route from Burntisland to London with a cargo of coal, she hit one of 34 mines laid by *U-74* (Weisbach), and sank. The survivors were picked up by the Dutch steamship *Noord Holland*, 15 minutes after abandoning their ship, and were landed at North Shields.

Lloyd's World War One Losses gives the position as 5607N, 0218W, while *British Vessels Lost at Sea 1914–18* describes the position for the loss as 7 miles SE by S from the May Island (i.e. 145° from the May Island).

An unknown wreck was reported on 24 March 1919 at 560310N, 021650W PA, 8 miles, 70° from Dunbar. Local fishermen found the wreck about 800 metres to the NW at 5603.560N, 0217.090W. The wreck lies north of the *Halland* in 55 metres to the seabed. Her bow points north, but is flattened, with a huge anchor and two large winches. The holds are on an even keel, and contain the cargo of coal, The midships section is twisted and listing to starboard. About 10 metres aft of the bridge area the hull seems to have been bent to starboard, at about 60° to the main body of the wreck. The bend area is the highest part of the wreck, rising 7 metres above the seabed. There is one boiler, lying transverse to the line of the ship. The stern is intact, and almost upright, but split from the main part of the wreck. It rises to 46 metres, and contains a spare propeller. Trawls are draped around the highest parts of the wreck.

CYCLOPS

Wreck No: 56		Date sunk: 21 February 1924
Latitude: 56 03 28.1 N		Longitude: 02 32 04.2 W
GPS Lat: 5603.461 N	**WGS84**	GPS Long: 0232.148 W
Location: 3 ½ miles NNE of Dunbar		Area: Dunbar
Type: Dredger		Tonnage:
Length: 180 ft	Beam: 25 ft	Draught: 7 ft
How Sunk: Foundered		Depth: 42 metres

The dumb dredger *Cyclops* (i.e. with no means of self-propulsion) capsized on 21 February 1924 while under tow by the tug Sunderland from Queensferry to Sunderland to be scrapped. She floated for a couple of hours before sinking, and is now lying almost upside down, in a rather broken condition in about 41 metres, standing up 5–6 metres from the bottom, and lying NNE/SSW. Her bucket and gantry system are clearly visible.

The position given in 1924 was 560415N, 023330W, about 2.8 miles, 96° from Bass Rock light. This position is somewhat inaccurate, and the wreck charted at 560343N, 022938W, 3½ miles NNE of Dunbar, was assumed to be the *Cyclops*. It is now known, however, that this is a First World War U-boat. In 1993 an East Lothian diver, who thought he was descending on the *Cyclops*, must have been very surprised to find a submarine on the bottom. The *Cyclops* is 1¾ miles west of the U-boat, at 5603.468N, 0232.067W (OSGB36). One of the transits for this wreck is the left edge of Tantallon Castle in line with St.Baldred's Boat. The other transit is a prominent grey building on the shore immediately west of Dunbar, midway between two pylons situated further inland.

UNKNOWN – WW2 ? OR SCOTIA ?

Wreck No: 57		Date Sunk: Pre–April 1945
Latitude: 56 03 00 N PA		Longitude: 02 20 54 W PA
GPS Lat: 5603.900 N		GPS Long: 0220.900 W
Location: 5½ miles NW of Barns Ness		Area: Dunbar
Type:		Tonnage:
Length:	Beam:	Draught:
How sunk:		Depth: 50 metres

An unknown Second World War wreck is thought to lie in this position. One possibility is that this may be the 50-ton iron dredger *Scotia* which foundered about seven miles off Dunbar on 21 September 1893 while en route from Eyemouth to Granton in a force 6 northeasterly. The *Scotia* was a dumb vessel – i.e. she had no means of self-propulsion.

The wreck here stands three metres up from the bottom, and was first reported on 7 April 1945 at 560400N, 022100W PA. In 1960 the position was given as 560354N, 022054W. In fact there may not be a wreck here at all, as it has been established that there is a big rock at 5603.993N, 0221.129W.

CRADOCK

Wreck No: 58		Date Sunk: 8 November 1941
Latitude: 56 05 00 N PA		Longitude: 02 00 00 W PA
GPS Lat: 5605.000 N		GPS Long: 0200.000 W
Location: 11 miles NNE of St Abbs Head		Area: Dunbar
Type: Trawler		Tonnage: 204 grt
Length: 115.4 ft	Beam: 22.2 ft	Draught: 12.1 ft
How Sunk: Bombed		Depth: 55 metres

The steam trawler *William Chalmers* was built in 1919 by Hawthorns & Co. of Leith (Yard No. 170, "Strath" class) for The Admiralty. As the First World War had ended by the time she was launched in January 1919, she was surplus to the Admiralty's requirements, and was sold to L.C. Cockrell of Wivenhoe, who renamed her *Cradock* (H14). The *Cradock* was registered in Lowestoft (LT591) in December 1919, but fished from Milford Haven between the years 1921–1938. Although she changed hands several times during her fishing career, her name remained *Cradock*. In December 1933 she was sold to Shields Engineering & Dry Dock Co. Ltd., North Shields and registered at Shields as SN8. She was bombed and machine-gunned by a German Ju-88 aircraft at 1830 hours on 8 November 1941.

British Vessels Lost at Sea 1939-1945 gives the position of attack as 14 miles NE of St Abbs Head. According to *Lloyd's* she was abandoned 12 miles NE of St Abbs Head and is presumed to have sunk. The nine crewmen were all saved.

The sinking position was estimated at 560500N, 020000W PA, 11 miles NNE of St Abbs Head, but a wreck found two miles further north at 5607.965N, 0200.433W was assumed to be the *Cradock*. This wreck was finally dived in April 2008, and found to be the steamship *Boyne Castle*. One of the two steam trawlers that have not yet been positively identified (see wrecks 59 and 60) might be the *Cradock*.

UNKNOWN STEAM TRAWLER 1

Wreck No: 59	Date Sunk:
Latitude: 56 05 20 N	Longitude: 02 24 53 W
GPS Lat: 5605.333 N	GPS Long: 0224.883 W
Location: 6 miles NE of Dunbar	Area: Dunbar
Type: Steam trawler	Tonnage:
Length: Beam:	Draught:
How Sunk:	Depth: 47 metres

The wreck in this position is 100 feet long. When dived in June 2003 it was found to be a steam trawler, intact and upright, oriented 170/350°. The bow lies pointing almost due south. Depth to the seabed is 50 metres, and the wreck rises three metres up from the bottom.

On 1 January 1928 the Leith-registered steam trawler *Eber* sprang a leak in heavy weather and foundered about 16 miles north of St Abbs Head. The crew of seven took to their little boat, and after being buffeted for about two hours, were picked up in an exhausted condition by a passing steamer inward bound to the Forth. The unidentified steam trawler found at 5605.333N, 0224.883W is 15 miles north of St Abbs Head, and may perhaps be the *Eber*.

UNKNOWN STEAM TRAWLER 2

Wreck No: 60	Date Sunk:
Latitude: 56 06 12 N	Longitude: 02 25 18 W
GPS Lat: 5606.217 N	GPS Long: 0225.300 W
Location: 6.8 miles NNE of Dunbar	Area: Dunbar
Type: Steam Trawler	Tonnage:
Length: Beam:	Draught:
How Sunk:	Depth: 46 metres

An unidentified wreck found in 1968 at 560600N, 022500W PA, was thought to originate from the Second World War. A more accurate position has since been established and the wreck is now charted at 560612N, 022518W, 6¼ miles, 150° from the May Island.

In 1977 it was reported that the least depth of this wreck was 45.6 metres in a general depth of 47 metres. Height of the wreck was 2.5 metres, length 30 metres, lying 000/180°. A magnetometer survey appeared to indicate that there is only about 50 tons of metal here, suggesting that the wreck may possibly be a fishing vessel. In 2003 the wreck was dived by Martin Sinclair, who confirmed that it is the wreck of a steam trawler. The wreck is intact, and sitting upright, with the bows pointing south.

MORESBY ?

Wreck No: 61	Date Sunk: Pre-1919
Latitude: 56 06 01 N	Longitude: 02 31 07 W
GPS Lat: 5606.020 N	GPS Long: 0231.120 W
Location: 4 miles E of Bass Rock	Area: Dunbar
Type: Steamship	Tonnage:
Length: Beam:	Draught:
How Sunk:	Depth: 40 metres

On 24 March 1919 the Senior Naval Officer at Granton reported that the wreck of a vessel named *Moresby* was in this position. A wreck is charted at 5606.062N, 0231.211W (WGS84), but no wreck has been found here, and no information has come to light about any vessel named *Moresby* sinking here.

BELLAX

Wreck No: 62	Date Sunk: 10 February 1917
Latitude: 56 06 00 N PA	Longitude: 02 18 00 W PA
GPS Lat: 5606.000 N	GPS Long: 0218.000 W
Location: 10 miles SE of May Island	Area: Dunbar
Type : Steamship	Tonnage: 1107 grt
Length: 227.4 ft Beam: 36.6 ft	Draught: 15.7 ft
How Sunk: By submarine *UB-22*	Depth:

The Norwegian wooden steamship *Bellax* (ex-*Adjutor*) was built in 1914 by Akers MV of Kristiania. While en route from Frederikstad to Havre with a cargo of timber she was reportedly sunk by a U-boat 10 miles south-east of the May Island on 10 February 1917.

This suggests an approximate position for the attack as 560600N, 021800W, but there is reason to be wary of the position description "10 miles South East of May Island," as according to a Norwegian source, the *Bellax* was intercepted and blown up by the German submarine *UB-22*, 150 miles south-west of Lister, while en route from Fredrikstad to Le Havre loaded with timber. This would place the sinking at about 5610N, 0412E, 225 miles east of May Island, in the middle of the North Sea, half way to Denmark!

UNKNOWN

Wreck No: 63		Date Sunk:
Latitude: 56 09 00 N		Longitude: 02 10 49 W
GPS Lat: 5609.000 N		GPS Long: 0210.822 W
Location: 14 miles N of St Abbs Head		Area: Dunbar
Type:		Tonnage:
Length:	Beam:	Draught:
How Sunk:		Depth: 53–58 metres

The wreck here was found in 1979. It is reported to be 30 metres long by 12 metres wide and standing up 5 metres high. It is considered to be an upright, intact wreck lying 075/255°, with its bows pointing towards the SSW. This is 14 miles, 52° from Dunbar, and 14 miles north of St Abbs Head.

I am more than a little suspicious about the supposed dimensions of this wreck. It seems most unlikely that a ship 100 feet long would have a beam of 40 feet. These figures seem disproportionate. A length of 100 feet might indicate that this wreck could be another lost trawler – but not with a beam of 40 feet. It is possible that neither of the alleged dimensions is correct. One might be too low and the other too high.

UNKNOWN

Wreck No: 64		Date Sunk:
Latitude: 55 58 56 N		Longitude: 02 12 38 W
GPS Lat: 5558.926 N		GPS Long: 0212.640 W
Location: 4.7 miles NW by N from St Abbs Head		Area: Dunbar
Type:		Tonnage:
Length:	Beam:	Draught:
How Sunk:		Depth: 58–63 metres

An unidentified wreck 25 metres long by 12 metres beam and standing up 5 metres from the seabed has been found in this position, which is 10.3 miles, 99° from Dunbar, or 4.7 miles, 328° from St Abbs Head. The wreck is apparently intact, and is oriented 160/340°.

PATHFINDER

Wreck No: 65		Date Sunk: 5 September 1914
Latitude: 56 07 18 N		Longitude: 02 09 20 W
GPS Lat: 5607.094 N		GPS Long: 0210.049 W
Location: 14 miles ESE of May Island		Area: Dunbar
Type: Light Cruiser		Tonnage: 2940 grt
Length: 379 ft	Beam: 38.5 ft	Draught: 13 ft
How Sunk: Torpedoed by *U-21*		Depth: 55–65 metres

HMS Pathfinder *(Author's collection)*

The light cruiser HMS *Pathfinder* was built by Cammell Laird of Birkenhead in 1904. At the outbreak of the First World War in 1914 she was leader of the 8th Flotilla, which consisted of 20 destroyers and 12 torpedo boats. The duty assigned to the Flotilla was to patrol the entrance to the Firth of Forth. The outer line from St Abbs Head – Bass Rock – May Island was patrolled by *Pathfinder*, the inner line by the destroyers and torpedo boats. At her full speed of 25 knots, *Pathfinder* burned an excessive amount of coal, and her bunker capacity was small. In order to maintain her patrol for five days a week, and have full speed available at ten minutes' notice, she could only steam at six knots while on patrol.

On the fine sunny afternoon of Saturday, 5 September 1914 a torpedo track was sighted off the starboard bow at a range of 2000–3000 yards. The Officer of the Watch, Lt. Cdr. Favell, rang down for the starboard engine to be put astern, and the port engine full ahead, while the wheel was turned in attempt to turn towards the torpedo track. At only six knots, however, the ship barely had steerage way, and at approximately 1550 hours, the torpedo hit the starboard side of *Pathfinder* under her bridge. The torpedo explosion sparked off the cruiser's forward magazine, blowing off her bows. Most of the ship forward of the bridge was blown off, and as the majority of the crew were below decks in that area at the time, they must all have been killed outright.

The forward part of the ship was well down. The foremast and No. 1 funnel had gone. Water was washing around the base of No. 2 funnel, which was badly holed, and there was a great amount of black smoke and burnt cordite smoke over the ship.

The Captain was not sure if the explosion had been seen by those on the May Island, 17 miles to the north-west, and ordered a blank round to be fired from one of the ship's after 4-inch guns. The gun support must have been weakened by the torpedo/magazine explosion, because when the gun was fired the mounting carried away, and the gun careered around the quarterdeck till it fetched up in the after screen and quietly dropped over the side.

The ship hardly listed at all. After a few minutes, the bulkheads carried away, and the ship gave a heavy lurch, and took an angle of about 40° down by the head. The ship settled down slowly at first, but the speed of sinking rapidly increased as more bulkheads collapsed, until only the stern was sticking out of the water at an angle of about 60°, before it finally disappeared beneath the surface.

The survivors could not see the nearest land from water level, but at 1715 hours, two destroyers, the *Stag* and the *Express*, which had headed for the pall of smoke, arrived and picked up most of those who still remained alive. A few others were picked up by two torpedo boats and local fishing vessels which had also headed to the scene. One of the crew described how, after he had been blown into the water, he reached out to grasp a rope, only to discover that the "rope" was actually human intestines.

The torpedo had been fired by the *U-21* (KL Otto Hersing) and *Pathfinder* sank in four minutes with the loss of 259 of the 268 crew. She was the first warship ever to be sunk by a torpedo fired from a submarine.

The 1919 report gave the approximate position as 560800N, 020500W, but the wreck charted at 560718N, 020920W is known to local fishermen as the *Pathfinder*. WGS84 5607.290N, 00209.483W or 5607.350N, 0209.267W.

As a direct result of this disaster to the *Pathfinder*, Royal Navy ships were henceforth ordered to maintain a speed of at least 15 knots while on patrol, so that they never lost the ability to steer.

The first merchantman sunk by a submarine (but not by torpedoing), was the British steamship *Glitra* (ex-*Saxon Prince*), 866 grt, 215 × 31 × 14 ft, built in 1895 by R. & W. Haw-

HMS Pathfinder *sinking (Author's collection)*

thorn of Newcastle, and belonging to Christian Salvesen of Leith. On 20 October 1914, while en route from Grangemouth to Stavanger and awaiting a pilot 14 miles WSW of Skudesnes, she was captured by the *U-17* (KL Johannes Feldkirchner), who appeared on the surface.

In strict accordance with the prize rules, the crew were given ten minutes to leave the ship before she was scuttled by the Germans after the *Glitra*'s crew were safely in their lifeboats. It was not until 30 January 1915 that the *Tokomaru* (British, despite her Japanese name) became the first merchantman to be sunk by a torpedo fired by a submarine. (That was in the English Channel.) Interestingly, that submarine was the *U-20*, commanded by KL Otto Schweiger who, five months later, gained everlasting notoriety by torpedoing the *Lusitania* off the south of Ireland.

Hersing's action in sinking the *Pathfinder* was later credited to a German agent, Carl Hans Lody who was spying on the British fleet in the Firth of Forth. Lody sent a telegram to his contact in Stockholm with the coded message that several large warships were leaving Rosyth. The light cruiser was intercepted by *U-21*, and 256 of her crew were killed. Lody, using a false American passport and calling himself Charles Inglis, was arrested by Scotland Yard on 2 October 1914. He denied spying, but his overcoat carried the mark of a Berlin tailor and the name "C.H. Lody" was sewn inside. Carl Hans Lody was found guilty of treason and executed by firing squad on 6 November 1914 in the Tower of London.

The wreck of the *Pathfinder* is lying on an even keel at about 55 metres. The bow is missing, and the decking has mostly rotted away, but at least five of the ship's nine 4-inch guns are still in place, one of them lying on its side. She was originally armed with 10 × 12-pounder QF[1], 8 × 3-pounder QF and 2 × 18-inch TT[2] but not long after completion two additional 12-pounder guns were added and the 3-pounder guns were replaced with 6 × 6-pounders. In 1911–12 she was rearmed with 9 × 4-inch guns. Shells are still stacked next to the guns and shell casings are strewn about. Lots of portholes are visible. The stern of the ship is intact with the propellers visible at 65 metres. Underwater visibility is around 10 metres, although a bit dark. The wreck is home to many lobsters and wolfish, and a trawl net is snagged on the forward section of the wreck, but it is not considered to pose a problem to divers.

BOYNE CASTLE

Wreck No: 66		Date Sunk: 7 February 1917	
Latitude: 56 07 58 N		Longitude: 02 00 26 W	
GPS Lat: 5607.965 N		GPS Long: 0200.433 W	
Location: 14 miles N by E of St Abbs Head		Area: Dunbar	
Type: Steamship		Tonnage: 245 grt	
Length: 118.8 ft	Beam: 23.1 ft	Draught: 6.6 ft	
How Sunk: By *UB-22* - gunfire		Depth: 47–53 metres	

The steamship *Boyne Castle* was en route from Macduff to Sunderland in ballast on 7 February 1917. At 9.50 a.m. a submarine was sighted about two miles on the starboard

1   QF – quick firing
2   TT – torpedo tubes

beam. The submarine submerged, but resurfaced much closer ten minutes later, and opened fire on the *Boyne Castle*. The fourth shell hit the ship. Her engine was stopped and the crew abandoned ship, which was now listing to port. The enemy then boarded the steamship, using one of the ship's boats and made the Chief Engineer open the seacocks. After firing two more shells into her water line, the submarine made off. The survivors made sail for land, but were picked up at 3.00 p.m. by a patrol vessel and landed at Granton.

The position of sinking was recorded as 12 miles N by E of St Abbs Head, which plots at 560700N, 020900W PA, and there are several unknown wrecks charted within a few miles of that position. The nearest charted wreck is less than half a mile away at 560718N, 020920W, but this is the *Pathfinder*. It had been assumed that the wreck at 5607.965N, 0200.433W was the steam trawler *Cradock*, which was lost after being attacked by a German aircraft in 1941. The wreck had never been dived until Marine Quest of Eyemouth took a party of divers to the wreck in their dive boat *North Star* at the beginning of May 2008.

The bell of the Boyne Castle
(Courtesy of Stevie Adams)

Conditions were perfect that day, with 20-metre horizontal visibility in the ambient light at 50 metres depth. The divers found the wreck to be a small steamship, sitting on a white sandy seabed at 53 metres. The bow and stern are intact, but the midships area has collapsed. The bow is lying on its port side, but the boiler and engine are still upright. The wreck is home to lots of extremely large lobsters, and many bottles, plates and jars were noted, along with brass items including portholes. Three of the divers from South Queensferry recovered the bell, enabling the wreck to be positively identified as the *Boyne Castle*, which was built by Dundee Shipbuilders in 1909 (Yard No. 207).

UNKNOWN

Wreck No: 67		Date Sunk:
Latitude: 56 07 24 N		Longitude: 02 29 06 W
GPS Lat: 5607.400 N		GPS Long: 0229.100 W
Location: 7 miles N of Dunbar		Area: Dunbar
Type:		Tonnage:
Length:	Beam:	Draught:
How Sunk:		Depth:

A fisherman's fastener was reported at 560724N, 022906W in 1974. Could this be the elusive *Moresby*? Another fastener was reported in the same year at 560736N, 022818W. These two fasteners are fairly close together and may be one and the same.

ZZ 12

Wreck No: 68		Date Sunk: 5 May 1946
Latitude: 56 09 00 N PA		Longitude: 02 13 07 W PA
GPS Lat: 5609.000 N	**WGS84 PA**	GPS Long: 0213.120 W
Location: 14 miles NNE of St Abbs Head		Area: Dunbar
Type: Minesweeper		Tonnage: 360 grt
Length: 145 ft	Beam: 30 ft	Draught: 2.5 ft
How Sunk: Foundered		Depth: 58 metres

The *ZZ12*, an A-class Lighter (Landing Craft), converted in late 1944 to a minesweeper, capsized in bad weather and sank while under tow on 5 May 1946. The position was given as 560900N, 021307W, but the wreck was not found there in searches made in the 1970s and again in 2004.

These lighters were powered by two diesel engines. Because of their shallow draught these lighters made ideal minesweepers for shallow waters, and were used to sweep rivers and canals in Europe, and even canals in Venice. They were fitted with the LL sweep for use against magnetic mines, and they were also equipped to deal with pressure mines.

UB-63

Wreck No: 69		Date Sunk: 28 January 1918
Latitude: 56 10 00 N PA		Longitude: 02 00 00 W PA
GPS Lat: 5610.000 N	**WGS84 PA**	GPS Long: 0200.000 W
Location: 15½ miles 16° from St Abbs Head		Area: St Abbs
Type: Submarine		Tonnage: 506 tons
Length: 182.2 ft	Beam: 18.9 ft	Draught: 12.2 ft
How Sunk: Depth-charged by HM trawlers		Depth: 57–60 metres

UB-63 *(Author's collection)*

UB-63 was a UBIII-class U-boat built by Vulcan, Hamburg. She displaced 508 tons surfaced, 639 tons submerged. This class of U-boat had an 88-mm gun mounted on the casing forward of the conning tower, four bow torpedo tubes and one stern tube. They had two propellers, and a prominent net cutter at the top of the bow. *UB-63* (Rudolf Gebeschus) was sunk on 28 January 1918. All 33 crew were killed. The position was recorded as 561000N, 020000W PA.

On 28 January 1918 two Granton-based trawlers, HMS *W S Bailey* and HMS *Fort George*, detected the sound of an enemy submarine on their hydrophones 14 miles E by S of May Island, and commenced tracking her. After hunting the submarine for some time, the *W S Bailey* went full astern to take the way off the ship, and shortly after sighted two periscopes only 20 yards away. The periscopes then went under water as the submarine dived, and the *W S Bailey* dropped a single depth charge right over the spot where the submarine had disappeared. The explosion resulted in a large quantity of oil and debris floating to the surface. For several days trawlers remained in the vicinity, and the *W S Bailey* swept the area with a chain sweep, which brought up more oil. It has been said that divers later confirmed the U-boat was *UB-63*, and that she had been destroyed with all hands. If this is true, one would have thought the position would be accurately known, but another position which has been given for the *UB-63* is 5617N, 0225W – allegedly confirmed by divers in 1918. This position is 6 miles E of Fife Ness, and 8 miles NE of May Island.

When dived in 1980 the wreck charted there (WGS84 5617.857N, 0224.167W) was found to be a twin-engine aircraft broken in two. It is certainly not *UB-63* – thus casting doubt about the report of divers confirming the identity of the U-boat. One wonders if the above version of events is another of the Auxiliary Patrol reports that should be taken with a large pinch of salt, as the German records apparently suggest an entirely different location for the loss of *UB-63*. According to the German records, Gebeschus left Germany on 14 January bound for the Irish Sea, via the Straits of Dover, but was never heard from again. It is considered possible that she may have been sunk in the Straits, while en route for the Irish Sea, but was more probably the victim of a depth-charge attack carried out by the trawler *Cormorant IV* and the drifter *Young Fred* off the north of Ireland on 27 January, or those carried out in the Irish Sea by *P-68* on 30 January or by the American destroyer *Allen* (DD-66) on 2 February.

During her service at Queenstown, Ireland from June 1917 until after the end of the war in 1918, *Allen* reported engagements with U-boats on ten separate occasions, but post-war checks of German records failed to substantiate even the most plausible of the supposed encounters.

KITTY

Wreck No: 70		Date Sunk: 9 May 1917
Latitude: 56 11 39 N PA		Longitude: 01 45 00 W PA
GPS Lat: 5611.650 N		GPS Long: 0145.000 W
Location: 25 miles ENE of St Abbs Head		Area: Dunbar
Type: Trawler		Tonnage: 181 grt
Length: 105 ft	Beam: 21 ft	Draught: 11.2 ft
How Sunk: By submarine *UC-42* – bomb		Depth: 52 metres

The steel steam trawler *Kitty* was built by Earle's Co., Hull in 1898 and registered in Fleetwood. She was captured by *UC-42* and sunk by explosive charge 25 miles ENE of St Abbs Head. Her skipper and chief engineer were taken as prisoners. *Lloyd's World War One Losses* gives 30 miles NNE of St Abbs Head.

The Hydrographic Department gives the approximate position of the *Kitty* as 560600N, 012600W, but the nearest charted wreck is at 561139N, 014500W PA, 21 miles ENE of St Abbs Head.

HARALD KLITGAARD

Wreck No: 71		Date sunk: 6 June 1917	
Latitude: 56 05 00 N PA		Longitude: 01 06 00 W PA	
GPS Lat: 5605.000 N		GPS Long: 0106.000 W	
Location: 28 miles N of Farne Islands		Area: Dunbar	
Type: Steamship		Tonnage: 1799 grt	
Length: 261 ft	Beam: 38 ft	Draught: 16 ft	
How Sunk: Torpedoed by *UC-77*		Depth: 34 metres	

The Danish vessel *Harald Klitgaard* (ex-*Fairfield*) was built by Richardson, Duck & Co. at Thornaby-on-Tees in 1884 for F. Binnington of Stockton (Yard No. 308). In 1895 she was renamed *Harald Klitgaard* when sold to Dansk Russiske Dampsk Selskab of Copenhagen. She was torpedoed and sunk by *UC-77* 28 miles north of the Farne Islands on 6 June 1917 while en route, in ballast, from Copenhagen to Seaham.

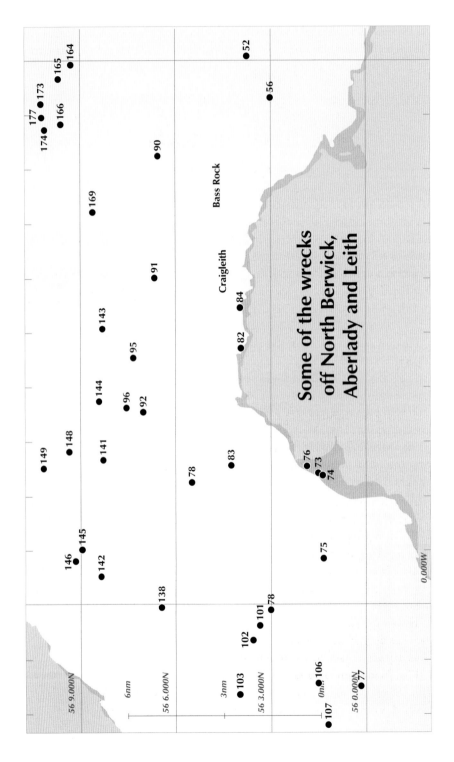

Some of the wrecks
off North Berwick,
Aberlady and Leith

3

North Berwick, Aberlady and Leith

BAYONET

Wreck No: 72	Date Sunk: 21 December 1939
Latitude: 55 59 50 N	Longitude: 03 09 54 W
GPS Lat: 5559.830 N	GPS Long: 0309.900 W
Location: ¾ mile NW of Leith Docks	Area: Leith
Type: Boom Defence	Tonnage: 605 grt
Length: 159.7 ft Beam: 30.7 ft	Draught: 13 ft
How Sunk: Mined	Depth: 8 metres

HMS *Bayonet* (ex-*Barnehurst*) was a Navy lifting vessel of the "Net" class, with bow "horns". She struck a mine and sank at 1500 hours on 21 December 1939, 21.5°, 6.56 cables from the Martello Tower – i.e. about three quarters of a mile north-west of Leith docks. She is reported to lie at 555950N, 030954W, but no wreck is charted in that position. An obstruction charted at 560010N, 030940W, quarter of a mile away, may be the remains of the *Bayonet*. The sound of the explosion of the mine was heard in Edinburgh, but its cause was not immediately apparent, and was at first thought to be a bomb. RAF fighters were despatched from Drem to search for German bombers, and two RAF Hampden bombers were shot down in error, one of them crashing into the sea off Gullane. The Hampdens were part of a flight from RAF Waddington. Apparently they should have had their landing gear down to indicate that they were friendly aircraft passing through the airspace controlled by another group. Some of the accompanying Hampdens from the Waddington flight landed at Drem, and the atmosphere in the mess that night was rather frosty. When the Hampdens departed the next day, they bombed the airfield with toilet rolls. The pilots who had shot the Hampdens down the previous day were made to go around and pick them up!

A third Hampden, attacked in error by Spitfires of 602 Squadron, crashed on to the Church of Christ, in Togston Terrace, Amble, Northumberland. The church was demolished. One person on the ground was killed and another was injured. One of the

HMS Burgonet – *a sister ship of HMS* Bayonet
(Courtesy of P. Ransome-Wallis)

bomber's crew was seriously injured and the rest were killed. According to *Axis Submarine Successes 1939-1945* the mine struck by *Bayonet* had been laid on 4 November 1939 by *U-21* (KL Fritz Frauenheim).

Admiralty documents state that *Bayonet* was working the boom when she struck one of 223 British defensive mines that had been laid in the South Inchkeith Channel by HMS *Plover* on 20 December 1939, 14 December 1939 and 16 December 1939. The mine she struck was at the southern end of one of the lines. The southern ends of two of the lines were cleared in April 1940 to let salvage work begin, and the rest of the field was cleared in July 1940. These large and uncontrolled minefields constituted a grave danger to British ships – the mines broke free in gales, the fields left no margin for error in navigation.

An unknown obstruction which may be a wreck or a rock, was reported by the receiver of wrecks at Leith in 1952. The position was given as 560010N, 030940W, slightly to the south of one of the three anchorage points (charted as L5) about one mile north of Leith docks. A submarine conning tower is said to have been found within the swing clearance circle of one of these anchorage points, the remainder of the submarine being assumed buried.

There are numerous stories of alleged submarines in various places around the coast of Britain, but I have not found any evidence pointing to the possible existence of any submarine near here. It is much more likely to have been wreckage left over from HMS *Bayonet*, e.g. her boiler.

UNKNOWN X-CRAFT 1

Wreck No: 73
Latitude: 56 01 22 N
GPS Lat: 5601.363 N

WGS84

Date Sunk: April 1946
Longitude: 02 52 46 W
GPS Long: 0252.861 W

Location: Aberlady Bay SSW concrete block
Area: Aberlady
Type: Submarine X-craft
Tonnage: 30 grt
Length: 51.6 ft
Beam: 5.8 ft
Draught: 7.4 ft
How Sunk: Scuttled
Depth:

This is the more complete of the two X-craft submarines, and lies 87 metres SSW of the concrete block.

UNKNOWN X-CRAFT 2

Wreck No: 74
Date Sunk: April 1946
Latitude: 56 01 28 N
Longitude: 02 52 42 W
GPS Lat: 5601.459 N
WGS84
GPS Long: 0252.798 W
Location: Aberlady Bay
Area: Aberlady
Type: Submarine X-craft
Tonnage: 30 grt
Length: 51.6 ft
Beam: 5.8 ft
Draught: 7.4 ft
How Sunk: Scuttled
Depth:

This one is in a much more deteriorated state and lies 103 metres NNE of the concrete block, which is at 5601.405 N, 0252.827 W. The remains of two X-craft midget submarines lie fairly close together in Aberlady Bay.

The X-craft were designed for use against the German battleships *Tirpitz* and *Scharnhorst*. They were towed, submerged, behind conventional submarines, to a position within range of the target. They then made their way, under their own power – a Gardner diesel engine for propulsion on the surface, and an electric motor for use while submerged – to lay charges under the target ship. On close examination of these wrecks, there seems to be barely enough room inside for one crewman, but the operational X-craft had a crew of four: commanding officer, first lieutenant, engineer and diver. The passage crews used

The remains of an X-craft midget submarine in Aberlady Bay
(Author's collection)

An X-craft underway on the surface
(Author's collection)

during Operation Source – the *Tirpitz* raid – consisted of three men only, as it was not necessary to have a diver on board while the X-craft was under tow.

The width dimension given above is for the X-craft without its two side charges, each of which contained about two tons of explosive, detonated by clockwork time fuses. They were attached to the submarine by a threaded bolt. This was released from inside the hull by turning a hand wheel. The craft would manoeuvre close to its target, release the side cargoes and move away before the charge exploded.

The X-craft were also fitted with a wet-and-dry compartment that made it possible for a diver to swim from the boat to attach limpet mines to enemy vessels, and then return to re-enter the submerged craft. On Operation Source, the targets for the X-craft were: X-5: *Tirpitz*; X-6: *Tirpitz*; X-7: *Tirpitz*; X-8: *Lützow*; X-9: *Scharnhorst*; and X-10: *Scharnhorst*.

The two midget submarines were placed in Aberlady Bay in 1946, to be used as bombing or rocket targets for practice by low-flying aircraft, in the same way as the destroyer HMS *Ludlow*, a few miles further east. They were moored at either side of a huge concrete block which is still there, between the submarines.

Some years ago the non-ferrous metal was salvaged by someone who drove a tractor over the sands to the submarines, which almost dry out completely at low tide, but the bulk of both submarines still lies there, partially buried in the sand. They are now in a very deteriorated condition, but around 1960 – almost 50 years ago – when they were very much more intact, the author Nigel Tranter, who lived nearby, used the westernmost of the two submarines as a hide while wildfowling in Aberlady Bay, and became trapped inside when the hatch seized shut. To effect an escape, he used the barrels of his shotgun as a lever to prise the hatch open again before the incoming tide completely engulfed the submarine! He incorporated this incident in a fictionalised account described in his novel *Drug on the Market*, published in 1962. In the book, he describes these submarines as Japanese, but they are in fact British, and of the same type used to attack the German battleship *Tirpitz* in September 1943.

The identities of these two submarines remain something of a mystery, but they have been positively identified as two of the XT-crafts – the training version of the midget submarines. Towards the end of 1993 Commander John Lorimer, DSO, who was one of the crew of the *X-6* in Operation Source, and therefore familiar with X-craft during the war, examined these wrecks and noticed that they were fitted with a device for releasing a smoke charge to divulge their submerged position. They also lack the release mechanism for the side charges. The induction mast is a fixed structure which cannot be lowered, and they did not have a night periscope. In these respects they differ slightly from operational X-craft, and also in their bow mooring arrangements, which were examined in March 1995, by digging away the sand with a spade, to confirm that they are in fact XT-craft – the training version. There was a report that after the war, all six XT-craft were experimentally lowered to crush depth in Loch Fyne. Five of them were raised and taken to Rosyth for scrapping. These wrecks must presumably, therefore, be two of those five.

UNKNOWN

Wreck No: 75		Date Sunk: 1920–1939 ?
Latitude: 56 01 24 N		Longitude: 02 57 24 W
GPS Lat: 5601.400 N		GPS Long: 0257.400 W
Location: 3 miles WNW of Aberlady Bay		Area: Aberlady
Type: Drifter		Tonnage:
Length:	Beam:	Draught:
How Sunk:		Depth: 13 metres

The wreck charted at 560124N, 025724W, 3 miles WNW of Aberlady Bay is reported to be a drifter sunk between the two wars. Wreckage found in 1970 stood 15 feet high on the seabed, and measured about 40 × 20 feet.

UNKNOWN

Wreck No: 76		Date Sunk:
Latitude: 56 01 52 N		Longitude: 02 52 20 W
GPS Lat: 5601.870 N		GPS Long: 0252.330 W
Location: Aberlady Bay		Area: Aberlady
Type:		Tonnage:
Length:	Beam:	Draught:
How Sunk: Ran aground		Depth:

One of the Earls of Wemyss used to buy old fishing boats from the fishermen of Cockenzie, and dumped them off Kilspindie Point, at the south side of Aberlady Bay, "to improve the view." Paintings of the Aberlady Bay area, dated around 1940, show these vessels. The remains of eight of these Fifie sailing fishing vessels, giving a snapshot of boats engaged in the Scottish fishing industry at the turn of the 20th Century, have been protected as Maritime Scheduled Ancient Monuments. They are designated Kilspindie Hulks Nos. 1–8, and described as "rare 19th–early 20th century 'Fifie' sailing fishing vessels."

At 560152N, 025220W, in Aberlady Bay, the remains of the keel and ribs of a wooden vessel partially buried in the sand, uncover at low water. This might be one of these old fishing boats, although it does seem to have been a somewhat larger vessel. The remains of several old wooden boats lie partially buried in the sands of Aberlady Bay, to the west of Gullane Point. Aberlady Bay has gradually filled up with sand over the years.

In 1547 Henry VIII sent up a fleet to try to relieve the English force beseiged in Haddington, but these vessels were repelled by the cannon of French mercenaries based at Luffness Castle, at the head of the bay, and had to go over to Fife instead, to wreak vengeance there. Whether any of these ships were sunk is not recorded, but Henry's anger was such that he ordered Luffness to be "spoiled" after the English won the battle of Pinkie (Musselburgh) two years later.

SAPPHO

Wreck No: 77		Date Sunk: 5 March 1900
Latitude: 56 00 09 N PA		Longitude: 03 04 30 W PA
GPS Lat: 5600.150 N		GPS Long: 0304.500 W
Location: South Craig Rocks (Craigwaugh)		Area: Leith
Type: Steamship		Tonnage: 1275 grt
Length: 231 ft	Beam: 33 ft	Draught: 16.5 ft
How Sunk: Ran aground		Depth: 7 metres

Before setting off on her maiden voyage from Burntisland to Rotterdam with a cargo of coal, the British Steam Navigation Company's new steamship *Sappho*, built by Ramage & Ferguson of Leith, ran her trials entirely satisfactorily during the afternoon of Monday, 5 March 1900. At 7.00 p.m., the party of guests on board were transferred to another vessel in Leith Roads, and the *Sappho* then proceeded on her voyage in clear weather and a calm sea. About an hour later, she ran on to South Craig Rocks at 11 knots. It was soon realised that the vessel was in a dangerous position, and the 16 crew collected their belongings, left the steamer, which was lying bow down at low water, and landed at Leith. It was feared that she would break in two and become a total wreck. In an attempt to save the vessel, deck fittings were stripped off, but within a few days, the *Sappho* settled stern first on the bottom.

LCA 672 ? OR LCA 811 ?

Wreck No: 78		Date Sunk: 2 April 1944
Latitude: 56 02 58 N		Longitude: 03 00 15 W
GPS Lat: 5602.970 N		GPS Long: 0300.250 W
Location: South Channel		Area Aberlady
Type: Landing Craft		Tonnage: 13.5 disp.
Length: 41.5 ft	Beam: 10 ft	Draught: 2.2 ft
How Sunk: Foundered		Depth: 14 metres

Charted as a wreck at 13.5 metres in a general depth of 17 metres, and classified by the Navy as a Landing Craft which sank in 1944. In 1975 divers estimated her to be standing about 8 feet above the seabed. Landing Craft *LCA 845* of 13.5 tons displacement was also sunk at 560527N, 025312W on 29 January 1944, during exercises off Leith, East Scotland. *LCA 552* was wrecked on 9 February 1944 during exercises off East Scotland. *LCA 672* and *LCA 811* foundered during exercises off East Scotland on 2 April 1944.

It is interesting that the word "wrecked" was used in respect of *LCA 552*. This can usually be interpreted as "ran aground", while the word "foundered" was used to describe the circumstances of loss for LCAs *672* and *811*. This wreck is therefore likely to be either *LCA 672* or *LCA 811*. These two landing craft were converted with strengthened hull frames, and were equipped to explode minefields in the path of an assault landing, for which purpose they were armed with 24 mortars in four rows of six.

PODEROSA

Wreck No: 79	Date Sunk: 27 November 1896
Latitude: 56 03 00 N PA	Longitude: 02 36 30 W PA
GPS Lat: 5603.000 N	GPS Long: 0236.500 W
Location: Seacliff, Scougall Rocks	Area: North Berwick
Type: Steamship	Tonnage: 1183 grt
Length: 249.8 ft Beam: 32.9 ft	Draught: 19.9 ft
How Sunk: Ran aground	Depth: 7 metres

The iron steamship *Poderosa* was built in 1875 by Cole Bros. Of Newcastle-upon-Tyne. She ran aground while en route, in ballast, from Grimsby to Grangemouth. The position has also been estimated as 560230N, 023630W.

ELTERWATER

Wreck No: 80	Date Sunk: 6 August 1927
Latitude: 56 03 06 N	Longitude: 02 36 48 W
GPS Lat: 5603.100 N	GPS Long: 0236.800 W
Location: The Rodgers, Scougall Rocks	Area: North Berwick
Type: Steamship	Tonnage: 2126 grt
Length: 280.5 ft Beam: 42.9 ft	Draught: 9.9 ft
How Sunk: Ran aground	Depth: 7 metres

The Newcastle steamship *Elterwater* ran aground in dense fog about three quarters of a mile SE ½ S of South Carr Beacon on Saturday, 6 August 1927. She had been bound from Antwerp to Grangemouth with a cargo of pig iron. Two women and two men went ashore in the vessel's own boats. Dunbar lifeboat was called out and stood by the steamer, but the remaining crew refused to leave, hoping that their vessel might be refloated. The *Elterwater* was badly holed and her fore part was almost awash at high water. Although the pumps were kept going, the water level in the ship continued to rise, and eventually the boiler fires were extinguished. The Master, and his crew then abandoned the ship and went ashore. The Court of Enquiry found that the cause of the stranding was the vessel being set in towards the land by an abnormal current from the north and east, unknown to the Master, and his neglect to verify the position of the vessel by the use of the lead in thick weather. As the stranding and loss of the *Elterwater* were caused by default of the Master, Arthur Stanley Coates, he was severely reprimanded by the Court and ordered to pay £25 towards the expenses of the investigation. The vessel subsequently became a total wreck. Salvage operations to recover the cargo were put in hand, but divers were not able to handle the pig iron with any great speed, so new methods were adopted.

A giant electro-magnet, manufactured by GEC, capable of dealing with heavy weights, was used to raise the sunken cargo, and this unusual method attracted considerable attention at the time. Memories of shipwrecks obviously fade fairly quickly, however, and are not recorded as well as they might be, as only 32 years later, in 1959, this was reported as an unknown stranded and heavily salvaged wreck at Seacliff, south of North Berwick.

VALHALLA

Wreck No: 81		Date Sunk: 27 February 1900
Latitude: 56 03 20 N PA		Longitude: 02 38 45 W PA
GPS Lat: 5603.330 N		GPS Long: 0238.750 W
Location: Near Tantallon Castle		Area: North Berwick
Type: Barque		Tonnage: 477 grt
Length:	Beam:	Draught:
How Sunk: Ran aground		Depth: metres

The Norwegian iron barque *Valhalla*, en route from London to Dundee in ballast, was driven ashore near Tantallon castle by a force 10 northeasterly storm on 27 February 1900.

LUDLOW

Wreck No: 82		Date Sunk: 5 July 1945
Latitude: 56 03 55 N		Longitude: 02 45 58 W
GPS Lat: 5603.920 N		GPS Long: 0245.970 W
Location: Broad Sands, Dirleton		Area: North Berwick
Type: Destroyer		Tonnage: 1020 grt
Length: 315.5 ft	Beam: 31.5 ft	Draught: 11.5 ft
How Sunk: Aircraft rocket target		Depth: 7 metres

HMS *Ludlow* (ex-USS *Stockton*, DD-73), a Caldwell-class destroyer built in 1917 by William Cramp & Sons, was one of 50 First World War destroyers given to Britain in 1940 by the USA, in exchange for the U.S. having the right to establish military bases in

HMS Ludlow *(Author's collection)*

various British possessions, mainly in the Caribbean, Bermuda and Newfoundland, under an agreement of 2 September 1940. In Royal Navy service, these old destroyers were given names of towns common to both Britain and the United States.

USS *Stockton* (Destroyer No. 73), a torpedo boat destroyer, was laid down on 16 October 1916 by William Cramp & Sons at Philadelphia, Pa. She was launched on 17 July 1917 and commissioned in the US Navy on 26 November 1917, Cmdr. H.A. Baldridge in command.

She spent the last year of the First World War assigned to convoy escort and antisubmarine duty, operating out of Queenstown, Ireland. During that time, she engaged an enemy U-boat on at least one occasion. On 30 March 1918 she and *Ericsson* (Destroyer No. 56) were escorting the troopship *St. Paul* on the Queenstown–Liverpool circuit, when *Ericsson* opened fire on a German submarine. Almost immediately, the U-boat

USS Stockton *at Queenstown, Ireland in 1918*
(Courtesy of Tony Cowart)

USS Stockton *at anchor, c.1919–1922 (Courtesy of U.S. Navy)*

fired a torpedo at *Stockton*, which the destroyer narrowly evaded. The two destroyers dropped patterns of depth charges, but the U-boat managed to evade their attack and escaped. Later that night *Stockton* collided with SS *Slieve Bloom* near South Sark Light. The destroyer had to put into Liverpool for repairs and the merchantman sank.

Stockton returned to the United States in 1919 and for three years continued to serve with the fleet. On 26 June 1922 she was placed out of commission and laid up at Philadelphia, Pa.

After having been laid up in reserve for 22 years, USS *Stockton* (DD73) was recommissioned on 16 August 1940 and shuttled to Halifax, where she was decommissioned on the 23rd and turned over to the United Kingdom under the provisions of the Lend Lease agreement.

She sailed for the UK on 31 August with a raw and inexperienced British crew. There followed a protracted refit at Devonport from 17/9/40 to 1/3/41, when considerable alterations were made, including changing the forward gun to a British 12-pounder HA, the removal of her after torpedo tubes, the fitting of depth-charge throwers, and the installation of asdic. On completion she came out of her refit as HMS *Ludlow* G75, and joined Rosyth Command, in which she served throughout the war, escorting East Coast convoys. After decommissioning and paying off at Rosyth in May 1945, the old ship was stripped and then towed to Broadsands on 6 June 1945, to be used as a rocket target by the RAF. She was sunk by the very first rocket fired at her, but because the water was so shallow, she did not disappear, and continued to be used as a target until July, when the sunken wreck was passed to the British Iron & Steel Company (BISCO) for disposal. The wreck was extensively salvaged by Easingwoods of Dunbar, and the remains lie partly buried in sand a few hundred yards off the beach at Dirleton. Parts of the wreck are still visible above the surface at low water.

Six Caldwell-class destroyers, DDs 69–74, were ordered in 1916 and began entering US Navy service the following year, armed with four 4-inch guns, one 3-inch gun and

Damage to USS Stockton *after her collision with SS* Sleive Bloom
(Courtesy of Robert M Cieri)

two triple 21-inch torpedo tubes. Their hulls were designed to be stronger than previous raised-forecastle ships, resulting in a "flush" weather deck, sloping continuously from bow to stern. They retained the same freeboard forward and aft as the "broken deckers" – as did the standardized mass-production destroyers of the following Wickes and Clemson classes. All but three flushdeckers had four stacks and two screws. DDs 71–73, *Gwin*, *Conner* and *Stockton* had three stacks; *Conner* and *Stockton* also had three screws.

The six Caldwells were designed for 18,500 shp and 30 knots, but differed from one another in other respects: *Caldwell*, *Craven* and *Manley* had four stacks; the others three. *Conner* and *Stockton* had three screws; the others two. USS *Stockton* was one of only two three-funnelled, triple-screwed units given to the Royal Navy. She had the same unusual stern form as the others, but had three shafts with direct drive turbines.

Parts of HMS Ludlow *break the surface at low water, with the islands of Lamb, Craigleith and the Bass Rock in the distance (Author's collection)*

Seagulls seem to like the wreck! (Author's collection)

DD-72 *Conner* 1918/1940 UK HMS *Leeds* 3 stacks, 3 screws.

DD-70 *Conway* 1918/1940 UK HMS *Lewes* 3 stacks, 2 screws.

DD-73 *Stockton* 1917/1940 UK HMS *Ludlow* 3 stacks, 3 screws.

CHESTER II

Wreck No: 83		Date Sunk: 29 February 1916
Latitude: 56 04 16 N		Longitude: 02 52 15 W
GPS Lat: 5604.270 N		GPS Long: 0252.250 W
Location: Gullane Bay		Area: Aberlady
Type: Trawler		Tonnage: 143 grt
Length: 104 ft	Beam: 21 ft	Draught: 11 ft
How Sunk: Collision		Depth: 17 metres

The iron-hulled steam trawler *Chester II* was built in 1896, and owned by the Consolidated Steam Fishing & Ice Co. Ltd. She was sunk in a collision on 29 February 1916, 2.98 miles, 267.5° from Fidra light. The wreck is intact, and the holds are full of silt. There are strong currents in this area.

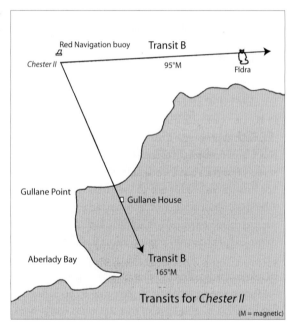

TRANSITS:

A) Left end of Fidra in line with the highest part of the Bass Rock.

B) Left wall of Fidra light in line with right shoulder of the Bass Rock.

C) Hopetoun monument in line with V-shaped tree to right of Gullane House.

BULL

Wreck No: 84		Date Sunk: 6 December 1893
Latitude: 56 03 57 N		Longitude: 02 43 36 W
GPS Lat: 5603.958 N	**WGS84**	GPS Long: 0243.600 W
Location: 300 metres W of N Berwick harbour		Area: North Berwick
Type: Steamship		Tonnage: 568 grt
Length: 175.6 ft	Beam: 25.6 ft	Draught: 14.3 ft
How Sunk: Collision with *Rosslyn*		Depth: 5 metres

On 6 December 1893 the steamship *Bull* was en route from Grangemouth to Middlesbroug̲ with four passengers, but otherwise in ballast, when she was struck amidships in a collisio̲ with the Leith steam trawler *Rosslyn* about one mile from North Berwick. One membe̲ of *Rosslyn*'s crew was lost.

A weather report in the *Fifeshire Advertiser* of 6 December 1893 noted that a violent storm of west wind had been blowing over this district during the greater part of the week, accompanied by drizzling rain.

The collision was said to have occurred between Craigleith and Lamb, but the wreck lies on one of the reefs just outside North Berwick harbour, about 40 metres in front of the Craig-n-tuch rock, about 300 metres west of the harbour, at a depth of only 5 metres.

There is very little left – just a skeleton. The wreck is well flattened, with plates and girders covering a very wide area on a sand and rock seabed, making it impossible to pick up anything distincitive on a sounder. There is plenty of life including crab, lobster and conger.

UNKNOWN – 1905

Wreck No: 85		Date Sunk: 1905	
Latitude: 56 04 45 N PA		Longitude: 02 38 30 W PA	
GPS Lat: 5604.750 N		GPS Long: 0238.500 W	
Location: Close NW of Bass Rock		Area: North Berwick	
Type:		Tonnage:	
Length:	Beam:	Draught:	
How Sunk:		Depth: 30 metres	

This wreck was first reported in the *Underwater World* magazine of May 1967, lying in 30 metres, off the north-west corner of the Bass Rock, suggesting that she may have struck the Bass. The position has also been recorded as 560442.5N, 023830W.

Statistical details of ships lost around Scotland in 1905 were published in Parliamentary papers dated 1907. Appended to these papers is a map showing the positions of the 1905 losses. One of the wreck positions is marked immediately adjacent to the Bass Rock, but unfortunately, the map is of such a small scale that it is not possible to determine the exact position, and the vessel is not identified in the accompanying text.

The wreck was found by Craig Hunter in May 2001, well out from the bottom of the cliff off the north-west of the Bass. It lies on a slight slope from 25–27 metres – very exposed to strong currents! The engine block is the highest remaining point – approximately two metres proud, but impossible to distinguish from surrounding large rocks by echo sounder, although there should be enough metal to obtain a reading by magnetometer. The main wreckage is about 8 metres long. It has obviously been a wooden vessel. Very little wood remains but some keel pins were found lying around. There are a few brass items, including sections of scattered pipework, but no propeller.

UNKNOWN

): 86   Date Sunk: Pre-1979
  56 05 14 N   Longitude: 02 49 43 W
t: 5605.230 N   GPS Long: 0249.720 W
 n: 1½ miles NW of Fidra   Area: North Berwick
Steamship   Tonnage: grt
h: Beam: Draught:
Sunk: Depth: 28 metres

/reck was first located on 14 December 1979, and is reputedly a collier lost off Fidra
1930s. (I wonder if this could be a reference to the *Stjernvik*?) It is reported in the
fisher Book of Tows Vol. 1 in Decca Chain 3, as Green C 38.90, Purple C 61.00.

BARGE G4

Wreck No: 87   Date Sunk: Pre-1953
Latitude: 56 05 15 N   Longitude: 02 55 10 W
GPS Lat: 5605.250 N   GPS Long: 0255.170 W
Location: 3½ miles NNW of Gullane Point Area: Aberlady
Type: Barge   Tonnage:
Length: Beam: Draught:
How Sunk: Depth: 33 metres

The barge *G4* was first located by HMS *Scott* in 1959 in position 560515N, 025513W,
standing up 12 feet from the bottom, with a least depth to the wreck of 110 feet. The
position was given as 560501N, 025503W in 1968, but is now charted at 560515N,
025510W. The barge was reported to be salvaged in 1953, but it was located by HMS
Scott in 1959!

LCA 845

Wreck No: 88   Date Sunk: 29 January 1944
Latitude: 56 05 27 N   Longitude: 02 53 12 W
GPS Lat: 5605.450 N   GPS Long: 0253.200 W
Location: 5 miles N of Gullane Point   Area: Aberlady
Type: Landing Craft   Tonnage: 14 grt
Length: 41.5 ft   Beam: 10 ft Draught: 2.3 ft
How Sunk: Foundered   Depth: 38 metres

See Wreck No. 78 (on pages 80–1) at 560258N, 030015W. *LCA 845* became waterlogged
and sank during exercises off Leith. She was constructed of wood and armour plating. The
wreck could not be found during a survey in 1960.

SHAKESPEARE

Wreck No: 89	Date Sunk: 7 Feb.
Latitude: 56 11 58 N	Longitude: 01 54 27
GPS Lat: 5608.972 N	GPS Long: 0154.452 V
Location: 16 miles NNE of St Abbs Head	Area: North Berwick
Type: Trawler	Tonnage: 202 grt
Length: 111.3 ft Beam: 22.6 ft	Draught: 12.1 ft
How Sunk: Scuttled by *UB-22*	Depth: 48–54 metres

The Hull trawler *Shakespeare* was built by Earle's Co. Ltd. of Hull in 1908. Engine by Amos & Smith, Hull. Her owners were the Hellyer Steam Fishing Co. Ltd., Hull.

On 7 February 1917 she was captured by the German *UB-22*, and the crew were forced to abandon their vessel, after which the U-boat's crew sank the trawler with scuttling charges.

The wreck was dived in October 2007 and found to be sitting on an even keel and fairly intact, although most of the decking and wheelhouse have rotted away, leaving the glass and brass lying about. It is 48 metres to the deck and 54 metres to the seabed.

She has a four-bladed propeller and a steam engine. There is nothing in the hold apart from a small amount of coal. A very obvious, sharp V-shaped indentation in the hull on the port side bow makes it look like the vessel was sunk due to being rammed, but this must have been the effect of the scuttling charge.

There is absolutely no doubt about the identity of the wreck as the bell was recovered. It is engraved: SHAKESPEARE 1908 HULL.

ROYAL FUSILIER

Wreck No: 90	Date Sunk: 3 June 1941
Latitude: 56 06 32 N	Longitude: 02 35 18 W
GPS Lat: 5606.530 N	GPS Long: 0235.300 W
Location: 2.4 miles NE of Bass Rock	Area: North Berwick
Type: Steamship	Tonnage: 2187 grt
Length: 290.2 ft Beam: 41.2 ft	Draught: 18 ft
How Sunk: Bombed	Depth: 44 metres

The *Royal Fusilier* was built in 1924 by Caledon of Dundee, for the London and Edinburgh Shipping Company. and registered in Leith. She was bombed by German aircraft at 5522N, 0121W, seven miles east of Amble, Northumberland while en route from London to Leith with a cargo of 50 tons of rice and 70 tons of paper. The ship started taking in water and developed a list. Amble lifeboat was called out, and 15 of the crew were taken on to the lifeboat. When it became clear that the *Royal Fusilier* was not about to sink, these crewmembers were put back on the ship again.

The damaged vessel was taken in tow towards the Forth by one of the two destroyers which were in attendance, but she capsized and sank at 4.18 p.m. at 560648N, 023500W,

4 miles north-east of the Bass Rock, off North Berwick. Her crew of 27 were all saved.

The wreck of the *Royal Fusilier* is intact, but lying on its port side, half buried in the mud, in 42–46 metres of water. Her stern is approximately two-thirds embedded in the seabed. It is swept by tides, and even at this depth is covered in marine growths, including a brilliant profusion of orange and white plumose anemones. Underwater visibility varies. It can be as much as ten metres with a green tinge in the water, but is more usually five metres in darkness.

With the hull of the ship being uppermost, parallel rows of brass port-holes, complete with intact glass, are very noticeable, and are a most impressive feature of this wreck. The portholes cannot be removed from outside the hull. The structure is still very strong, and it would be necessary to enter the hull to get at the fastenings from the inside. At this depth, however, this is a daunting prospect, especially as the bridge area is totally covered in net, some of which is floating quite high up, and part of the starboard companionway has a trawl net draped over it. Any removal would be a long slow process of repetitive dives – well beyond the patience of most divers, and relatively few divers visit the wreck. This is a very exposed stretch of water where conditions can change very rapidly. Calm weather is essential for diving here. However, when conditions are calm along this stretch of coastline, low-lying fog can rapidly reduce surface visibility to almost zero.

At the stern, the wreck protrudes only three metres from the seabed, which is at 46 metres. Dropping over the anemone-infested railings at the side of the hull, the deck now stands vertically in the water. The sterncastle and the remains of a derrick can be seen here. Moving forwards, a companionway runs along the starboard side of the ship, with doorways leading off into the interior. Entering enclosed cabins at this depth is not to be recommended as mud can be easily stirred up, instantly reducing visibility to zero, and making it difficult to find the way out again. There is a fair amount of debris on the sea floor, and ropes which look extremely thick due to dense colonisation by marine growths. The bridge juts out horizontally from the vertical deck, with a smaller raised bridge on top.

Royal Fusilier *(Courtesy of Kenneth King)*

From the side of the bridge the hull sweeps down in a large curve to the deck level. Forward of the bridge is another large crane, and the foremast lies on the sea floor. Towards the bow the side of the hull rises up to the fo'cs'le, with the anchor winch and bollards. As the bow curves round, it sinks into the mud before the stem of the ship can be seen.

UNKNOWN

Wreck No: 91		Date Sunk:	
Latitude: 56 06 38 N		Longitude: 02 41 59 W	
GPS Lat: 5606.633 N		GPS Long: 0241.983 W	
Location: 3 miles N of North Berwick		Area: North Berwick	
Type:		Tonnage:	
Length: 132 ft	Beam: 23 ft	Draught:	
How Sunk:		Depth: 47 metres	

On 18 August 1993 wreckage, 40 metres by 7 metres in size, (132 ft × 23 ft) was found at 560638N, 024158.9W. The least echo sounder depth was 46 metres in a general depth of 47 metres, but side-scan sonar indicated a height of 4 metres.

The identity of this wreck has yet to be established. The apparent size very closely matches the Swedish steamship *Stella*, (which measured 135.3 ft × 23.1 ft), but the *Stella* has been found 2¼ miles south-east of this wreck.

DUNA ?

Wreck No: 92		Date Sunk: 3 February 1902	
Latitude: 56 06 59 N		Longitude: 02 49 18 W	
GPS Lat: 5606.980 N		GPS Long: 0249.300 W	
Location: 2.7 miles NNW of Fidra		Area: North Berwick	
Type: Schooner		Tonnage: 119 grt	
Length: 91.8 ft	Beam: 23.3 ft	Draught: 10.7 ft	
How Sunk: Collision with *Chancellor*		Depth: 51 metres	

This wreck was first located by HMS *Scott* in 1959, and charted in the above position in 55 metres of water. It stands up 4 metres from the bottom, and therefore its least depth is 51 metres. This position is 4 miles SSW of Elie, but it is also 2.7 miles NNW of Fidra. The magnetic variation in the area would have been much greater in 1902, and at that time the bearing would have been nearer to NW of Fidra.

On 3 February 1902 the Norwegian schooner *Duna* was sunk in collision with the Granton steam trawler *Chancellor* about 3 miles NW of Fidra. The *Duna* was en route, in ballast, from Egersund to West Wemyss, and two of her crew were lost.

Captain Gabrielsen of the *Duna*, and some of his crew, managed to jump on board the trawler, but as their vessel remained afloat, they were put on board again, and the schooner was taken in tow by the *Chancellor*, which was proceeding to Granton. About one mile east of Inchkeith, however, the schooner suddenly foundered, and the crew only just managed to board their small boat as the schooner sank. In attempting to rescue the men, the trawler ran down the boat, throwing the men into the water, and it took half an hour for the trawler to rescue Captain Gabrielsen and three very exhausted men.

The 60-year-old mate, Lars Wilhelmsen, and a 20-year-old seamen named Meyar, sank before the trawler could pick them up again, and were drowned. A sad feature of the disaster was that a short time prior to the collision Captain Gabrielsen had sent a telegram ashore to be forwarded to Stavanger stating that they had arrived safely and were all well.

On 30 April the badly decomposed body of a man evidently 45–50 years of age and about six feet in height was washed ashore on Inchkeith. It was presumed to be one of the seamen belonging to the schooner which had been lost after being run into by the trawler about two months previously. A doctor examined the body, which was far too decomposed to be identified, and stated that death had been due to drowning. The remains were interred in Kinghorn cemetery. The body was almost certainly that of the mate.

UNKNOWN

Wreck No: 93	Date Sunk:
Latitude: 56 07 00 N	Longitude: 02 45 42 W
GPS Lat: 5607.000 N	GPS Long: 0245.700 W
Location: 2.7 miles NNE of Fidra	Area: North Berwick
Type:	Tonnage:
Length: Beam:	Draught:
How Sunk:	Depth: 56 metres

An unknown wreck with at least 28 metres over it in about 56 metres. Possibly the *Kinloch*?

ELIZA

Wreck No: 94	Date Sunk: 2 October 1899
Latitude: 56 03 24 N PA	Longitude: 02 37 30 W PA
GPS Lat: 5603.400 N	GPS Long: 0237.500 W
Location: South Carr Beacon, Seacliff	Area: North Berwick
Type: Barque	Tonnage: 447 grt
Length: 171.4 ft Beam: 26.5 ft	Draught: 16.2 ft
How Sunk: Ran aground	Depth: 7 metres

The Danish iron barque *Eliza* struck the rocks at the South Carr Beacon, off Seacliff on 2 October 1899, with the loss of ten lives. She had been en route from Bremerhaven to Methil in ballast.

MUNCHEN

Wreck No: 95   Date Sunk: 17 September 1921
Latitude: 56 07 18 N   Longitude: 02 46 22 W
GPS Lat: 5607.300 N   GPS Long: 0246.370 W
Location: 2.9 miles N of Fidra   Area: North Berwick
Type: Light Cruiser   Tonnage: 3756 grt
Length: 364.7 ft   Beam: 43.7 ft   Draught: 18.4 ft
How Sunk: Torpedo experiment   Depth: 48-58 metres

Built by A.G. Weser, Bremen, in 1905, the German light cruiser *Munchen* was armed with ten 4.1-inch guns, two machine guns and two submerged 17.7-inch torpedo tubes. She could also carry 108 mines. Her deck armour was two inches thick but the deck ends were less than an inch thick, and she had no belt armour. She saw service under Commander Bocker in the 4th Scouting Group at the Battle of Jutland in May 1916, when she was extensively damaged. The ship was decommissioned and disarmed, and reduced to a barrack ship until 1918. She was stricken from the German Navy on 5 November 1919, and given up on 6 July 1920 as part of the war reparations (British prize Q). It had been intended that she should be broken up, but it is doubtful if any scrapping work was actually carried out before she was expended in a torpedo experiment on 17 September 1921.

The wreck of the *Munchen* is charted in the above position with a clearance of at least 28 metres in about 56 metres depth. The wreck is lying in its port side, orientated 090/270° in 58 metres, and projects 10 metres up from the seabed of mixed gravel, sand, mud and shell over rock. Because of the depth, it would be best to dive the *Munchen* at a low neap tide, when the starboard side of the hull should then be at 48 metres.

The German cruiser Munchen *(Author's collection)*

In good underwater visibility, green light extends a long way down before the water turns black. The *Munchen* is completely covered in large orange and white plumose anemones. The stunning encrustation of the *Munchen* by soft corals at this depth suggests that the tide runs fast and hard over the wreck. Dropping down the now-vertical deck, the bridge superstructure is still in place. On top of this is the ship's wheel, encrusted in anemones and marine growth.

Heading towards the bow, a number of interesting brass items can be seen below the deck by torchlight, especially where the forward gun turret once was. The turret and its armament were removed before the sinking, leaving a large hole in the deck. This was not part of any scrapping work carried out by the British. The disarming of the ship was carried out by the Germans themselves in 1916, and no doubt they had rather pressing alternative use for the guns in the middle of the First World War.

The *Munchen* carried 400 tons of coal to fire her ten boilers and two triple expansion engines. Looking down from deck level, pipes can be seen running the length of the ship.

Following the starboard rail and taking in the immensity of the vessel, past air vents, bollards and hawse pipes, with the anchor chains running out from them, the clean, straight edge of the bow, fringed by large plumose anemones, slopes down into the darkness. To explore this area further involves going deeper than 50 metres, and entering the wreck below decks at this depth would be extremely dangerous.

There are dive boats operating out of North Berwick, but air divers wishing to visit the *Munchen* should note that not all the local skippers will drop you on to it, as some impose a 50-metre maximum-depth policy on air. They cannot guarantee that the shotline will land on the wreck, so there is the possibility of it landing on the sea floor at 58 metres. Trimix is the obvious solution, but if you plan to dive the *Munchen* on air, check with your skipper first to avoid later disappointment.

STJERNVIK

Wreck No: 96		Date Sunk: 12 April 1928	
Latitude: 56 07 31 N		Longitude: 02 49 06 W	
GPS Lat: 5607.520 N	WGS84	GPS Long: 0249.070 W	
Location: 3½ miles SSW of Elie		Area: North Berwick	
Type: Steamship		Tonnage: 1174 grt	
Length: 240 ft	Beam: 34.2 ft	Draught: 14.1 ft	
How Sunk: Collision with *British Ambassador*		Depth: 36 metres	

The wreck at 5607.520N, 0249.070W, 3.41 miles, 339° from Fidra lighthouse (159° to Fidra) was first located in 1935 (WGS84 5607.515N, 0249.142W). It is known to local fishermen as *Tommy Littles*, and is charted with a least clearance of 36 metres in about 49 metres total depth.

HMS *Scott* reported in 1959 that it had a least depth of 120 feet, and stood up some 34 feet above the sea bed, indicating that it must be a fairly substantial vessel – compare the reports of the *Avondale Park* (2878 grt, standing up 32 ft from the bottom), and the *Rolfsburg* (1825 grt, standing up 40 ft).

Its position is in a direct line with the approach to (or departure from) the Fairway buoy, and it would be quite logical to describe it as "off Fidra." (It could also be descibed as 3½ miles SSW of Elie.) The chart indicates that the seabed here is fine sand.

The 1174-grt iron steamship *Stjernvik* (ex-*Louise*, ex-*Balbus*) was built in 1883 by Barrow S.B. Co., and registered in Sweden. She was in collision with the steamship *British Ambassador* in dense fog off Fidra while en route from Ridham Dock to Burntisland in ballast on 12 April 1928. The Swedish vessel was badly damaged, and the crew took to their boats, where they remained until the *Stjernvik* disappeared. They were then taken aboard the *British Ambassador* and landed in Leith. The *British Ambassador* was en route, in ballast, from Grangemouth to the Tyne, and was able to continue on its voyage.

The wreck was located and dived by Craig Hunter, Scott Maxwell and Jonathan Phillips on 7 October 2001 at 5607.520 N, 00249.172 W (WGS84). A porthole and the ship's compass, inscribed with the words "G.W. Lyth   Stockholm", were recovered. The bell, inscribed "Louise Malmö" was recovered on 14 October 2001. Malmö was the Swedish port where the vessel was first registered.

The wreck is intact and upright, oriented 105/285°, and stands up 8–10 metres from the seabed. At low water the depths are 46 metres to the seabed, 40 metres to deck and 36 metres to the highest part of the wreck – the engine room skylight and bridge. She is a centre island ship, very similiar in layout and size to the *Wallachia* in the Clyde, with two holds forward of the bridge, and one behind. Both bow and stern are covered in nets, the bow extensively so. The raised fo'cs'le has partially collapsed, allowing the nets to penetrate this at deck level from the starboard side of the bow. The decks are still com-

The bell from the Stjernvik *(Courtesy of Scott Maxwell & the author)*

plete, and between the fo'cs'le and the bridge are two cargo holds, with a winch between holds No. 1 and No. 2. The top level of the bridge has partially collapsed. The roof is missing, but it is otherwise generally intact. There is a large kettle and griddle still in the galley. Aft of the bridge is the funnel and engine room skylight, then another hold. A spare three-metre diameter, four-bladed propeller lies forward of the raised canopy at the stern (again similiar to the *Wallachia* in curved shape and type), with the auxiliary steering wheel and the remains of an iron or steel binnacle on the starboard side. Collision damage is obvious on the starboard side, at the after end of hold No. 3, towards the stern. The engine room is full of silt to the top of the very large diameter two-cylinder engine, and boiler, although it is possible to transit the area. A lot of the portholes and fittings are made of iron or steel, rather than brass. Her main propeller is also four-bladed.

METANOL

Wreck No: 97		Date Sunk: 5 January 1974
Latitude: 56 04 00 N PA		Longitude: 02 46 00 W PA
GPS Lat: 5604.000 N		GPS Long: 0246.000 W
Location: Off Broad Sands, Dirleton		Area: N.Berwick
Type: Tanker		Tonnage: 803 grt
Length: 224 ft	Beam: 33 ft	Draught: 14 ft
How Sunk: Foundered		Depth: 12 metres

The Spanish chemical tanker *Metanol* sank off Broad Sands, Dirleton on 5 January 1974 after her cargo of nitric acid leaked into her double bottom and ate through the steel plating of her hull. She was raised in June 1974, and beached between Lamb and Fidra, and is now reported to be completely broken up in 12 metres on a seabed of sand and rock.

On the other hand, I have also been informed that the raised wreck was taken to Leith for scrapping, and that her stainless steel tanks were able to be reused. There may well be some residual wreckage remaining on the seabed where she was beached.

STELLA

Wreck No: 98		Date Sunk: 8 December 1903
Latitude: 56 08 19 N		Longitude: 02 44 44 W
GPS Lat: 5608.310 N		GPS Long: 0244.730 W
Location: 3½ miles SE of Elie		Area: N.Berwick
Type: Steamship		Tonnage: 341 grt
Length: 135.3 ft	Beam: 23.4 ft	Draught:
How Sunk: Collision with *Waterland*		Depth: 48–52 metres

This wreck was first located in 1959 by the survey ship HMS *Scott*, standing up 4 metres in 52 metres. The site is known locally as "Law to Craig". This local name probably indicates that the wreck lies on the transit North Berwick Law – Craigleith.

Side-scan sonar indicated a height of 7 metres, length 38 metres (115 feet), and breadth 10 metres (32 ft). The site is a well-defined wreck lying with its keel orientated 075/255°.

The least echo sounder depth was 48 metres in a general depth of 52.1 metres. By 1993 the least echo sounder depth was 45.6 metres in a general depth of 50.9 metres. A scour pit measured a depth of 51.2 metres.

In 2006 the recovery of the bell enabled this wreck to be identified as the Swedish steel steamship *Stella*, which was built in 1888 by Motala MV of Oskarshamn, and owned by Angfartygs A/B Stella (Ahrenberg), Gothenburg. She was 341 grt, and measured 135.3 ft by 23.4 ft – somewhat different from the apparent size of the wreck as indicated by side-scan sonar. Three hours after leaving Brucehaven, Limekilns, bound for Haugesund, Norway, with a cargo of coal, *Stella* was sunk in a collision with the Dutch steamship *Waterland* "near the Bass Rock" on 8 December 1903. Three of her crew were lost.

UNKNOWN – PRE 1945

Wreck No: 99
Latitude: 55 58 12 N
GPS Lat: 5558.200 N
Location: 1 mile NW of Musselburgh
Type:
Length: Beam:
How Sunk:

Date Sunk: WWII
Longitude: 03 01 32 W
GPS Long: 0301.530 W
Area: Leith
Tonnage:
Draught:
Depth: 7 metres

This is thought to be an unknown Second World War wreck, and was reported as 2½ miles west of Cockenzie on 14 November 1945. She could not be found in the charted position in 1960, but a good echo was obtained three cables to the east of this position.

IVANHOE

Wreck No: 100
Latitude: 55 59 30 N PA
GPS Lat: 5559.500 N
Location: 4 cables, 38° Martello Tower
Type: Trawler
Length: 112.2 ft   Beam: 19.8 ft
How Sunk: Ran aground

Date Sunk: 3 November 1914
Longitude: 03 10 00 W PA
GPS Long: 0310.000 W
Area: Leith
Tonnage: 190 grt
Draught: 9.9 ft
Depth: 1 metre

British Vessels Lost At Sea 1914–18 merely states "wrecked in Firth of Forth". *Ivanhoe*, (Trawler No.664), was stranded 4 cables, 38° from the Martello Tower half a mile east of Leith Docks. Her masts, funnel and wheelhouse were visible above water for a time after she ran aground.

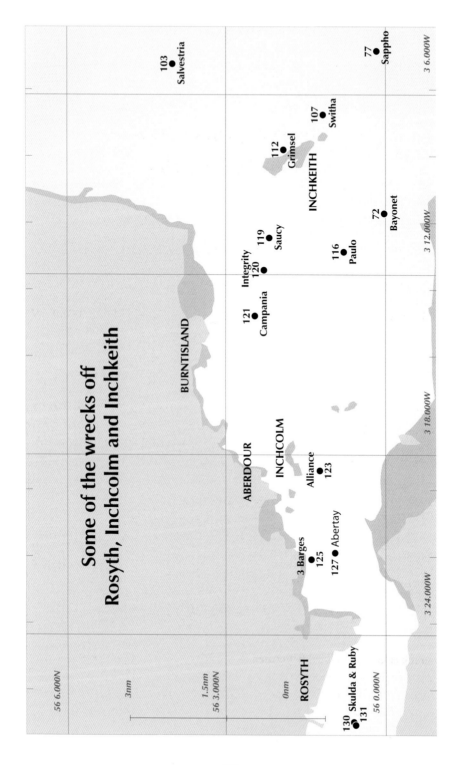

Some of the wrecks off
Rosyth, Inchcolm and Inchkeith

4

Rosyth, Inchcolm
and Inchkeith

MEDUSA

Wreck No: 101	Date Sunk: 13 December 1974
Latitude: 56 03 20 N	Longitude: 03 01 04 W
GPS Lat: 5603.330 N	GPS Long: 0301.070 W
Location: 3½ miles E of Inchkeith Light	Area: Inchkeith
Type: Tug	Tonnage:
Length: 45 ft Beam:	Draught:
How Sunk: Foundered	Depth: 22 metres

The Leith tug *Medusa* sank in gale force winds on Friday, 13 December 1974. The two crewmen were never found, depite a search by the Anstruther and South Queensferry lifeboats, a Royal Navy tug, and an RAF helicopter. The wreck is intact, 4 miles, 265° to the north tip of Inchkeith, 5½ miles, 175° to the west chimney at Cockenzie power station.

BOY ANDREW

Wreck No: 102	Date Sunk: 9 November 1941
Latitude: 56 03 31 N	Longitude: 03 01 55 W
GPS Lat: 5603.520 N	GPS Long: 0301.920 W
Location: 5 miles SE of Kirkcaldy	Area: Inchkeith
Type: Drifter	Tonnage: 97 grt
Length: Beam:	Draught:
How Sunk: Collision with *St.Rognvald*	Depth: 27 metres

This wreck is known to local fishermen as the *Mussels Wreck*, and is very close to the approximate position given for the sinking of the *Boy Andrew* in 1941 (560342N, 030136W PA). It could not be found during a search around that PA in 1960. The drifter *Boy Andrew* (ex-*Sunburst*) was built in 1918 by John Lewis & Sons of Aberdeen.

She was used as an Admiralty Drifter during the First World War. In 1940 she was requisitioned again, for use as an auxiliary patrol vessel, and renamed *Boy Andrew*.

On the morning of 9 November 1941 the steamship *St.Rognvald* was overtaking the *Boy Andrew* in a swept channel when the drifter suddenly went to starboard across the course of the *St.Rognvald*. The drifter was pushed bodily under water and all her crew of 13 were drowned.

The Court of Enquiry took the view that the *St.Rognvald*'s course was too close to the *Boy Andrew*, and that this was not good seamanship. She could have given the *Boy Andrew* a wider clearance, but both vessels, by faulty navigation, contributed to the disaster, the apportionment of blame being two-thirds to the *Boy Andrew* and one-third to the *St.Rognvald*. This decision was upheld by a court of appeal in 1947.

While searching for this wreck in 1990, we manoeuvred alongside a fishing boat trawling very close to this position. The trawler skipper pointed out the wreck position a short distance off his course, and we dropped a shot line on the wreck when it appeared on our echo sounder. While kitting up and waiting for the trawl net to pass safely before putting divers in the water, however, our shot line was caught in the trawl and swept away – after we had thought it was past! MORAL: Beware of trawlers! Their nets can extend an awfully long way behind the vessel!

SALVESTRIA

Wreck No: 103		Date Sunk: 27 July 1940
Latitude: 56 04 03 N		Longitude: 03 04 07 W
GPS Lat: 5604.074 N		GPS Long: 0304.804 W
Location: 2.77 miles NE of Inchkeith Lt.		Area: Inchkeith
Type: Whale Factory Ship/Tanker		Tonnage: 11938 grt
Length: 500.3 ft	Beam: 62.4 ft	Draught: 42.6 ft
How Sunk: Mined		Depth: 27 metres

The steamship *Cardiganshire* was built in 1913 by Workman, Clark & Co. at Belfast for the Royal Mail Steam Packet Co., but was allocated to their Shire Lines subsidiary for the Far East run. At 9426 grt and with a length of 500 ft and a beam of 62 ft 5 ins, she was the largest and fastest ship on that route. In September 1914 she was used to ferry units of the British Expeditionary Forces across the Channel, and in February 1915 was taken over by the Admiralty for a voyage to Zeebruge with troops and war supplies. As the ship approached Zeebruge the Belgian pilot ordered full speed ahead and steered her into the mole causing damage to the bow. The pilot was subsequently arrested, investigated and shot for sabotage. In April 1915 she participated in the Dardenelles campaign. She was chased by a submarine in the Mediterranean on 14 January 1917, but her 14-knot speed enabled her to escape. Later that year she crossed the Atlantic and brought US troops to Britain.

Salvestria *(Courtesy of Christian Salvesen)*

In May 1929 she was sold to Christian Salvesen's South Georgia Co. who had her converted into a whale factory ship, and renamed *Salvestria*. The conversion included the fitting of a stern ramp, for pulling the whales inboard. The rest of the conversion resulted in her gross weight being increased by 2512 tons to 11938 grt.

As a whaling factory ship, she was obviously equipped for very long voyages, and able to remain at sea for months at a time. She was also fitted with large capacity tanks to contain whale oil. Her extremely large tank capacity enabled her to act as a pretty useful tanker.

Inward-bound from Aruba with 12000 tons of fuel oil in her cargo tanks, she arrived off Methil on 27 July 1940, and anchored in Largo bay, close to Elie Ness, to await a pilot to guide her upriver to to Grangemouth. At 1630 Pilot Thomas Flockhart came aboard

The whale factory ship Salvestria *(Courtesy of John Marsh collection)*

and Captain John Jamieson immediately weighed anchor and got under way. Proceeding towards Inchkeith by the swept channel, she was following three or four other ships. The *Salvestria* was the deepest draught ship amongst them, and was keeping as close as possible to the buoys with white flags marking the centre of the channel. Steaming to westward and to starboard of the centre line of the channel at 7.5 knots, she was about to make a turn on to the last leg of the channel approaching Inchkeith East Gate, (i.e. the antisubmarine barrier gate operated by boom defence vessels), when at 1755 hours a magnetic mine detonated under No. 7 and No. 8 cargo tanks abaft the engine room. The *Salvestria* was then in 042°, Inchkeith Lighthouse 2.8 miles. Captain Jamieson, who was on the starboard wing of the bridge, heard only one explosion, which seemed to be directly under his ship. Looking aft he saw a column of smoke and flame rising to about 100 feet. *Salvestria* moved just 75 yards after the explosion. According to Jamieson she immediately settled by the stern, and when the stern touched the bottom after only about one minute, she listed to port. Her bow stayed afloat for about 20 minutes after the explosion. She was the first Salvesen ship to be sunk during the war, and ten of the 57 crew were lost. The survivors were taken off by HM drifter *Betty Brodie* and *HMS Norna*.

Captain G. H. Lang of the Royal Artillery on Inchkeith said that dense clouds of black smoke rose 300 feet from the burning tanker. As he approached the wreck in a boat from Inchkeith, he noted a thick scum of sticky oil on the surface of the river. Oil from the *Salvestria* washed ashore on both sides of the Forth.

It had been thought that the *Salvestria* must have strayed out of the swept channel, but the Court of Enquiry found no evidence to support this. Captain Jamieson and Pilot Flockhart both confirmed that they passed within 100 feet of the swept channel buoys. At the time of the explosion, however, there was a westerly set to the tidal stream, and the buoys became displaced either to east or west of the charted position, according to the direction of the tidal stream. The court pointed out that when ships are using swept channels, the centre line of which is marked by buoys, there is a definite danger of them paying more attention to the buoys than to the correct channel.

The *Salvestria* measured 500.3 by 62.4 by 42.6 feet, and is one of the largest wrecks in the Forth. The wreck is charted with a clearance of 14.4 metres. It may have been only 14.4 metres at one time, but salvage efforts have since reduced it to a large pile of scrap metal at 27 metres. The steam engine and condensers were salvaged by Whites of Burntisland at the end of the war, and the wreck dispersed with depth charges. The highest point stands 5 metres off the sandy bottom. As this wreck is very popular with sea anglers, there is lots of fishing tackle, grapnels, etc. entangled in the wreckage.

IRIS

Wreck No: 104
Latitude: 56 04 00 N PA
GPS Lat: 5604.000 N

Date Sunk: 27 April 1912
Longitude: 03 04 00 W PA
GPS Long: 0304.000 W

Location: 5 miles E by N of Inchkeith   Area: Inchkeith
Type: Steamship   Tonnage: 149 grt
Length: Beam: Draught:
How Sunk: Collision with *Cayo Manzanillo*   Depth:

The Danish wooden steamship *Iris* left Dysart on 27 April 1912, bound for Treguier, France, with a cargo of coal, but was sunk in a collision with the London steamship *Cayo Manzanillo* 5 miles E by N of Inchkeith.

GOOD DESIGN

Wreck No: 105   Date Sunk: 23 November 1940
Latitude: 56 02 56 N   Longitude: 03 06 20 W
GPS Lat: 5602.930 N   GPS Long: 0306.330 W
Location: 1¼ miles NE of Inchkeith   Area: Inchkeith
Type: Drifter   Tonnage: 21 grt
Length: 45 ft   Beam: 15 ft   Draught:
How Sunk: Mined, towed to Granton   Depth: 25 metres

The drifter *Good Design* was built by Walter Reekie of St Monans in 1936, and was a well-known Pittenweem fishing vessel until requisitioned by the Admiralty for patrol work during the Second World War.

Two of the six crew of the *Good Design* were killed when the vessel struck a mine, and broke in two at 1155 hours on 2 November 1940, 073° Inchkeith 3.1 miles. (560256N, 030620W).

There are extremely strong currents in this area – far stronger than the chart suggests, and it was not until after I had spent a considerable time abortively looking for the wreck, that I discovered the two halves were towed to Granton. There is no wreck in the above position.

VIGILANT

Wreck No: 106   Date Sunk: 28 December 1882
Latitude: 56 01 26 N   Longitude: 03 04 20 W
GPS Lat: 5601.430 N   GPS Long: 0304.330 W
Location: ½ mile N of North Craig   Area: Inchkeith
Type: Brig   Tonnage: 303 grt
Length: 125.4 ft   Beam: 25.4 ft   Draught: 14.9 ft
How Sunk: Ran aground/foundered   Depth: 6 metres

The three-masted Norwegian brig *Vigilant* had loaded a cargo of coal at Wemyss and was lying at anchor in Leith roads on the night of 27 December 1882, waiting for daylight the next morning to sail for Christiania (Oslo).

In the late evening a strong gale sprang up from the west. The gale increased in force to become a W by N force 10 storm. The *Vigilant* dragged her anchor for some time, until at about 1 a.m., the anchor cable broke, causing the vessel to drift helplessly before the storm. At 2 a.m. she struck a reef of rocks at the south end of Inchkeith, about three quarters of a mile mile from the lighthouse. The eight crew took to their small boat, and succeeded, with great difficulty, in making a landing on the east side of the island. The men reached the lighthouse in an exhausted state at 4 a.m. The *Vigilant* remained on the rocks for a short time before drifting off in a damaged state, and finally foundered about two miles east of the island. At low water the next day, the greater portion of the ship's masts could be seen protruding above water, and the wreck was considered likely to become a source of danger to vessels frequenting the vicinity of Inchkeith. The crew of the wrecked vessel had lost all their clothes, and were taken to Leith by a steam tug.

A foul at 5.9 metres is charted at 560117N, 030442W, and in 1966 it was reported that a fairly large wreck standing up 4 metres in 10 metres depth was located at 560126N, 030420W. This is two miles south-east of Inchkeith Light, or one mile east of Herwit Rock. The position of this wreck and the water depth in the area would seem to be consistent with that report, and this wreck is likely to be the *Vigilant*.

SWITHA

Wreck No: 107		Date Sunk: 31 January 1980	
Latitude: 56 01 11 N		Longitude: 03 06 38 W	
GPS Lat: 5601.180 N		GPS Long: 0306.630 W	
Location: Herwit Rock, S of Inchkeith		Area: Inchkeith	
Type: Isles class trawler		Tonnage: 573 grt	
Length: 178 ft	Beam: 30 ft	Draught: 15 ft	
How Sunk: Ran aground		Depth:	

HM Fisheries Protection vessel *Switha*, (ex-*Ernest Holt*), was built in 1948 by Cochrane & Sons of Selby. Despite radio warnings that she was running into danger, she ran aground on the Herwit Rock about a mile south of Inchkeith, in rough seas and gale force winds at 4.40 a.m. on 31 January 1980.

The Anstruther lifeboat took over two hours in the prevailing stormy conditions to cover the 18 miles to the wreck. All 25 aboard were airlifted to safety by a Sea King helicopter from RAF Boulmer in Northumberland. Attempts to refloat her were unsuccessful, and on 7 February explosives were used to release, and burn her remaining fuel oil to avoid further pollution. The wreck remained perched on Herwit Rock, and her back was soon broken by subsequent wave action. Despite being almost completely broken in two, she remained prominently visible above water at all states of the tide for 20 years.

Storms over the years gradually took their toll, particularly one in early January 1992, which significantly widened the gap between the bow section, which lay on its starboard

The trawler Ernest Holt, *which became HMS* Switha *(Author's collection)*

HMS Switha *perched on Herwit Rock (Author's collection)*

HMS Switha *perched on Herwit Rock (Author's collection)*

Very little of HMS Switha *now remains visible above the surface (Author's collection)*

side, and the remainder of the wreck which was upright, but with a slight list to starboard. The wreck collapsed and disappeared beneath the surface in 2001. All non-ferrous items are long gone.

IONA

Wreck No: 108		Date Sunk: 2 February 1882
Latitude: 56 01 24 N		Longitude: 03 06 48 W
GPS Lat: 5601.400 N		GPS Long: 0306.800 W
Location: Little Herwit Rock		Area: Inchkeith
Type: Steamship		Tonnage: 909 grt
Length:	Beam:	Draught:
How Sunk: Ran aground / raised		Depth: 5 metres

While inward-bound from London to Leith, the steamship *Iona* ran aground on Little Herwit Rock at 5.25 a.m. on 2 February 1882. Visibility was hazy, and although Inchkeith light could be seen, the vessel's distance from the light was misjudged, and because the sea was so smooth, no sound was heard from either of the buoys marking the Herwit Rock. The *Iona* was not too badly damaged, and signals for assistance were made. Two tugs attempted to drag her off the rocks, but without success.

The fine weather continued over the next ten days, during which the vessel's cargo was removed to lighten her, in order to make it easier to tow her off. The cargo was taken to Leith in steam lighters. Just as preparations were being made to float the *Iona* off the rocks, however, a severe WSW gale blew up on 12 February, and immediate attempts to refloat her had to be abandoned. On the morning of the 13th, it was seen that the *Iona*'s stern had sunk into deep water, while her forepart was still fast upon the rock.

She remained in that position, lying on her starboard side, and was considered a total loss until, in September 1882, she was refloated by the Dundee Salvage Company, and taken to Leith.

DEERHOUND

Wreck No: 109	Date Sunk: 25 March 1885
Latitude: 56 01 12 N	Longitude: 03 06 38 W
GPS Lat: 5601.200 N	GPS Long: 0306.630 W
Location: Herwit Rock, S of Inchkeith	Area: Inchkeith
Type: Steamship	Tonnage: 112 grt
Length: 99 ft Beam: 16.5 ft	Draught: 9.7 ft
How Sunk: Ran aground	Depth: 5 metres

The Leith-registered iron-hulled paddle-wheel steam trawler *Deerhound* (LH1087) was wrecked in fog at Inchkeith on 25 March 1885. She obviously struck the Herwit Rock and broke her back. The forward section of the wreck lies on the north side of Herwit Rock, very broken up, with the bows pointing north. Part of this forward section includes two radially-corrugated cylinders, about two feet in diameter, and 5 or 6 feet long, lying at an angle of about 30°. The after part of the forward section of the wreck was almost touching the starboard side of the *Switha*, before the *Switha* finally collapsed on to it. Her boiler breaks the surface at low water springs, immediately to the south of Herwit Rock.

QUICKSTEP

Wreck No: 110	Date Sunk: 15 October 1907
Latitude: 56 01 12 N PA	Longitude: 03 07 24 W PA
GPS Lat: 5601.200 N	GPS Long: 0307.400 W
Location: Briggs Reef, S of Inchkeith	Area: Inchkeith
Type: Steamship	Tonnage: 936 grt
Length: 210.3 ft Beam: 51 ft	Draught: 15.4 ft
How Sunk: Ran aground	Depth:

Shortly after leaving Leith on 15 October 1907 with a cargo of 1200 tons of coal for Rochester, the steamship *Quickstep* ran on to rocks south of Inchkeith.

All the efforts of the crew to call for assistance went unnoticed, and as their vessel was perched above water across a ledge of submerged rock, with about two metres depth of water forward, and ten metres aft, she soon broke her back. Attempts were made to launch a boat, but it was found that this could not be done without incurring even greater danger than would be experienced by remaining aboard throughout the stormy night.

The following morning, the wreck was discovered by the tug *Transit*, which was visiting Inchkeith, and took off the 16 crew and landed them at Leith. The *Quickstep* ran on to Briggs Reef, and the Hydrographic Department has recorded her at 560130N, 030745W PA.

She was built in 1889 by J. Priestman, engine by North East Marine, and registered in Sunderland.

OSCAR II

Wreck No: 111	Date Sunk: 16 November 1888
Latitude: 56 01 24 N PA	Longitude: 03 07 30 W PA
GPS Lat: 5601.400 N	GPS Long: 0307.500 W
Location: Long Craig, S of Inchkeith	Area: Inchkeith
Type: Barque	Tonnage: 520 grt
Length: Beam:	Draught:
How Sunk: Ran aground, but towed to Leith	Depth:

The Norwegian barque *Oscar II* was en route from Sundswall to London with a cargo of firewood when the weather started to blow up, and she entered the Forth to seek shelter until the storm abated. While the vessel was wind bound, lying at anchor in Leith roads, a violent SW storm, force 10, broke out (the Inchkeith lighthouse keepers report describes the wind as SW, blowing a hurricane), and like many other ships that morning, during the height of the gale the ship's anchors failed to hold. The ship consequently drifted on to a reef of rocks at the south end of Inchkeith, about a quarter of a mile from the lighthouse. At 11.30 a.m., on 16 October 1888, the lighthouse keepers observed the ship on the rocks with the sea apparently making a clear breach over it, but they could render no assistance to the crew.

At noon, word reached Leith that a large vessel was dragging her anchors near Inchkeith. Captain Thomson, Assistant. Dock master at Leith, seeing the perilous position of the vessel, at once got together a volunteer crew to man the lifeboat, which was towed out to the distressed vessel by the steam tug *William Fenwick*. Before the lifeboat had time to reach the scene, the vessel had stranded on the Herwit Rocks, which lie three quarters of a mile SSE of Inchkeith.

Hundreds of people had assembled on the West Pier at Leith, eagerly watching the lifeboat as it made its way to the wreck, and anxiously awaiting its return with the crew of the vessel. The gale was now raging with great fury, and the sea was running very high. Three times the lifeboat went adrift from the tug, but at last succeeded in reaching the stranded vessel, which proved to be the 520-ton Norwegian barque *Oscar II*, Captain Andersen, bound from Sundsval to London with firewood. Her masts were gone, and the waves were dashing over her with great force. The lifeboat with her volunteer crew was nearly swamped in getting alongside the wreck, and experienced the greatest difficulty in getting the eleven crew off the barque, along with their clothing and effects. After the men were rescued from their dangerous position, the lifeboat, assisted by the steam tug, conveyed them safely to Leith.

On the morning of the 28th the Inchkeith lighthouse keepers observed that the vessel had floated off the rocks into deep water. A tug arrived and towed her into Leith in a broken down condition.

GRIMSEL

Wreck No: 112	Date Sunk: 12 October 1889
Latitude: 56 01 54 N	Longitude: 03 07 48 W
GPS Lat: 5601.900 N	GPS Long: 0307.800 W
Location: E Side of Inchkeith	Area: Inchkeith
Type: Steamship	Tonnage: 1398 grt
Length: 251 ft Beam: 34.2 ft	Draught: 17.5 ft
How Sunk: Ran aground in fog	Depth: 4 metres

The South Shields steamship *Grimsel* was built in 1880 by J. Redhead & Co. En route from Salonica to Leith with a cargo of rye and five passengers, she took a pilot on board as she passed St Abbs Head at midnight on 11 October 1889. As the vessel proceeded north towards the Forth, visibility deteriorated as she encountered an increasingly thick fog, although the lights on the Bass Rock, May Island and Fidra were seen. Passing within a few miles of Fidra, they continued at full speed towards Inchkeith, in the hope that they would also see its light. At about 4.20 a.m., with the vessel still going full speed ahead, the island suddenly came in sight, dead ahead, but the light could not be seen through the fog.

Despite immediately going full astern, the *Grimsel* struck the rocks on the east side of the island with great force, and stuck fast. The sea entered several compartments of the ship. Later, in an effort to save their ship, the owners employed a large number of men to discharge the damaged cargo into lighters, and take it to Leith, but the *Grimsel* could not be saved, and the wreck was auctioned on 31 October.

The broken remains of the keel from the bows to the bridge lie covered in kelp in shallow water close to the shore at 560154N, 030748W. Brass bell dolphins almost a metre long have been recovered, along with the bell clapper, but the diver who recovered them in 1990 could find no trace of the bell itself. The stern section with the engine and boiler were presumably scrapped.

GIHDO

Wreck No: 113	Date Sunk: 21 December 1900
Latitude: 56 01 30 N PA	Longitude: 03 08 00 W PA
GPS Lat: 5601.500 N	GPS Long: 0308.000 W
Location: Long Craig, S of Inchkeith	Area: Inchkeith
Type: Schooner	Tonnage: 159 grt
Length: Beam:	Draught:
How Sunk: Ran aground	Depth:

The Russian schooner *Gihdo* had discharged a cargo of pit props at Grangemouth, and had then loaded a cargo of coal at St Davids for Riga. She then lay at anchor, wind bound in the Forth, for over a week. The wind worsened to a SSW storm on 21 December 1900. When the storm was at its height, she parted from her anchor and was blown on to the rocks south of Inchkeith at 1.30 a.m. Her distress signals were seen from the lighthouse, but when the keepers went down to the south end of the island, they could see that no assistance could be given, but the crew could get ashore at low tide, which they subsequently did, bringing their belongings with them. It had been thought that if the weather moderated before the vessel got too much damage, it might be saved, but this turned out not to be the case.

JEHU

Wreck No: 114		Date Sunk: 25 January 1890
Latitude: 56 01 30 N PA		Longitude: 03 07 30 W PA
GPS Lat: 5601.500 N		GPS Long: 0307.500 W
Location: Long Craig, S of Inchkeith		Area: Inchkeith
Type: Barquentine		Tonnage: 198 grt
Length:	Beam:	Draught:
How Sunk: Ran aground		Depth:

The barquentine *Jehu* had loaded a cargo of coal for France at Grangemouth, and was towed down to Leith roads, where she was lying at anchor on 25 February 1890, when a severe SW gale broke out. As the evening wore on, the gale increased in strength, and eventually her starboard anchor cable parted.

The remaining anchors failed to hold the her, and at 8.00 p.m. the vessel drifted helplessly on to the reef of rocks at the south end of Inchkeith, about 300 yards from the lighthouse. The sea then made a clean breach across the ship as she lay on the rocks, and as the crew had no small boat in which to attempt an escape, they were forced to take to the rigging until 3.00 p.m. the following day – a period of some 19 hours! – when a tug was finally able to approach their stranded vessel and take them off.

PAUL

Wreck No: 115		Date Sunk: 16 November 1888
Latitude: 56 01 57 N PA		Longitude: 03 08 18 W PA
GPS Lat: 5601.950 N		GPS Long: 0308.000 W
Location: West landing, Inchkeith		Area: Inchkeith
Type: Schooner		Tonnage: 135 grt
Length:	Beam:	Draught:
How Sunk: Ran aground		Depth:

During the morning of 16 November 1888, while the German brig *Paul* was lying at anchor about a mile and a half west of Inchkeith, waiting for an opportunity to enter the harbour at West Wemyss to load a cargo of coal, a severe WSW gale blew up. Three anchors were deployed, in the hope of riding out the gale, but at about 11.30 a.m. the anchor cables parted, and the vessel was blown ashore in the little bay on the west side of Inchkeith, a short distance from the landing jetty. The captain and six crewmen remained aboard their vessel for a short time after the vessel struck, although the waves soon made a clean breach over her. Meanwhile, the five soldiers on the island had hurried down to the shore to render asststiance. A line was thrown on shore, and by means of it, a stout rope was made fast to a rock from the mast of the ship, but the crew seemed most unwilling to leave. After waiting for more than an hour they resolved to come on shore by the rope through the surf, a distance of about 40 yards. The first to venture was a young lad, who on getting about half way, fell from exhaustion into the sea. Two of the soldiers immediately rushed into the water, nearly up to their necks, and saved him. Timing their movements by the waves, the other men also came ashore hand over hand, and were caught by the soldiers standing waist deep in the water. The shipwrecked men were taken to the light keepers houses, where their needs were attended to.

During the night, when the tide was out, the seamen went on board their vessel, which was lying high and dry, and recovered their belongings. Next day, the vessel began to break up, and by the 19th her masts, sails and hull lay in a mass of confusion on the rocks.

Captain Brebens of the *Paul* set out in a sail boat that day and landed at Kinghorn to report the wrecking of his vessel. The crew were picked up from the island by the tug *Stephenson* and taken to Leith on the 21st.

PAOLO

Wreck No: 116		Date Sunk: 20 October 1898
Latitude: 56 01 24 N		Longitude: 03 11 00 W
GPS Lat: 5601.400 N		GPS Long: 0311.000 W
Location: 1½ miles West of Inchkeith		Area: Inchkeith
Type: Steamship		Tonnage: 1039 grt
Length: 224.4 ft	Beam: 33 ft	Draught: 13.2 ft
How Sunk: Ran aground		Depth: 16 metres

The iron steamship *Paolo* was registered in West Hartlepool. She left Burntisland for Hamburg on Saturday, 15 October 1898, but, in the vicinity of the May Island, was badly damaged in the severe easterly force 9 gale, and her lifeboat was carried away. The captain decided to put back to Burntisland. It appears that a number of other vessels in the area obscured his view of the West Gunnet Ledge buoy, and the captain, mistaking the east one for it, sailed right between the two, and struck on the reef, one and a half miles west of Inchkeith. The accident was witnessed by the pilot boat *Mary Thomas* of Newhaven, which went immediately to the rescue. The last of the 18 crew had just reached the *Mary Thomas* when the steamer lurched back and sank in three fathoms of water and became a total loss.

Gunnet Ledge is at 560124N, 031030W. An anchor chain runs from the south side of Gunnet Ledge and disappears into the mud, but the wreck has not been found. The rocky area is not too large to search, although if she has completely broken up, it might be difficult to distinguish wreckage from rock with an echo sounder. The 20-ton drifter *Persevere* was mined 75 yards, 074° from East Gunnet Ledge buoy on 27 October 1940 (560122N, 031024W).

GRASSHOLM

Wreck No: 117		Date Sunk: 7 September 1911
Latitude: 56 01 30 N PA		Longitude: 03 10 00 W PA
GPS Lat: 5601.500 N		GPS Long: 0310.000 W
Location: West Gunnet Ledge		Area: Inchkeith
Type: Fishing boat		Tonnage: 40 grt
Length:	Beam:	Draught:
How Sunk: Collision with *Sir Walter Scott*		Depth:

The steam trawler *Grassholm* was heading for Granton from the fishing grounds, and was rounding the West Gunnet Ledge between midnight and 1.00 a.m. on 7 September 1911 when she was run into by the steamship *Sir Walter Scott*[1], which was out-bound from Leith to Hamburg. The collision was so great that the trawler sank in six minutes, and two of the crew were drowned.

LY 120

Wreck No: 118		Date Sunk: 2 December 1974
Latitude: 56 03 42 N		Longitude: 03 10 42 W
GPS Lat: 5603.700 N		GPS Long: 0310.700 W
Location: Pettycur Bay		Area: Inchkeith
Type: Hopper barge		Tonnage:
Length:	Beam:	Draught:
How Sunk: Ran aground		Depth:

The American hopper barge *LY 120* broke loose while her cargo of 838 tons of wood pulp was being discharged. She was driven ashore in Pettycur Bay. Attempts to refloat her were unsuccessful.

SAUCY

Wreck No: 119	Date Sunk: 4 September 1940
Latitude: 56 02 10 N	Longitude: 03 10 33 W
GPS Lat: 5602.173 N	GPS Long: 0310.741 W

---

1   On one page of the Inchkeith lighthouse keeper's report the name of the colliding vessel is given as *Sir William Wallace*, while on another page it is correctly named *Sir Walter Scott*.

The search and rescue tug HMS Saucy *(Author's collection)*

Location: 1½ miles W of Inchkeith Light   Area: Inchkeith
Type: Tug   Tonnage: 579 grt
Length: 155.3 ft   Beam: 31.1 ft   Draught: 15.7 ft
How Sunk: Mined   Depth: 14 metres

The steel tug *Saucy* was built in 1918 by Livingston & Cooper of Hessle. Her engine was by Bellis & Morcom of Birmingham. In 1939 she was requisitioned as a search and rescue tug for use in the Second World War.

On 3 September 1940 she left Aberdeen with the damaged Dutch MV *Delftdijk* (10220 grt) in tow for the Forth. At 1955 hours on 4 September, shortly after casting off the tow of the *Delftdijk*, *Saucy* struck a mine one and a half miles west of Inchkeith, and sank with the loss of 26 crew members. It was said that there were five survivors.

The vessel had sunk 277°, 2560 metres from Inchkeith Light and was marked by a buoy laid 300°, 90 metres from the wreck. In 1945 the wreck was dispersed to give a least depth of water over the wreck of 13.6 metres and the buoy was removed, although the area was still regarded as 'foul'.

The wreck was not found during a survey in 1967, and it was considered to have been buried in the silt. In 1971 the wreck was again searched for with sonar and not found. In 1992, however, the wreck was located at 560210N, 0031033W, using Decca. The wreck was found to be sitting upright in 14 metres of water, substantially intact, and covered with anemonies. Most of the superstructure, and the anchors are still in place, and a gun is mounted near the bows.

The conversion from Decca to latitude/longitude must have been slightly inaccurate, as on 9 August 1993 HMS *Sandown* located an uncharted wreck at 560212N, 031044W. The least echo sounder depth was 11.2 metres in a general water depth of 15 metres. The vessel was dived upon and found to be a tug of the First World War era with a 3.5-inch gun forward. The vessel is upright with its masts lying alongside on the seabed. The bow is complete and stands 4 metres high in a scour pit, but the stern has broken up.

The wreck was reported to be 40 metres long by 10 metres beam, oriented 338/158°, with the bow to the NW, standing about 4 metres above the seabed at 560211.5N, 0031045W.

Anywhere upriver from Inchkeith is prone to silting, so underwater visibility here varies with the state of the tide and the weather. Unfortunately, it is almost always very poor.

INTEGRITY

Wreck No: 120		Date Sunk: 7 October 1879
Latitude: 56 02 16 N		Longitude: 03 11 48 W
GPS Lat: 5602.270 N		GPS Long: 0311.800 W
Location: 1½ miles SE of Burntisland		Area: Inchkeith
Type: Tug		Tonnage:
Length:	Beam:	Draught:
How Sunk: Collision with John Stirling		Depth: 31-36 metres

The steam trawler *Integrity* sank in five minutes after being in collision with the 427-ton iron paddle steamer *John Stirling*, which was on her usual route from Granton to Burntisland in thick fog. The trawler's crew of seven were picked up and taken to Burntisland by the John Stirling. Compensation of £870 plus costs was made by the North British Railway Co. who owned the *John Stirling*. The wreck is 165 feet long, and is oriented 075/255°.

CAMPANIA

Wreck No: 121		Date Sunk: 05 11 1918
Latitude: 56 02 26 N		Longitude: 03 13 20 W
GPS Lat: 5602.430 N		GPS Long: 0313.330 W
Location: 1 mile S of Burntisland		Area: Inchkeith
Type: Aircraft Carrier		Tonnage: 18000 displ.
Length: 622 ft	Beam: 65.2 ft	Draught: 26 ft
How Sunk: Collision with HMS *Glorious*		Depth: 27 metres

The 12950-grt Cunard liner *Campania* was built by Fairfield Shipbuilding Co., Glasgow in 1893. After trials off Skelmorlie she made her maiden voyage on 22 April 1893 from Liverpool to New York. At that time the *Campania* was the largest and fastest ship afloat. On the return voyage, in May 1893, she captured the 'Blue Riband' for a record voyage from Sandy Hook, New York to Queenstown, Ireland in 5 days, 17 hours and 27 minutes, with an average speed of 21.9 knots. In June 1893 the record passage from Liverpool to New York was also beaten. Then in August 1894 she made her fastest crossing in 5 days, 9 hours, and 21 minutes at an average speed of 21.59 knots. It was not until 1898 that the Norddeutscher Lloyd ship, *Kaiser Wilhelm der Grosse*, took all the Atlantic records and the Blue Riband.

Although she remained on Cunard's Liverpool–New York service, she was converted into an armed merchant cruiser, and represented Cunard at Queen Victoria's Diamond Jubilee Review at Spithead in 1897.

In July 1900 the *Campania* was involved in a serious collision at sea. Whilst returning from New York she ran into thick fog 207 miles west of Queenstown, Ireland. She reached Roches Point, outside Queenstown, but had to wait for the fog to lift before attempting to enter the harbour. On the morning of 21 July, while travelling at 10 knots in dense fog about 26 miles north-east of Tuskar, the *Campania* collided with the Liverpool barque *Embleton*, and sliced clean through it. The forward half of the sailing ship sank immediately, and the aft part swung around and damaged the *Campania*'s starboard side. Lifeboats were only able to save seven of the *Embleton*'s crew of 18. The *Campania*, which had been steaming at her minimum speed to maintain steerage way, reached the Mersey without any further incident.

In 1901 she was fitted with wireless. The captain of the Cunard liner *Lucania*, from New York, reported that on September 25, in latitude 48.15 North, longitude 38.39 West, communication by Marconi's wireless telegraphy was established at a distance of 33 miles, with the same company's steamer *Campania*, outward bound to New York, and messages were exchanged between the two vessels until a distance of 65 miles had separated them.

In 1904 a rogue wave swept five passengers overboard. This was the first time the Cunard Line lost passengers through an accident.

On 14 April 1914 she completed 250 round voyages across the Atlantic. She was then chartered to the Anchor Line for five more voyages, after which she was temporarily recalled from August to October 1914 while *Aquitania* served as a troop ship. *Campania* was then taken out of service, and on 15 October 1914 she was sold to T.W. Ward for scrapping.

At that time the Royal Navy had three small seaplane carriers – the converted cross-channel steamers *Empress*, *Engadine* and *Riviera*. These ships were too small (they could only accommodate three or four aircraft each), lacked endurance, and were too slow to keep up with the fleet. The Grand Fleet had requested a larger and faster ship.

Someone at the Admiralty decided that the *Campania* would be ideal for conversion to a large seaplane carrier. Fast enough at 22 knots to accompany the battleships of the Grand Fleet, and with sufficient coal to cross the Atlantic (she burned 12 tons per hour), the Royal Navy purchased her from the shipbreakers on 27 November 1914. Breaking work had progressed only to the stripping of deck fittings, and she was taken to Cammell Laird at Birkenhead for conversion into an aircraft carrier. The first simple conversion was completed fairly quickly, and the 18000 tons displacement HMS *Campania* entered Royal Navy service on 17 April 1915. She joined the Grand Fleet in Scapa Flow on 30 April, with Charles Lightoller, senior surviving officer of the *Titanic*, as her First Lieutenant.

The aircraft she was to operate was a new Fairey seaplane, also called the Campania. This was the first aircraft designed for carrier use. A total of sixty-two were built, and used until 1919.

The Cunard liner Campania *(Courtesy of Glasgow University Archives)*

The aircraft carrier HMS Campania *after first conversion*
(Courtesy of Clydesite, www.clydesite.co.uk)

The aircraft carrier HMS Campania *after second conversion*
(Author's collection)

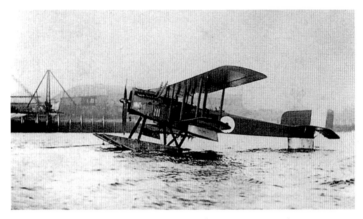

Fairey Campania seaplane (Author's collection)

The aircraft took off from a 200-foot wooden ramp which was built from the forefunnel to the bow, using wheeled trolleys placed under the floats. *Campania* was the first Royal Navy vessel to launch aircraft whilst underway. It was soon found that this runway was too short, and her aircraft capacity was too small to be worthwhile (only 2–3 aircraft). A second conversion, carried out by Cammell Laird between November 1915 and March 1916, improved the design considerably. She re-entered service in April 1916 with a much longer flying-off platform forward. In order to lengthen the runway, her forefunnel was removed, and replaced with twin uptakes set as far apart as possible. Additionally, the aft superstructure was removed to make space for a seaplane working deck, additional derricks were fitted, and other improvements were made. She was much more useful in this configuration, and could now carry ten aircraft. She could also operate balloons, but there is no record of her doing

A Fairey Campania aircraft on HMS Campania *(Author's collection)*

so. She was the largest and fastest of the wartime conversions, but was never considered to be completely successful.

The *Campania* operated with the Grand Fleet as a scouting aide, but missed the Battle of Jutland due to a communications failure. At 2010 hours on 30 May 1916 a signal was sent to all the Grand Fleet ships at Scapa Flow, ordering them to be ready to leave harbour at 2130 hours. Captain Oliver Swann[2], never received the signal to sail, and weighed anchor two hours late, at 2345. (Due to an administrative oversight, the 2010 signal had not been sent to *Campania*). Admiral Jellicoe had been wrongly informed that *Campania* could only do 19 knots, rather than her actual 22 knots, and had calculated that at 19 knots she would never arrive in time for her aircraft to be of any use. In fact the carrier was rapidly gaining on the battle fleet, and could have caught up with the Grand Fleet at approximately 1330 hours on 31 May, but at 0437, Jellicoe ordered her back to Scapa rather than continue, unescorted, at risk of attack by U-boat.

Her ancient machinery, already worn out when she was purchased, presented continual maintenance problems, and eventually she was reduced to training duties in 1918, due to her persistent machinery problems.

On 4 November 1918, very near the end of the war, she was moored off Burntisland with a number of Royal Navy battleships. She was lying to a single anchor – her starboard anchor – and at three hours notice for steam. By then Captain Swann had been replaced by Captain J. C. H. Lindsay. At 2230 hours on the 4th, when Captain Lindsay retired to bed for the night, there was a light WSW wind and it was raining. It was a very dark night. The barometer was falling slowly, but not enough suggest any unusually severe weather to come. At 0330 hours on the 5th, the anchored ships were suddenly hit by a very violent

2   Born with the surname, Schwann, Captain Swann anglicised it in 1917 after making a forced landing on Scarborough racecourse in a German *Mars* aeroplane. With a German sounding name, flying a German aircraft still in its German markings, he was very nearly shot by local army personnel. His flying career started before WWI, when he was involved in the development and construction of the Navy's first airship. When airship development was halted he turned to heavier-than-air machines. Despite not having a pilot's licence, he bought himself an Avro biplane, fitted it with floats and carried out the first take off by a British pilot from salt water. He obtained a pilot's licence the following year.

As captain of *HMS Campania*, he was advised to prepare to accompany the Grand Fleet on the eve of the Battle of Jutland, but never received the signal ordering the ship to set sail. Two hours after the main fleet sailed Swann gave orders to follow, only to be ordered back to port by Admiral Jellicoe. As a result the Grand Fleet was deprived of a potentially valuable reconnaissance facility, which may have produced a totally different outcome to the battle. Captain Swann was responsible for creating the first training establishment to train pilots and observers in fleet co-operation techniques, and his interest in aviation led to him becoming Deputy Chief of the Air Staff in 1918. In 1920 he was removed from the Navy Lists on being awarded a Permanent Commission in the RAF, and later became Air Vice-Marshal Sir Oliver Swann KCB, CBE.

force 10 squall. *Campania* was struck on the beam, and swung round. Her anchor immediately started to drag, and the ship was blown at a considerable speed across the stem of the nearest anchored battleship.

There was initially some confusion about the identity of the ship invoved in the first encounter. When Captain Lindsay had turned in for the night, HMS *Glorious* was the nearest anchored ship. He was unaware that while he was asleep, HMS *Royal Oak* had arrived, and anchored between the *Campania* and *Glorious*.

When he was wakened at 0330 hours, he saw that his ship was almost under the bows of what he assumed to be the *Glorious*. It was, in fact, the *Royal Oak*.

Attempts were made to arrest the drift by hauling on the anchor and dropping a second anchor, but this failed to halt the ship. On drifting down sideways into *Royal Oak*'s bows, the *Royal Oak* too, started to drag – the combined effects of both ships being too much for the *Oak*'s one anchor to hold. In the heavy squalls, both ships were dragging uncontrollably towards the battleship *Royal Sovereign*, but in a very few minutes, the *Royal Oak* struck the *Glorious*, the *Glorious*'s stem hitting *Royal Oak*'s port side at a fine angle. *Royal Oak* then drifted down *Glorious*'s starboard side, with *Campania* still across her ram. When the *Royal Oak*'s bows came abreast of *Glorious*'s stem, *Campania* was then impaled on the latter's projecting forefoot and was released from the *Royal Oak*, whose anchors then held. *Campania* was then pivoted around *Glorious*'s stem by the wind, and swung round to drift down *Glorious*'s port side, bow to stern.

Captain Lindsay's immediate concern was to get *Campania* clear of *Glorious*. Orders had been given to raise steam, and despite the fact that the boiler room was on three hours notice for raising steam, this was achieved in only half an hour from the time the order was given – a most creditable performance.

A searchlight illuminates the scene just before dawn

As soon as steam was ready, *Campania* went slow ahead and hove in on both anchor cables. Her starboard anchor was found to have hooked *Glorious*'s anchor cable, which was being drawn up under *Royal Oak*'s bows. That anchor was then buoyed and slipped, while the port anchor was hauled in, and *Campania* finally got clear of *Glorious* at 0534 hours.

By this time there was a lot of water in *Campania*'s engine room, and in response to radio signals asking for assistance, several other vessels had arrived on the scene, including the tugs *Neptor*, *Volcano* and *Merrimac*, and the destroyer HMS *Grenville*. All the ship's company were put aboard the destroyer, except for a few seamen and the watch of stokers, who were kept on board in case they could still be of some use. The tugs were asked if they could take the sinking *Campania* in tow to shallower water, but they all said it would be impossible on account of her, by now, very pronounced draught, against the wind and tide. In addition, other anchored ships, particularly HMS *Royal Sovereign*, were in the way, between *Campania* and the shore. *Campania*'s bilge pumps were running at full power, but the water level was rapidly increasing. An electric submersible pump was useless, as there was no electric power, due to her dynamo room being flooded. By about 0600 hours there was 20 feet of water in each engine room. Captain Lindsay was concerned that the foremost bulkhead could carry away at any moment, in which case the ship would sink in a very few minutes. For that reason, he was keen to get all the ships crew off. All except about 20 men were put on the destroyer and one of the tugs. It was then reported that water was rising in the after stokehold, so orders were given to draw the boiler fires. When this had been done, Captain Lindsay and all the remaining men boarded the tug *Merrimac*, and remained alongside the sinking ship. *Campania* was by then drawing about 45 feet of water aft. Just at that time the salvage vessel *Mariner* arrived from Leith, and the weather appeared to moderate a little. *Mariner* went alongside *Campania*'s port side and Captain Lindsay went aboard her. An attempt was made to get *Mariner*'s submersible pump aboard *Campania*. Before the pump could be got aboard, however, *Campania* was drawing about 50 feet of water aft, and the upper deck of the ship was awash as far as the engine room. The salvage officer was wading up to his knees on *Campania*'s deck, when the ship lurched heavily to port. *Mariner*'s captain and his men got back aboard their own vessel, and as *Mariner* went astern, *Campania* heeled over towards them and sank at 0835 hours.

A series of photographs (shown opposite) was taken as she sank.

HMS *Campania* is the largest ship sunk in the Forth, and although she sank in 100 feet of water, the ship was of such a size that for a time after she sank she was a hazard to navigation, with her masts showing above the surface.

A salvage company was contracted to clear the obstruction, and by 1921 the wreck had been demolished to what was at that time considered a safe depth. She was eventually dispersed to give a clearance of 6.5 fathoms (12 metres) in 1947. It is also reported that salvage of metals took place during the late 1940s and again in the 1960s.

Campania *settles by the stern*

Campania *further down by the stern*

Campania *sinking by the stern*

Campania *going down by the stern*

The wreck lies in 20–30 metres on a muddy bottom about one mile south of Burntisland harbour, between 560226N, 031320W and 560220N, 031324W. It is about 150 yards from the green navigation buoy No. 9, and rises up about 15 metres from the bottom. It can be easily found by echo sounding around the buoy. One of the highest peaks of the wreck lies NNE of the buoy (200° magnetic to the buoy), and another to the SSW (20° magnetic to the buoy). I had previously been given erroneous information that the *Campania* was broken in two pieces, but side scan sonar images show that the wreck is, in fact, complete and in one piece, although in a state of collapse.

The wreck has been declared a site of historic importance, and is designated as a Protected Wreck under Section One of the Protection of Wrecks Act 1973. A licensed diver must accompany groups interested in diving the *Campania*. (I believe only Mark Blyth of The Dive Bunker, Burntisland Watersports, and MC Diving of Dalgety Bay are currently licensed.) A strict no-touch policy is in force for this wreck.

Campania *sitting on the seabed outside Burntisland harbour*

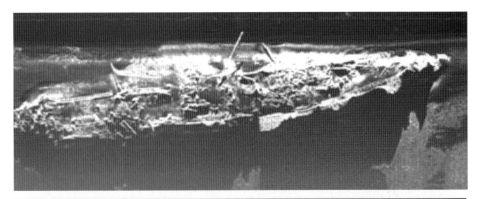

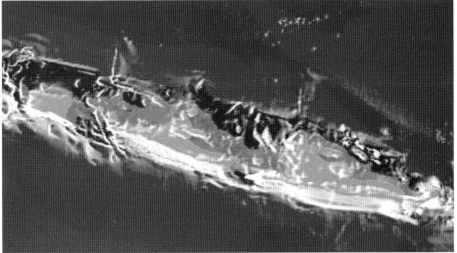

Side-scan sonar images show that the wreck is complete, but in a state of collapse

Underwater visibility in this area is usually very bad, making it difficult to know which part of the wreck you are on. (The best underwater visibilty here is said to be about five metres, but in my experience, I think five centimetres would be the norm!)

PORTHCAWL

Wreck No: 122
Latitude: 56 01 36 N PA
GPS Lat: 5601.600 N
Location: 200-300 yds W of Inchcolm
Type: Steamship
Length: 298.5 ft   Beam: 44 ft
How Sunk: Ran aground

Date Sunk: 1 Febraury 1926
Longitude: 03 18 36 W PA
GPS Long: 0318.600 W
Area: Inchcolm
Tonnage: 2481 grt
Draught: 21.2 ft
Depth: 4 metres

The steel steamship *Porthcawl* was built at Burntisland in 1923, and registered in Cardiff. Her engine was made by D. Rowan & Co. of Glasgow. According to *The Scotsman* newspaper, the *Porthcawl* went ashore on the west side of Inchcolm on 1 February 1926, shortly after leaving Grangemouth with a cargo of 4000 tons of coal for Genoa.

On 4 February, despite continuous pumping, the ship was still firmly on the rocks with serious bottom damage, the sides showing signs of strain, and some of the deck plates buckled, although it was hoped to make an attempt to refloat her in a day or two. The following day it was reported that her back was broken in front of the bridge, and that salvage had been abandoned. In addition to the 4000 tons of cargo coal, a further 380 tons of coal was in her bunkers.

The *Porthcawl* had grounded between two reefs with her bow high and dry, and her hull buckling with a severe list to port. In daylight she could be seen from the shore. Despite pessimistic reports about the condition of the ship, due to the extensive damage she had sustained, Leith Salvage & Towage Company persevered in their efforts, and were finally rewarded with success in refloating the *Porthcawl*. The severely damaged ship was then towed to the back of the West Pier at Leith, where she was beached. She still had a large quantity of coal in her holds, and this was to be removed to lighten the ship before taking her into the dry dock.

ALLIANCE ?

Wreck No: 123	Date Sunk: 22 March 1905
Latitude: 56 01 14 N	Longitude: 03 18 27 W
GPS Lat: 5601.230 N	GPS Long: 0318.450 W
Location: 0.4 miles S by W of Inchcolm	Area: Inchcolm
Type: Steamship	Tonnage: 326 grt
Length: 145.2 ft Beam: 23.1 ft	Draught: 9.9 ft
How Sunk: Ran aground	Depth: 25 metres

When this wreck was found in 1967 it was judged to be about 160 feet long, and lying N/S. The iron steamship *Alliance*, belonging to the North Eastern Shipping Co. of Aberdeen, was en route from Inverkeithing to London with a cargo of stones from Carlingnose quarry, when she went on the rocks close to Inchcolm when starting her voyage in foggy conditions on the night of Wednesday, 22 March 1905. The vessel sank and the crew landed on the island.

There is some doubt about this wreck being the *Alliance*, in view of its position in the deep water of the main shipping channel, 0.4 miles S by W from Inchcolm. It would seem much more likely that this is the wreck of a vessel that either foundered or sank in a collision. The *Alliance* is perhaps more likely to be near where the *Porthcawl* ran aground, close to 560136N, 031836W, just off the west of Inchcolm. There are extremely strong currents here in very silty water, right in the middle of the very busy shipping channel, making this a very dangerous place to investigate at close hand.

GIRL MARY

Wreck No: 124
Latitude: 56 01 40 N
GPS Lat: 5601.670 N
Location: 255°, 4 cables from Inchcolm Tower
Type: Drifter
Length: 50 ft   Beam:
How Sunk: Explosion

Date Sunk: 10 October 1940
Longitude: 03 18 40 W
GPS Long: 0318.670 W
Area: Inchcolm
Tonnage: 80 grt
Draught:
Depth: 13 metres

The steel drifter *Girl Mary* was built by Walter Reekie of St Monans in 1933, and was registered in Arbroath (AH 37). She was requisitioned for Admiralty use during the Second World War, and on 10 October 1940 she sank after an explosion, in 7 fathoms (13 metres), 255° 4 cables from Inchcolm Tower, in an area of very poor underwater visibility amongst a tangle of discarded anti-submarine boom netting. Five of the crew were saved, but two were lost. According to Naval records, the explosion was caused by the vessel striking a mine.

3 BARGES

Wreck No: 125
Latitude: 56 01 24 N
GPS Lat: 5601.408 N
Location: 1 mile E of Carlingnose
Type: 3 Barges
Length: Beam:
How Sunk:

Date Sunk: 1955
Longitude: 03 21 24 W
GPS Long: 0321.400 W
Area: Inchcolm
Tonnage:
Draught:
Depth: 5 metres

Three steel Thames-type barges carrying concrete ballast were sunk in 1955, and were reported in 1967 to have least depths of 62 feet and 50 feet. Their positions are: 560124N, 032112W / 560124N, 032115W and 560124N, 032124W.

In 1974 divers reported that one of the barges was lying on top of another, and the third barge lay close by. Apparently these barges did have names. One was *Jimmy Piper*, and another was *Alice Piper*. The name of the third barge is not known.

TURO

Wreck No: 126
Latitude: 56 00 03 N PA
GPS Lat: 5600.050 N
Location: Inchgarvie
Type: Schooner
Length: 89.3 ft   Beam: 21.3 ft
How Sunk: Ran aground

Date Sunk: 13 November 1901
Longitude: 03 23 00 W PA
GPS Long: 0323.000 W
Area: Rosyth
Tonnage: 164 grt
Draught: 10.5 ft
Depth:

In a severe easterly gale on 13 November 1901 the Swedish schooner *Turo* was driven on to Inchgarvie, on which the central piers of the Forth Bridge rest. As she was inward bound from Halmstad to Methil with a cargo of pit props, she was obviously driven before the storm for some considerable distance beyond her intended destination before finally striking the rocks. Inchgarvie is a narrow, elongated rock with a rather pointed eastern end, and the waters of the Forth were lashing against the island with terrific fury when the schooner stranded. The seven crewmen made a gangway of pit props from the vessel to the rocks, and all reached the island safely. The North Queensferry Coastguards had noticed lights on the island during the morning, and at 7.00 a.m., one of the Coastguards went along the Forth Bridge and descended one of the ladders which connects the bridge with Inchgarvie. *Turo's* crew were led off the island, and taken to the Albert Hotel at North Queensferry. The *Turo* was badly damaged, but was being kept afloat by her cargo. It had been hoped to tow her to Dysart for repairs, but I do not know if she lasted long enough for that to be achieved.

(There is some doubt about the correct spelling of the name of this vessel. *Turo* – ex-*Karreboek* – seems most likely, but it has also been written as *Thura* and as *Ture*. She is not in Lloyd's Register for 1901).

ABERTAY ?

Wreck No: 127		Date Sunk: 10 October 1892	
Latitude: 56 00 57 N		Longitude: 03 21 12 W	
GPS Lat: 5600.950 N		GPS Long: 0321.200 W	
Location: 1 mile E of Carlingnose Point		Area: Inchcolm	
Type: Steamship		Tonnage: 635 grt	
Length: 222.3 ft	Beam: 33.3 ft	Draught: 12.8 ft	
How Sunk: Collision with *Iron Duke*		Depth: 18 metres	

There may be two wrecks here, or perhaps one wreck in two parts, possibly sunk as the result of a collision. The steel steamship *Abertay* looks a likely candidate for the wreck charted in this position.

On 10 October 1892 she sank after colliding with the anchored battleship HMS *Iron Duke* near the Forth Bridge. The *Iron Duke* was was lying at her usual moorings, not far west of the Forth Bridge. The night was fine, and the waters of the Forth were almost without a ripple. *Iron Duke's* bow had swung round to point west, due to the flow of the out-going tide, and as darkness fell, her lights were switched on. Shortly after 7.00 p.m. the *Abertay*, outward bound from Grangemouth to Rostock with a cargo of 1200–1300 tons of coal, ran into the *Iron Duke*, and subsequently sank.

Divers reported that one of the plates on *Iron Duke's* port bow, close to the ram, about 10 feet under water, was slightly indented, and a rivet had been knocked out of place. The *Abertay* obviously also sustained damage, and would likely be carried further east by the out-going tide before foundering. On the other hand, it has been recorded that *Abertay* sank on the west side of Inchgarvie. This would suggest a position of about 5600.070N, 0323.410W.

TELESILLA

Wreck No: 128		Date Sunk: 14 September 1896
Latitude: 56 00 22 N		Longitude: 03 24 12 W
GPS Lat: 5600.370 N		GPS Long: 0324.200 W
Location: Mackintosh Rock, Forth Road Br.		Area: Rosyth
Type: Steamship		Tonnage: 1174 grt
Length: 230.0 ft	Beam: 31.6 ft	Draught: 17.3 ft
How Sunk: Ran aground		Depth: 13 metres

The British iron steamship *Telesilla* was built in 1877 by E. Withy & Co. of Hartlepool.

Shortly after leaving Grangemouth on the night of 14 September 1896, bound for Hamburg with a cargo of coal, she ran on to Beamer Rock then drifted off to sink adjacent to Mackintosh Rock, which is the rock on which the north towers of the Forth Road Bridge are constructed.

Wreckage of the *Telesilla* was discovered during the construction of the Road Bridge during 1959–1962. A fairly substantial amount of wreckage, including a 10-inch diameter propshaft and prop tunnel, was again encountered during maintenance work on the bridge piers in the late 1990s. This wreckage had to be removed at that time to allow piling work to be undertaken.

ELCHO CASTLE

Wreck No: 129		Date Sunk: 30 October 1919
Latitude: 56 01 00 N		Longitude: 03 24 48 W
GPS Lat: 5601.000 N		GPS Long: 0324.800 W
Location: Ashore close to Rosyth Docks		Area: Rosyth
Type: Steamship		Tonnage: 33 grt
Length: 56.1 ft	Beam: 16.4 ft	Draught: 5.8 ft
How Sunk: Foundered		Depth:

The wooden steamship *Elcho Castle* foundered in the fairway to Rosyth dockyard shortly after the First World War. The date given by the Hydrographic Department is 11 March 1921, but another source gives the date as 30 October 1919.

She sank after springing a leak while on passage from Inverkeithing to Ostend with a cargo of coal. Why did she sink upriver of her point of departure, when logic dictates that she should have been going the other way? Apparently she was being towed from Inverkeithing to Ostend by the steam hopper *Queensferry*. Off Leith the leak was discovered, and she was then towed back upriver to Rosyth, which was the nearest port with a dry dock and repair facilities, but the *Elcho Castle* sank just before reaching there.

She was raised and moved out of the way (perhaps this was achieved on 11 March 1921) to a position 1000 feet, 300° from Cultness. That would place her in the mud close to the shore at 560100N, 032448W, adjacent to the entrance to the dockyard (position 560106N, 032432W has been recorded), and she would presumably have been scrapped at that site, as there does not seem to be any further record of her, and there is no sign of wreckage in that area.

RUBY

Wreck No: 130		Date Sunk: 10 October 1905
Latitude: 56 00 34 N		Longitude: 03 26 50 W
GPS Lat: 5600.570 N		GPS Long: 0326.830 W
Location: Off Rosyth		Area: Rosyth
Type: Steamship		Tonnage: 481 grt
Length: 175 ft	Beam: 26.6 ft	Draught: 10.5 ft
How Sunk: Collision with *Prudhoe Castle*		Depth: 18 metres

The iron steamship *Ruby* was built in 1888 by Scotts of Bowling, and registered in Glasgow. While en route from Middlesbrough to Grangemouth with a cargo of pig iron on 10 October 1905, she sank two miles west of the Forth Bridge after colliding with the steamship *Prudhoe Castle*. The *Ruby* was reported to lie upside down in 13 fathoms (24 metres), and salvage was abandoned.

Just over a year later, however, on 8 November 1906, it was reported that the wreck of the *Ruby* was being removed as she was a danger to shipping. That report must be somewhat inaccurate, as salvage had already been abandoned, and if she was lying upside down, her masts and funnel can hardly have been a danger (The report must have been intended to refer to the *Skulda*).

The wreck is charted as 17.9 metres in 22 metres, although the scour pit around the wreck is 29 metres deep. The wreck lies oriented 340/160°. The higest point of the wreck is at N5600.575N, 0326.933W.

SKULDA

Wreck No: 131		Date Sunk: 9 October 1906
Latitude: 56 00 34 N		Longitude: 03 26 56 W
GPS Lat: 5600.567 N		GPS Long: 0326.933 W
Location: 1.3 miles W of Beamer		Area: Inchcolm
Type: Steamship		Tonnage: 1177 grt
Length: 227 ft	Beam: 33 ft	Draught: 14.8 ft
How Sunk: Collision with *Tento*		Depth: 25 metres

The steamship *Skulda* was built in 1882 by S. & H. Morton of Leith for J.T. Salvesen of Grangemouth. She sank in collision with the Norwegian steamship *Tento*, in the Firth of Forth, while en route from Grangemouth to Stockholm with a general cargo. According to the *Fife Free Press* of 13 October 1906 the collision took place about 100 fathoms (600 feet) west of Beamer Rock. Reports in *The Scotsman* newspaper give various distances averaging about 1.3 miles upstream from the Beamer.

The *Skulda* was hit practically amidships, near the engine room, and immediately began drifting. Her hatches blew off, and it was seen that there was no chance of keeping the vessel afloat. A boat from the *Tento* took off some of *Skulda*'s 17 crew, while others managed to get away in one of *Skulda*'s own boats. The chief officer, who was below at the time of the collision, could not be reached, and went down with the ship, which sank in nine minutes. The *Tento*, which was built in 1871, was on her way from Norway to Alloa with a cargo of pit props. She sustained considerable damage to her stem, but was able to proceed, and landed the 16 *Skulda* survivors at Grangemouth.

The sunken wreck was a danger to navigation, in about 14 fathoms of water one mile, three cables in a westerly direction from the Beamer beacon. Her masts still projected above water, and the Commissioners of Northern Lights vessels *Pharos* and *May* acted in turn as lightships marking the danger. On 19 October they were replaced by the fishing boat LH850, moored to the NNE of it, from which were exhibited at night three fixed white lights on a yard about twenty feet above the sea, two placed vertically at one end, and one at the other, the single light being on the side nearest the wreck. By day three balls were displayed in a similar arrangement. During fog or thick weather a gong and a bell would be sounded alternately in quick succession, at intervals of not more than one minute. A wreck buoy was also moored to the SSW of the wreck. An examination of the wreck by a diver showed that the collision impact had been so strong that the ship had been cut amidships right to the coaming of the hatch. Naturally the cargo had been disturbed, and the hatchway was jammed by barrels.

On 26 October the *Skulda*'s masts and funnel were removed by blasting, to give a clearance of seven fathoms over the wreck. The attendant fishing boat and the wreck buoy were then removed. It was noted that the *Skulda* had sunk in practically the same position as the *Ruby* had sunk exactly a year before.

SOPHIE WILHELMINE

Wreck No: 132	Date Sunk: 14 October 1898
Latitude: 56 01 30 N	Longitude: 03 33 04 W
GPS Lat: 5601.500 N	GPS Long: 0333.070 W
Location: 1¼ miles S of Crombie Point	Area: Rosyth
Type: Schooner	Tonnage: 105 grt
Length: Beam:	Draught:
How Sunk: Collision with *Perth*	Depth: 5 metres

The Norwegian wooden schooner *Sophie Wilhelmine*, outward bound from Bridgeness to Nykjsking with a cargo of coal, was sunk in collision with the Glasgow steamship *Perth* about 2 miles E by N of Bridgeness Pier on 14 October 1898. A foul charted as 4.7 metres in about 5.4 metres at 560130N, 033304W is the right distance and direction from the east pier at Bo'ness.

GLEN

Wreck No: 133	Date Sunk: 22 November 1940
Latitude: 56 02 00 N	Longitude: 03 34 03 W
GPS Lat: 5602.000 N	GPS Long: 0334.070 W
Location: 1¼ miles SW of Crombie Point	Area: Rosyth
Type: Steam lighter	Tonnage: 130 grt
Length: Beam:	Draught:
How Sunk: Mined	Depth: 6 metres

The steam lighter *Glen* was thought to have hit a mine between Grangemouth and Crombie on the night of 22 November 1940, while carrying 5¼-inch ammunition to Rosyth. The position of this wreck, just south of the main channel to Grangemouth, fits the description of the location of its loss 1¼ miles SW of Crombie Point.

The 46-ton vessel *Triumph VI* is reported to have been sunk in a collision in the Rosyth area on 15 December 1944. Three of the crew of the patrol launch *Mesme* were lost when she was sunk in collision with the submarine *Sunfish* off Grangemouth at 2130 hours on 1 September 1940.

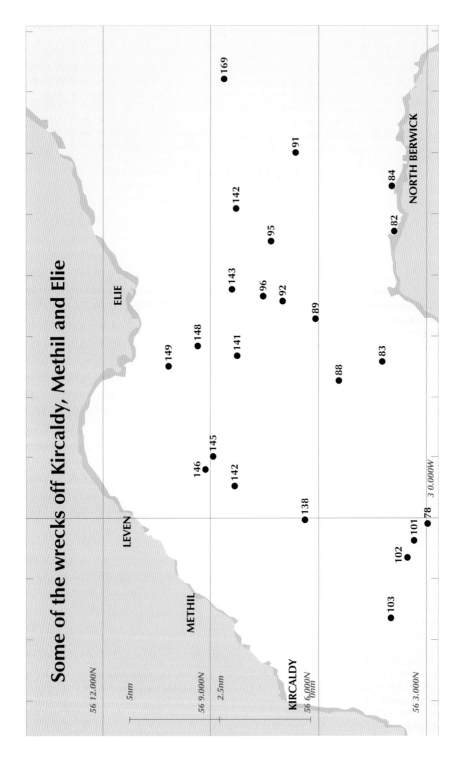

Some of the wrecks off Kircaldy, Methil and Elie

5

Kirkcaldy,
Methil and Elie

KINLOCH

Wreck No: 134
Latitude: 56 07 30 N PA
GPS Lat: 5607.500 N
Location: 4 miles SW of Elie Point
Type: Steamship
Length: Beam:
How Sunk: Foundered

Date Sunk: 29 November 1921
Longitude: 02 53 00 W PA
GPS Long: 0253.000 W
Area: Elie
Tonnage: 64 grt
Draught:
Depth:

The steam coaster *Kinloch* of Peterhead foundered four miles SW of Elie Point on 29 November 1921, while en route from Leith to Inverness with a cargo of manure. The vessel was built in 1904. An obstruction was reported in 1960 at 560648N, 025206W, which is four and a half miles SW of Elie Ness.

WEARBRIDGE

Wreck No: 135
Latitude: 56 11 00 N PA
GPS Lat: 5611.000 N
Location: Chapel Ness, Elie
Type: Steamship
Length: 360 ft   Beam: 49 ft
How Sunk: Ran aground in tow / salvaged

Date Sunk: 23 January 1936
Longitude: 02 50 18 W PA
GPS Long: 0250.300 W
Area: Elie
Tonnage: 4014 grt
Draught: 26.9 ft
Depth:

Treacherous seas prevailed on 23 December 1936 when the vessel *Wearbridge* of Hartlepool, which was built in 1911, was being towed from the Tyne to Rosyth to be broken up by Metal Industries. Opposite Inchkeith, the towing hawser snapped, and the vessel broke adrift in the early hours of the morning. The anchor was immediately dropped, but between 4 a.m. and 5 a.m., the coastguard at the lookout station saw the vessel dragging her anchor, and making towards the shore. Anstruther lifeboat was called out about 9 a.m., but by the time it arrived at the scene, after a difficult launch due to there being only four feet of water at the harbour mouth at the time, Elie Life Saving Brigade had already taken the seven crewmen off the *Wearbridge* by breeches buoy, just as the vessel struck the rocks at Chapel Ness. It was feared that if the gale continued, the vessel would become a wreck. Two tugs were called to try to pull her off, but they were unsuccessful.

The *Wearbridge* remained aground for six months while salvage work was carried out. She was eventually refloated on 12 June 1937, and towed to Rosyth, arriving there about 23 June. As she was holed internally, it was not safe to break her up while still afloat alongside a quay. She was therefore taken into one of the drydocks at Rosyth where final demolition work commenced on 30 June. No wreckage remains in the area.

KAREN

Wreck No: 136		Date Sunk: 5 February 1940
Latitude: 56 11 04 N		Longitude: 02 58 45 W
GPS Lat: 5611.070 N		GPS Long: 0258.750 W
Location: 1 mile E of Methil		Area: Methil
Type: Aux Motor Schooner		Tonnage: 341 grt
Length: 130.1 ft	Beam: 29 ft	Draught: 13 ft
How Sunk: Explosion and fire		Depth: 5 metres

The wooden three-masted Danish auxiliary motor schooner *Karen* (ex-*Havet*, ex-*Willem-oes*) was built by Christensen of Kolding in 1920. She suffered an explosion, and was set on fire off Methil on 5 February 1940.

ADAM SMITH

Wreck No: 137		Date Sunk: 26 December 1884
Latitude: 56 05 36 N PA		Longitude: 03 09 00 W PA
GPS Lat: 5605.600 N		GPS Long: 0309.000 W
Location: Long Craig Rock, Kirkcaldy		Area: Kirkcaldy
Type: Steamship		Tonnage: 185 grt
Length: 150.3 ft	Beam: 22.1 ft	Draught: 12 ft
How Sunk: Ran aground		Depth:

The iron steamship *Adam Smith* was built at Port Glasgow in 1876. When returning to her home port from London on Boxing Day, 26 December 1884, she ran on to Long Craig Rock, a little over a mile south of Kirkcaldy harbour, and became a total loss. Although no lives were lost, this event must have dampened the crew's Christmas somewhat!

ROYAL ARCHER

Wreck No: 138		Date Sunk: 24 February 1940
Latitude: 56 06 26 N		Longitude: 02 59 56 W
GPS Lat: 5606.430 N	**WGS84**	GPS Long: 0300.123 W
Location: 5 miles ESE of Kirkcaldy		Area: Kirkcaldy
Type: Steamship		Tonnage: 2266 grt
Length: 290.5 ft	Beam: 41.2 ft	Draught: 18 ft
How Sunk: Mined		Depth: 24 metres

The steamship *Royal Archer* was built in 1928 by Scotts of Greenock for the London and Edinburgh Shipping Company. Along with her two sister ships *Royal Fusilier* and *Royal Scot*, she sailed up and down the east coast of Britain, ferrying passengers and cargo between London and Leith. She had been running continuously between the Forth and London since the war began, often as Commodore ship of FS and FN convoys.

On 24 February 1940, some 15 miles west of the May Island, and nearing the end of her voyage from London to Leith with 630 tons of general cargo, she struck a mine five miles east-south-east of Kirkcaldy. At that moment second engineer Thomson was easing his way carefully down the propeller shaft service tunnel to inspect the bearings. The tunnel was not quite high enough to allow him to stand upright, and it was dark and oily. The noise of the ships engines was all that he could hear. Suddenly the whole tunnel shook violently and Thomson, aware that all was not well, hurried aft to the shaft tunnel hatch. Captain Riper was just leaving the bridge to go to his cabin when a terrific explosion occurred towards the stem of the ship, and huge lumps of metal flew into the air. Three lifeboats were smashed and the wireless room was enveloped in clouds of steam from burst steam pipes. The captain ordered the ships siren to sound, and the three remaining lifeboats to be launched. The first of these capsized as it was launched, throwing William

Royal Archer *(Courtesy of P. Ransome-Wallis)*

Rendall, the ships quartermaster, into the sea. He could not swim, and drifted away to the stem of the vessel, supported by his lifejacket.

Meanwhile, other crewmembers assisted 2nd engineer Thomson from the prop shaft tunnel hatch, and helped the chief engineer, Loudon, whose leg had been fractured by the blast in the engine room, down into the remaining lifeboats. Twenty-eight of the 29 crew members (including one gunner), got into the lifeboats safely and the final member, quartermaster Rendall, was picked up by the trawler *Tourmaline* after 20 minutes in the water. *Tourmaline* landed all of the *Royal Archer*'s crew, including two injured men, at Leith.

The *Royal Archer* finally disappeared below the surface of the Forth some 30 minutes after the mine explosion. The mine she hit had been laid on 3 November 1939 by *U-21* (Frauenheim). Her position was reported as 6 miles, 44.5° from Inchkeith Lighthouse, and charted at 560618N, 025956W (14.4 metres in 24 metres). In 1949 the wreck was reported to have been dispersed.

It was dived on just west of the charted position in 1982, and was found to be in a somewhat broken up state. She is broken in large sections 3–4 metres high in general depths of 27 metres. The stern area is the most intact part of the wreck, with its companionways and hand-rails covered in plumose anemones. The centre section of the wreck is well broken up, with two boilers under a high mass of steel. To see the boilers you have to go inside the mass of steel from the port side. There is no sign of any of the steam engine or associated equipment, which suggests salvage work has been carried out at some time to recover these. The bow and stern sections are relatively intact. The forward hold contained bales of what appeared to be news sheet, and the stern hold full of vehicle chassis and axles.

A beautiful wooden compass binnacle, complete with compass was found on the stern. The bolts securing it to the deck were removed, and the binnacle carefully rigged to lift upright. Unfortunately, while lifting it aboard the salvage vessel, one of the crew inadvertently turned it upside down and the compass fell out! It is probably still lying buried in the mud off the port quarter of the wreck. The bell was recovered by Mark Blyth in August 2007.

Also mined at the same time and in the same position as *Royal Archer* were *Clan Morrison* in convoy FN102 and *Jevington Court* in convoy FS103, but neither of these ships sank. The cruiser HMS *Belfast* (11500 tons) was seriously damaged in the Firth of Forth, at 560648N, 025436W, between Inchkeith and the May Island on 21 November 1939 by a magnetic mine laid by *U-21* on 4 November.

UNKNOWN – PRE-1946

Wreck No: 139	Date Sunk: Pre-1946
Latitude: 56 07 23 N	Longitude: 03 05 23 W
GPS Lat: 5607.380 N	GPS Long: 0305.380 W
Location: 2 miles W of Kirkcaldy	Area: Kirkcaldy

Type: Barge   Tonnage:
Length: Beam: Draught:
How Sunk: Depth: 9 metres

In 1946, and again in 1947, the wreck of a barge was reported one mile east of Dysart and two miles from Kirkcaldy Pier at 560727N, 030518W. The barge was marked by a wreck buoy until it was dispersed in 1949. The position was corrected in 1959 to 560723N, 030523W. The remains stand only about two feet up from the bottom in about ten metres depth.

MARE VIVIMUS

Wreck No: 140   Date Sunk: 12 December 1925
Latitude: 56 08 00 N   Longitude: 02 51 00 W
GPS Lat: 5608.000 N   GPS Long: 0251.000 W
Location: 3¼ miles S of Kincraig Point   Area: Elie
Type: Trawler   Tonnage: 82 grt
Length: 78 ft   Beam: 19 ft   Draught: 9 ft
How Sunk: Foundered   Depth: 44 metres

The steam trawler *Mare Vivimus* sank in 1925. Although charted in 560800N, 025100W, this is obviously only an approximate position, and it was not found during an asdic search in 1960.

ROLFSBORG

Wreck No: 141   Date Sunk: 13 July 1945
Latitude: 56 08 13 N   Longitude: 02 52 03 W
GPS Lat: 5608.271 N   **WGS84**   GPS Long: 0252.006 W

The steam trawler Mare Vivimus *(Author's collection)*

Location: 3¼ miles SW of Elie
Area: Elie
Type: Steamship
Tonnage: 1831 grt
Length: 264.4 ft   Beam: 42 ft   Draught: 18 ft
How Sunk: Collision with *Empire Swordsman*   Depth: 27 metres

The steel collier *Rolfsborg* (ex-*Skard*, ex-*Kollskegg*) was built in 1915 at Fredrikstad, Norway. She sank following a collision with SS *Empire Swordsman* on 13 July 1945. Two WGS84 positions have been recorded: 5608.271N, 00252.006W and 5608.267N, 00251.976W.

In 1987 she was described as apparently intact, lying on her port side, and standing 12 metres high in 40 metres. Her uppermost, starboard side was at about 30 metres, and a very large brass eagle was fastened around the stern. When dived in 1993 the wreck was described as intact, except for collision damage near the port quarter. It has a 45° list to port and stands 8 metres high.

UNKNOWN

Wreck No: 142
Date Sunk:
Latitude: 56 08 18 N
Longitude: 02 58 21 W
GPS Lat: 5608.300 N
GPS Long: 0258.350 W
Location: 2¾ miles SSW of Methil
Area: Methil
Type: Steamship
Tonnage:
Length: Beam: Draught:
How Sunk: Depth: 29 metres

The wreck charted at 560818N, 025821W is obviously the remains of an old steamship, as wreckage including a boiler standing up three metres high in a general depth of 32 metres was found when dived in 1988.

MERLIN

Wreck No: 143
Date Sunk: 28 November 1884
Latitude: 56 09 00 N PA
Longitude: 02 42 00 W PA
GPS Lat: 5609.000 N
GPS Long: 0242.000 W
Location: Off May Island
Area: May
Type: Paddle steamer
Tonnage: 75 grt
Length: 82.6 ft   Beam: 17.1 ft   Draught: 9.1 ft
How Sunk: Destroyed by fire   Depth:

The wooden paddle steam tug *Blue Bonnet* was built in 1866. She was renamed *Merlin* (LH1054) in 1883, and was destroyed by fire 5 miles WSW of May Island on 28 November 1884. This may be the UNKNOWN at 560822N, 024851W, in 50 metres.

UNKNOWN – MERLIN ?

Wreck No: 144		Date Sunk: 28 November 1884
Latitude: 56 08 22 N		Longitude: 02 48 51 W
GPS Lat: 5608.383 N		GPS Long: 0248.733 W
Location: 2¾ miles S of Chapel Ness		Area: Elie
Type: Paddle Steamer		Tonnage:
Length:	Beam:	Draught:
How Sunk: Destroyed by fire		Depth: 50 metres

Two obstructions were reported in position 560833N, 024924W in 1939, but apparently a decision was taken in 1940 to record them as one wreck at 560830N, 024930W PA, which is a convenient, round number, but no wreck is marked on the chart in or near that position, and, in 1959, the survey vessel HMS *Scott* was unable to find any wreck there. A fishermans fastener known locally as *Rocky Mill* was reported in 1977 in Decca chain 3, Green C38.5, Purple 1C66.7, which converts to 560816N, 024851W. *Rocky Mill* has also been reported in Decca chain 3, Green C37.2, Purple 1C68.8. In 1984 an obstruction was located, but not investigated, at 560822N, 024851W.

It was finally investigated in 1999, and found to be a small iron or steel paddle steamer fitted with tug equipment. There are iron chains at the stern, but there is no super-structure. Despite the wreck being wrapped in a shroud of nets, in only two metres visbility, a compass was recovered. A diving reel and line were left behind, as it was considered far too dangerous to disentangle them, and the divers involved were in no hurry to rush back! About a year later another diver, who thought he was on a virgin wreck, found the line, and I think returned it to its owner.

Sonar readings suggest the wreck to be intact, and lying 090/270°, with the bow point-ing west. The dimensions appear to be 36 metres long by 12 metres wide, and standing up 3 metres from the bottom in a general depth of 53 metres. It is possibly *Merlin* (ex-*Blue Bonnet*), reported as lost by fire 5 miles WSW of May Island on 28 November 1884. This wreck is 9 miles WSW of May Island, but *Merlin* probably drifted, on fire, for some time. The wind at the time was NNW, force 2. On an incoming tide she could easily have been swept 4 miles south-westwards before finally foundering. Entangled nets would increase the apparent size of the wreck as judged by sonar image.

Is the obstruction located in 1984, and *Rocky Mill* one wreck broken in two pieces, or are there really two wrecks? If there are two wrecks, could one of them possibly be the *Kinloch*?

UNKNOWN

Wreck No: 145	Date Sunk: 1970–1971
Latitude: 56 08 58 N	Longitude: 02 56 57 W
GPS Lat: 5608.970 N	GPS Long: 0256.950 W
Location: 2¾ miles SW of Methil	Area: Methil

Type: Barge		Tonnage:
Length: 30 ft	Beam:	Draught:
How Sunk:		Depth: 24 metres

A wooden barge approximately 30 feet long, standing 2 metres high, laden with steel scaffolding, was reported to have sunk while engaged in repair work on a moored oil rig in 1970 or 1971.

CHARLES HAMMOND ?

Wreck No: 146		Date Sunk: 2 November 1918
Latitude: 56 09 05 N		Longitude: 02 57 31 W
GPS Lat: 5609.080 N		GPS Long: 0257.520 W
Location: 2½ miles SW of Methil		Area: Methil
Type: Trawler		Tonnage: 324 grt
Length:	Beam:	Draught:
How Sunk: Collision with *Marksman*		Depth: 22 metres

When dived on in 1988, the wreck charted in 26 metres at 560905N, 025731W was found to be an old steamship or steam trawler, with the highest point standing 4 metres up from the bottom. Could this be the steam trawler *Charles Hammond* which was sunk off Kirkcaldy in a collision with HMS *Marksman* on 2 November 1918?

UNKNOWN – PRE-1939

Wreck No: 147		Date Sunk: Pre-1939
Latitude: 56 09 17 N		Longitude: 02 52 51 W
GPS Lat: 5609.280 N		GPS Long: 0252.870 W
Location: 2 miles SSW of Kincraig Point		Area: Elie
Type:		Tonnage:
Length:	Beam:	Draught:
How Sunk:		Depth: 32 metres

In 1939 a non-sub contact was reported at 560912N, 025340W, 2 miles SSW of Kincraig Point. It was not located in that position in 1959 by HMS *Scott*, but a wreck was found at 560919N, 025340W, with a least depth of 27 metres, standing up 6 metres in a depth of 33 metres. As a result, it was charted as a wreck at 27 metres in that position.

Almost 30 years later, it could not be found there, despite repeated searches around the area in 1987 and 1988, but wreckage standing 3 metres high in a general depth of 38 metres was located half a mile to the east at 560917N, 025251W. These are all probably the same wreck, the differing positions stemming from the development over the years of more accurate position fixing equipment.

PHAEACIAN

Wreck No: 148		Date Sunk: 29 September 1943
Latitude: 56 09 20 N		Longitude: 02 52 32 W
GPS Lat: 5609.288 N	**WGS84**	GPS Long: 0251.655 W
Location: 2 miles S of Kincraig Point		Area: Elie
Type: Steamship		Tonnage: 480 grt
Length: 144.1 ft	Beam: 25.2 ft	Draught: 11.1 ft
How Sunk: Collision with *San Zotico*		Depth: 22 metres

The Harwich-registered steel three-masted steamship *Phaeacian* was built by Mistley S. B. & Rprg. Co. in 1920. On 29 September 1943 she was in a collision with the British steam tanker *San Zotico*, and sank shortly after being taken in tow by a tug. The position was originally recorded as 560924N, 025142W, but she is now charted at 560920N, 025132W, 2 miles south of Kincraig Point near Elie.

In 1986 she was reported to be broken into three parts which stand no more than 4 metres high in general depths of 30 metres. The wreck appears to have rolled over to port, with the bow section lying on its side, pointing towards the south-east, while the main body is lying upside down. In the early 1990s the hull was reported to be largely intact, but by 2001 the plates had started coming apart, and the inside spaces of the vessel could be seen. A split near the stern, which may be the collision damage, provides access to the engine room.

The wreck lies on a muddy bottom at a depth of about 32 metres. Because of the depth and the nature of the bottom, visibility can sometimes be poor. Plumose anemones make spectacular decorations hanging from the floor and roof of some of the compartments.

Three WGS84 positions, extremely close together, have been recorded for the *Phaeacian*: 5609.288N, 00251.655W / 5609.268N, 00251.658W / and 5609.270N, 00251.649W. Previous OSGB36 positions for the three parts were given as: 5609.650N, 0253.320W / 5609.700N, 0253.300W / 5609.720N, 0253.230W

ARIZONA

Wreck No: 149		Date Sunk: 29 September 1940
Latitude: 56 10 14 N		Longitude: 02 52 23 W
GPS Lat: 5610.203 N	**WGS84**	GPS Long: 0252.440 W
Location: 1 mile SSW of Kincraig Point		Area: Elie
Type: Motor Vessel		Tonnage: 398 grt
Length: 143.4 ft	Beam: 26.2 ft	Draught: 8.9 ft
How Sunk: Mined		Depth: 12 metres

The Dutch motor vessel *Arizona* was built in 1939 by van Diepen of Waterhuizen. She was mined on 29 September 1940, while en route from Blyth, via Methil, for Bridgewater with a cargo of 500 tons of coal. Five of the crew of eight were lost.

In 1993 the wreck was reported to be fairly broken up on a sand/shingle seabed at a depth of 17–18 metres. The highest points stand 4–5 metres up from the bottom, 204°, one mile SSW of Kincraig Point signal tower, or two miles south of Elie Ness. A small section of the bow is reasonably intact, lying on its starboard side. The centre section is very broken up. The stern section is slightly less broken, also lying over to starboard. The telegraph, propeller, some portholes and copper pipes from the engine room have been salvaged. There is lots of marine life on the wreck.

For many years it was rumoured that a possible sunken U-boat lies close to this position. All the local fishermen seemed to know about the German submarine, and other wrecks that had been sunk off Elie. Over a period of two years, Peter Grosch, a professional diver who lives in Anstruther, supplied two of the Elie fishermen and two Pittenweem fishermen with buoys, ropes and sinkers, for them to mark the wrecks off Elie Ness, including what one of the older fishermen thought was definitely the submarine. On all four occasions, when diving on the wreck that they had marked, he found the marker buoy was on the *Arizona*!

The WGS84 position of the Arizona has been variously recorded as: 5610.203N, 00252.440W, 5610.148N, 00252.389W, 5610.198N, 00252.488W, 5610.201N, 00252.452W.

ANTELOPE

Wreck No: 150	Date Sunk: 22 February 1888
Latitude: 56 10 30 N PA	Longitude: 03 00 45 W PA
GPS Lat: 5610.500 N	GPS Long: 0300.750 W
Location: Stranded at Methil	Area: Methil
Type: Steamship	Tonnage: 509 grt
Length: Beam:	Draught:
How Sunk: Ran aground	Depth:

The West Hartlepool iron steamship *Antelope*, en route from Methil to Aalborg, ran aground when leaving Methil harbour on 22 February 1888, and became a total loss.

VULCAN

Wreck No: 151	Date Sunk: 15 October 1882
Latitude: 56 05 18 N PA	Longitude: 03 09 00 W PA
GPS Lat: 5605.180 N	GPS Long: 0309.000 W
Location: Vows Rocks, Seafield, Kirkcaldy	Area: Kirkcaldy
Type: Steamship	Tonnage: 235 grt
Length: 141 ft Beam: 22.2 ft	Draught: 12.5 ft
How Sunk: Ran aground	Depth: 5 metres

The *Vulcan* was built in 1874 by R. Dixon of Middlesbrough. The iron steamship *Vulcan* was a regular visitor to the Forth, trading between Middlesbrough and Grangemouth with pig iron. On her inward run from Middlesbrough on 15 October 1882, no land had been seen after rounding St Abbs Head. The night was very dark and rainy, and a force 10 southerly storm was blowing. Inchkeith light was seen and recognised at about 10.30 p.m., but at midnight, the ship struck Vows Rocks, Seafield, near Kirkcaldy. (The Inchkeith lighthouse keeper's report does not specify whether the vessel hit the East or the West Vows, which are about a quarter of a mile apart, and only a few hundred yards offshore. The position given above assumes the latter.)

The ship's boat was smashed while it was being launched, but a second, smaller boat was successfully launched. This boat was only capable of taking nine of the 14 crew. These nine survivors pulled for the shore, and with great difficulty reached Kirkcaldy, where they sought help for the five crewmembers left behind on the stranded wreck. Because of the seas breaking heavily on the shore at Kirkcaldy, it was impossible to launch a boat from there to go to their rescue.

A messenger was consequently despatched to Burntisland for a tug to proceed to the wrecked vessel, but it was found, on arrival, that the *Vulcan* had slipped off the reef and sunk in deep water, taking with her the five men who had been left behind.

The *Fifeshire Journal* of 13 December 1860 carries a report that the stern of a vessel bearing the name *Vulcan* was found on the beach at Elie.

GRAF TOTLEBEN

Wreck No: 152		Date Sunk: 20 February 1912
Latitude: 56 10 50 N		Longitude: 02 50 00 W
GPS Lat: 5610.830 N		GPS Long: 0250.000 W
Location: At East Vows, Elie		Area: Elie
Type: Steamship		Tonnage: 1484 grt
Length: 246 ft	Beam: 33.3 ft	Draught: 17.6 ft
How Sunk: Ran aground/refloated		Depth: 3 metres

The Russian-owned iron steamship *Graf Totleben* (ex-*Skjold*) was built by Lobnitz of Renfrew in 1881. While en route from Methil to Riga with a cargo of 1800 tons of coal and one passenger, she went ashore near Chapel Point, Earlsferry between 3 a.m. and 4 a.m. on 19 February 1912. By firing a rocket and sounding her horn, she drew attention to her plight.

The local life saving brigade turned out with their rocket apparatus, and at the first attempt, succeeded in throwing a line across the vessel, which lay only 100 yards from the shore. The crew, however, did not take advantage of this line, and little was done until the first light of dawn, when it was seen that the vessel was high on the rocks, and her stern was knocking against them. The crew of 20, including Captain Martin Grieve and his wife, were busied bringing ashore their belongings. Two tugs and a lighter went alongside the following day, and a quantity of coal was brought ashore, but it was considered that the chances of getting the vessel off the rocks were very slim. Two days later, a southwesterly gale sprang up, and two small boats belonging to salvagemen who were working aboard the stranded vessel broke adrift and were dashed to pieces on the rocks on the Elie side of the bay. The life saving apparatus was called to rescue the salvagemen from the wreck. Three rockets were fired before a line landed within their reach, and the salvagemen were successfully brought ashore. The period of rough weather caused more damage to the vessel, virtually eliminating what little chance there had previously been of saving the ship, but the vessel was finally refloated in May of that year.

A large anchor, located to the west of the beacon on East Vows, may be from the *Graf Totleben*.

NO. 4 HOPPER

Wreck No: 153		Date Sunk: 7 December 1908
Latitude: 56 10 50 N PA		Longitude: 03 00 30 W PA
GPS Lat: 5610.830 N		GPS Long: 0300.500 W
Location: On rocks near Methil breakwater		Area: Methil
Type: Dredger		Tonnage: 265 grt
Length:	Beam:	Draught:
How Sunk: Ran aground		Depth: 1 metre

Steam dredger *No. 4* went ashore on rocks near Methil breakwater where she later broke up and became a total loss.

JUPITER

Wreck No: 154		Date Sunk: 24 September 1897
Latitude: 56 11 00 N PA		Longitude: 02 48 30 W PA
GPS Lat: 5611.000 N		GPS Long: 0258.500 W
Location: Elieness		Area: Elie
Type: Schooner		Tonnage: 326 grt
Length:	Beam:	Draught:
How Sunk: Ran aground		Depth:

The Russian schooner *Jupiter* was lost on the rocks at Elieness on 24 September 1897. She had been en route from Alloa to Riga, Latvia, with a cargo of coal when she ran ashore on the rocks to the east of Fish Rock, and the local life saving brigade were soon on the scene with their rocket apparatus.

Five of the crew of seven were taken off by breeches buoy, but the captain, who was the owner of the vessel, and the mate refused to leave, stating that they would prefer to go down with the ship, which lay in several fathoms of water, grinding heavily on the rocks.

Consideration was given to removing them forcibly from the vessel, but this was not resorted to, and it is not known whether the captain and mate subsequently changed their minds, or if they did go down with the ship.

THE BRODERS

Wreck No: 155
Latitude: 56 11 00 N PA
GPS Lat: 5611.000 N
Location: Elieness
Type: Lighter
Length: Beam:
How Sunk: Ran aground

Date Sunk: 7 October 1897
Longitude: 02 48 30 W PA
GPS Long: 0248.500 W
Area: Elie
Tonnage: 160 grt
Draught:
Depth:

The Grangemouth lighter *The Broders* was engaged in salvage work, and was moored over the wreck of the *Jupiter* at Elieness. During a WSW force 7 near gale on 7 October 1897, she was blown ashore at the same place as the *Jupiter*, and joined her on the bottom.

AXEL

Wreck No: 156
Latitude: 56 07 18 N PA
GPS Lat: 5607.300 N
Location: E of Noop Rock, Dysart harbour
Type: Barque
Length: Beam:
How Sunk: Ran aground

Date Sunk: 18 October 1898
Longitude: 03 07 12 W PA
GPS Long: 0307.200 W
Area: Kirkcaldy
Tonnage: 520 grt
Draught:
Depth:

The large Norwegian barque *Axel* of Friedrickstadt, was driven ashore at Dysart, in an easterly storm force 10, on 18 October 1898. Between 3 a.m. and 4 a.m. she was sighted by the coastguard station, drifting helplessly before the wind. Her rudder was evidently disabled and she had become unmanageable. In about half an hour, she was dashed on the rocks between the Noop and the harbour. Her crew of ten were all saved. The rock on which she was driven was shattered by the force of the impact, and her hull was seriously damaged. The *Axel* had left London about a fortnight previously for Christiansand with a cargo of 509 tons of coke.

She experienced very stormy weather in the North Sea, and made for the Forth for shelter. A large number of people visited the scene of the wreck during the day. Several even clambered on the deck and assisted in cutting away the masts. The grog keg was broached, with the result that one man had to be taken home in a cart, along with the boxes, ropes, etc. saved from the wreck.

ASHGROVE

Wreck No: 157
Latitude: 56 11 00 N
GPS Lat: 5611.000 N
Location: On sea wall at Methil
Type: Steamship
Length: 285.3 ft   Beam: 34.6 ft
How Sunk: Ran aground

Date Sunk: 16 January 1912
Longitude: 03 00 12 W
GPS Long: 0300.200 W
Area: Methil
Tonnage: 1702 grt
Draught: 17.7 ft
Depth: 1 metre

The iron steamship *Ashgrove* was built by Earle's Co., Hull, in 1882. While en route from Middlesbrough to Methil in ballast on 16 January 1929 she was driven on to the sea wall at Methil and became a total loss. Three of her crew were lost.

ANSGAR

Wreck No: 158
Latitude: 56 11 45 N
GPS Lat: 5611.745 N
Location: Near Ardross Castle, nr St.Monance
Type: Steamship
Length: 235.8 ft   Beam: 33.1 ft
How Sunk: Ran aground

Date Sunk: 13 February 1910
Longitude: 02 47 18 W
GPS Long: 0247.295 W
Area: Elie
Tonnage: 1347 grt
Draught: 15.8 ft
Depth: 6 metres

The Danish steamship *Ansgar* was built in 1879 by Burmeister & Wain of Copenhagen. While en route from London to Methil in ballast, she ran ashore near Ardross Castle at about 10.30 p.m. on Sunday, 12 October 1910 in a strong westerly wind. The rocket LSA was despatched to the scene, but when the first rocket was fired, the rope jammed amongst rocks, rendering it useless.

Anstruther lifeboat set out, first being rowed clear of the shore, then by sail, and reached the stranded steamer at about 3 a.m. Considerable difficulty was experienced in getting alongside

The Danish steamship Ansgar *(Author's collection)*

in the heavy seas, but within five minutes of closing the steamer, all 18 crew and a dog were taken aboard the lifeboat. The return trip, this time with the weather, did not take so long, and by 4 a.m. the shipwrecked crew were landed at Anstruther. The *Ansgar*'s stern was completely submerged, and although there was obviously little probability of being able to refloat her, it was thought that if calm weather prevailed, it might be possible to salvage some of her fittings.

GARELOCH

Wreck No: 159			Date Sunk: 18 August 1935
Latitude: 56 12 56 N			Longitude: 02 42 24 W
GPS Lat: 5612.939 N			GPS Long: 0242.404 W
Location: Billowness, Pittenweem			Area: Elie
Type: Trawler			Tonnage: 246 grt
Length: 125.6 ft		Beam: 22.1 ft	Draught: 12.1 ft
How Sunk: Ran aground			Depth: 4 metres

The Aberdeen steam trawler *Gareloch* (ex-*Lily Melling* of Fleetwood), ran aground near Anstruther bathing pool in dense fog on the morning of 18 August 1935. She had loaded over 100 tons of coal at Methil and was on her way back to Aberdeen with a skeleton crew when she ran aground and was badly holed. When the tide receded she heeled sharply over on her port side, and one member of the crew was thrown on to the rocks, sustaining two broken ribs. The trawler lay so close to the shore that a number of visitors to the swimming pool swam out and boarded the vessel. With the return of the high tide in the evening she could not be refloated.

A boiler at 5612.910N, 0242.430W recorded by Maritime Fife during the Coastal Assessment Survey for Historic Scotland, Kincardine to Fife Ness in 1996, may be all that remains remains of the *Gareloch*.

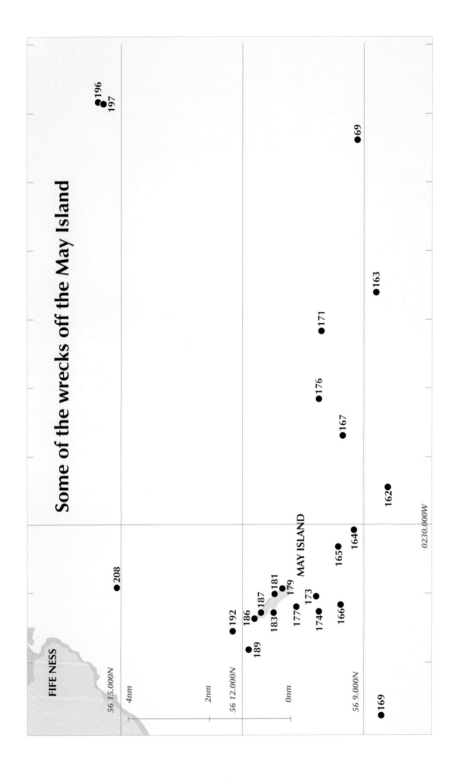

Some of the wrecks off the May Island

6

The May Island

ALEKTO

Wreck No: 160		Date Sunk: 18 September 1898
Latitude: 56 07 35 N PA		Longitude: 02 39 50 W PA
GPS Lat: 5607.580 N		GPS Long: 0239.830 W
Location: 5 miles WSW of May Island		Area: May
Type: Schooner		Tonnage: 91 grt
Length:	Beam:	Draught:
How Sunk: Collision with *Ben Macdui*		Depth: 40 metres

Outward bound from Bo'ness to Christiansand with a cargo of coal, the Norwegian schooner *Alekto* was run down by a steamship between the Bass Rock and May Island in the early hours of 18 September 1898. Although the steamer's lights had been plainly seen, the collision was of such a force that the schooner's bows were almost entirely smashed, and the foremast fell across the lifeboat on to the deck.

The steamer kept on its course after the collision, and Captain Anderson and his crew were taken off by another Norwegian schooner, which was also bound from the Forth to Christiansand with coal. Captain Anderson deemed it advisable to go to Leith to report the matter and try to identify the colliding steamer. With two members of his crew, he transferred to the inward-bound Granton steam trawler *St.Bernard*, the rest of his crew remained aboard their homeward-bound rescuer's vessel.

Shortly after boarding the *St.Bernard*, the *Alekto* foundered about 5 miles WSW of the May Island. The colliding vessel was subsequently identified as the Belgian steamship *Ben Macdui*.

UNKNOWN – PRE-1919

Wreck No: 161		Date Sunk: Pre-1919
Latitude: 56 08 18 N		Longitude: 02 32 40 W
GPS Lat: 5608.300 N		GPS Long: 0232.670 W
Location: 2½ miles S of May Island		Area: May
Type:		Tonnage:
Length:	Beam:	Draught:
How Sunk:		Depth: 45 metres

A wreck was reported here in 1919, but in 1960, and again in 1972, nothing was found within a radius of 1.3 miles of this position.

UNKNOWN

Wreck No: 162		Date Sunk:
Latitude: 56 08 30 N PA		Longitude: 02 28 18 W PA
GPS Lat: 5608.500 N		GPS Long: 0228.300 W
Location: 3½ miles SE of May Island		Area: May
Type:		Tonnage:
Length:	Beam:	Draught:
How Sunk:		Depth: 49 metres

Charted as Wk PA with at least 35 metres clearance in a general depth of 49 metres.

UNKNOWN – CRADOCK ?

Wreck No: 163		Date Sunk:
Latitude: 56 08 57 N		Longitude: 01 54 30 W
GPS Lat: 5608.950 N		GPS Long: 0154.500 W
Location: 16 miles, 38° St.Abbs Head		Area: May
Type:		Tonnage:
Length:	Beam:	Draught:
How Sunk:		Depth: 48 metres

One of the positions estimated in 1941 for the *Cradock* was 560900N, 020000W PA, which was described as 14 miles NNE of St Abbs Head. This wreck might, therefore, be the *Cradock*. (The other position estimated in 1941 for the *Cradock* was 560500N, 015700N, described as 12 miles NE of St Abbs Head.)

AVONDALE PARK

Wreck No: 164		Date Sunk: 7 May 1945
Latitude: 56 09 17 N		Longitude: 02 30 07 W
GPS Lat: 5609.280 N		GPS Long: 0230.120 W
Location: 1½ miles SE of May Island		Area: May
Type: Steamship		Tonnage: 2878 grt
Length: 320.1 ft	Beam: 49.5 ft	Draught: 23.1 ft
How Sunk: Torpedoed by *U-2336*		Depth: 45 metres

Avondale Park was built in 1944 by Foundation Maritime Ltd., of Pictou, Nova Scotia, Canada. All of the 'Park' ships were registered in Canada and owned by the Park Steamship Company. They were named after well-known national, provincial or municipal parks in Canada. The Company became a Canadian Government Crown Corporation in 1942

Chignecto Park – *a sister ship of* Avondale Park *(Courtesy of Shipsearch Marine, Canada)*

to own, manage and operate the ships allocated to it for the purposes of the war. The Park Steamship Company contracted the operation of the ships to private steamship companies and shipping agents, who assumed responsibility for the care of the ships, hiring of crew and officers as well as supplying the ships with fuel and supplies, the payment of all expenses and collection of revenues. Government wartime authorities determined how the ships were used and where they would sail. The *Avondale Park* was effectively leased to the British government, and operated as a British ship. The crew were all British.

The *Chignecto Park*, hull No. 11, and *Avondale Park*, hull No. 12, were both products of Foundation Maritime Ltd. yard at Pictou. The former became *Alexandre de Rhodes* in 1946 and *Tadjouri* in 1956. Hull No. 13 at that yard was the *Confederation Park*, which became *Gialong* in 1946, *Obokil* in 1956, *Tawau Bay* in 1961, and *Shin Chong* in 1966.

Shin Chong – *another sister ship of* Avondale Park *(Courtesy of Shipsearch Marine, Canada)*

The Norwegian steamship Sneland I *(Courtesy of Geir Jørgensen)*

SNELAND I

Wreck No: 165		Date Sunk: 7 May 1945
Latitude: 56 09 40 N		Longitude: 02 30 48 W
GPS Lat: 5609.646 N	**WGS84**	GPS Long: 0230.934 W
Location: 1½ miles SE of May Island		Area: May
Type: Steamship		Tonnage: 1791 grt
Length: 268 ft	Beam: 42.3 ft	Draught: 17 ft
How Sunk: Torpedoed by *U-2336*		Depth: 44 metres

The Norwegian steamship *Sneland I* (ex-*Ingeborg*) was built in Stettin in 1922 by Nuscke & Co. She was owned by D/S A/S Vestland (Richard Amlie & Co. A/S Managers).

On this last day of the war, 7 May 1945, the convoy system was still operating, and that evening, just after 2000 hours, convoy EN91 sailed from Methil for Belfast. (The convoy numbers ran from 01 to 100 and then started at 01 again. Arnold Hague gives the convoy number as EN491, hence this was presumably on the fifth cycle of 01 to 100.) The convoy consisted of five merchantmen escorted by three armed trawlers, *Angle*, *Valse* and *Leicester City*. The British *Avondale Park* and the Norwegian *Sneland I* were two of the merchant vessels in the convoy. *Avondale Park* was en route from Hull to Belfast, while *Sneland I* was en route from Blyth to Belfast with 2800 tons of coal. The other ships in the convoy were Norwegian ships *Rolf Jarl* and *Selvik*, and the British *Weybank*.

As the end of the European war was imminent, *Leicester City*'s radio operator had rigged a BBC speaker on deck so that no one would miss anything. Germany was to sign unconditional surrender, hostilities were to cease at midnight, Churchill was to speak and there was to be a two-day holiday from the following day. This last was received with some choice language from the ship's company. Altogether there was a feeling of buoyant excitement, perhaps slightly tinged with thoughts of being drafted to the Far East, but this looked like being the last convoy in home waters. There were only five merchant ships and three escorts. *Angle* was ahead, *Valse* on the port wing and *Leicester City* on the starboard.

At 2250 hours the convoy was about two miles south of the May Island when the *Avondale Park* was hit by a torpedo. The torpedo struck *Avondale Park* on her starboard side between the engine room and No. 3 hold, destroying the starboard lifeboat. As the ship settled by the stern, a raft from the poop was got away two and a half minutes before the vessel sank.

The Norwegian collier *Sneland I* was following, and in order to avoid the sinking vessel, *Sneland I* had to alter course to port, but just three minutes later when she drew level with the sinking *Avondale Park*, she was struck on the starboard side near No. 2 hatch and sank within two minutes.

Leicester City dropped a pattern of depth charges to deter further attacks, and then moved to pick up survivors from the stricken ships. *Avondale Park* had a crew of 28 and four gunners. Two of the *Avondale Park*'s crew were killed – namely Chief Engineer George Anderson of Newcastle, and Donkeyman Greaser William Harvey of South Shields, who were in the engine room when the torpedo struck.

Sneland I had a crew of 26 and three gunners. The First Mate, Nils Ingvald Nilsen, and the Third Mate, Alf Berentsen, attempted to launch the port lifeboat, but before they could get it in the water the ship capsized to starboard and the survivors ended up in the sea, clinging to a raft and debris until they were picked up by HM Trawlers *Valse* (T-151) and *Leicester City* (FY-223). Captain Johannes Lægland was drowned, five of the crew were reported missing and the 3rd engineer, Otto Skaugen, died while being brought ashore. An attempt was made to revive him, but he could not be saved. The survivors were later transferred to the Norwegian steamship *Selvik* which landed them in Methil on 8 May. A total of 55 survivors from both ships were landed at Methil.

Leicester City was 3000 yards on the starboard beam of the *Avondale Park*, the leading ship of the starboard column. Lt. John Wells R.N.V.R., C.O. of *Leicester City*, reported that the convoy course was 070°, wind NE force 1–2, sea and swell slight. At 2250/7 hours when the light was fading rapidly, the *Avondale Park*, was seen to have been hit. *Leicester City* immediately altered course towards her at full speed. At 2253 *Sneland I*, the second ship in the starboard column was also hit. A possible submarine contact was then established, 1550 yards to port, and one single depth charge was dropped at approximately 2300 hours, with the intention of disturbing the enemy in any further attempt to fire torpedoes at the remaining ships. Contact was still held but there was no movement or hydrophone effect. No star shells were fired as the light still seemed sufficiently good to detect a U-boat on the surface. The contact was attacked with a five-charge pattern at 2305. Lt. Philip Calvert, *Leicester City*'s First Officer recalled that the force of the explosions almost lifted

Leicester City out of the water, and blew all the main electric fuses, putting her asdic set out of action. All the lights in the ship had also been put out. The electrical switchboard had caught fire and was doused with sacks. Without electric power for the asdic the ship was unable to continue the search for the U-boat. Six-inch nails were put across the fuses to prevent further blows.

A small number of red dots could be seen in the sea, which were the lights on life jackets. While the asdic was being repaired a scrambling net was rigged over the side, and two of *Leicester City's* strongest crewmen went down on it to sea level, and began to haul the exhausted men inboard. They picked up about a dozen survivors who were in the near vicinity and also lowered a boat to search for others. At 2315 hours the asdic set was working again, but the ships lighting, including the binnacle lights, were still out of action. A square search was then commenced and at 2325 a single charge was dropped, again with the intention of keeping the U-boat down. At 2340 a further contact was gained in approximately the same position as the first one, and was attacked with three charges. A few minutes later a further four charges were dropped. No evidence was brought to the surface as a result of these attacks. Great difficulty was encountered in carrying out these last two attacks due to the failure of the binnacle lighting and to the fact that one officer and five ratings were absent as members of the boats crew.

The boat that had been lowered to look for survivors was *Leicester City's* lifeboat – an ordinary rowing boat with no engine, about 16 feet long. When it had been dropped into the sea it was very dark, and as soon as *Leicester City* moved off the boat's crew could see nothing. After rowing around, they saw what they thought was the conning tower of a U-boat awash, and the figure of the officer of the watch. The officer in charge of the boat brought his automatic rifle to the ready, but as there was no movement from the supposed U-boat he moved in closer to find that what appeared to be the U-boat was an upturned ship's lifeboat with a man sitting on top. The man was lucky to be alive, as he was very near to being shot! More survivors were picked up from the water. Some of them clinging to floating timber had to have their fingers prised and hammered before they would let go to be hauled into the boat.

A cry was heard from a heap of flotsam. This turned out to be from a Norwegian stewardess who was trapped in the debris. Leading Seaman George Ritchie tied a line around himself and swam across and under the flotsam to rescue her. By this time *Leicester City* was long out of sight, still hunting for the U-boat.

After drifting in the darkness, looking for further survivors, HMS *Angle* found the lifeboat. After taking aboard the crew and survivors, *Angle* proceeded to tow the empty lifeboat, but at such a speed that it overturned and all the gear was lost out of it. The boat and crew were returned to *Leicester City* some hours later. Twenty-two survivors from *Sneland I* were picked up by HM Trawlers *Valse* (T-151) and *Leicester City* (FY-223) and transferred to the Norwegian steamship *Selvik* which landed them at Methil. In the morning, before leaving the ship, the stewardess looked for George Ritchie, who had saved her, and presented him with a brooch as a keepsake.

As convoy EN91 was leaving the Forth, the Norwegian destroyer *Stord*, en route from Scapa Flow to Rosyth, was coming into the Forth just as the attack happened. She also immediately joined the search for the U-boat, and dropped a series of depth charges, but *U-2336* arrived at Kiel unharmed on 14 May. *Selvik*, *Rolf Jarl* and *Weybank* turned back to Methil after the *Avondale Park* and *Sneland I* were sunk.

Lloyd's War Losses – The Second World War Vol.1 gives position 560936N, 023124W for *Sneland 1*. In 1962 HMS *Scott* gave the position as 560940N, 023048W, and this is the charted position. I have position 5609.646N, 00230.934W (WGS84) recorded for *Sneland I*. The wreck lies oriented 085/265°. The forward section of the wreck has been reported to be lying on its side, while the aft section appears to be almost upside down in 58 metres.

According to *Lloyd's* the *Avondale Park* was sunk one mile SE of the May Island while en route from Hull to Belfast. She was the last British ship to be sunk in the Second World War. The wreck charted at 560917N, 023007W was first located by HMS *Scott* in 1959, and was reported in 1965 to have a least depth of 44.5 metres, standing some 10 metres above the seabed which is at 55 metres, and gave the impression of being a large wreck, about 350 feet long, lying 325/145° (NW by N/SE by S). I have three GPS positions recorded for the *Avondale Park*: 5609.271N, 00230.195W or 5609.283W, 00230.011W or 5609.261N, 00230.240W (all WGS84).

When dived in 1992 she was found to be lying with a list to starboard. The bows and bridge are upright, and standing eight metres high, but the stern lists to port and is severed from the hull. Two guns were observed. There were other guns on the towers and wing bridge.

The torpedoing by *U-2336* took place at almost 2300 hours, after the German surrender documents had been signed, but an hour before the time of their effect at midnight on the 7th, despite an order issued to U-boats on 4 May not to carry out any more attacks in view of the impending German surrender. The Type XXIII U-Boat, *U-2336* returned to its base at Kiel unscathed on 14 May 1945, and surrendered to the British, but it was not until October 1945, after BdU records had been examined, that it became apparent that *U-2336* was responsible for these two sinkings. Kapitänleutnant Emil Klusemeier, who had been on his first operational patrol as captain, claimed that he had not heard any order to cease fire broadcast by U-boat HQ on the 4th. He told Allied investigators that he had not heard the surrender order transmitted three days earlier.

One of the advantages of the Type XXIII boats was their ability to remain submerged for much longer periods than previous boats – up to three days continuously submerged – before having to come to the surface for fresh air and to recharge their batteries. At that time they were unable to either transmit or receive radio messages while submerged. This may account for the apparent non-receipt of the radio messages ordering a cessation of hostilities, as *U-2336* was a Type XXIII boat. On the other hand, she could not have made the passage from Kiel entirely submerged, as her range underwater was only 194 miles at 4 knots (2600 miles at 8 knots on the surface). Another possible factor is that Type XXIII coastal boats were very small submarines, and were equipped with a much smaller radio aerial than was carried by Type VII Atlantic U-boats. The smaller radio aerial resulted in a relatively poor radio performance – both transmitting and receiving.

Klusemeier revealed that he had been in the vicinity of the May Island between 2000 hours on 7 May and 0600 hours on the 8th, and that after the attack he circled the May Island. This caused great consternation as his approach had apparently gone undetected by the indicator loops. The loops to the north of May were controlled from the Fixed Defence Station on the island, and those to the south were controlled from Canty Bay, North Berwick. While the records for Canty Bay had by then been destroyed, those for the May Island revealed that *U-2336* had indeed been detected passing eastwards over No. 4 Loop at 0452 hours on the 8th, and No. 13 Loop at 0516 hours on the 8th, but her passage had been ignored, or had gone unnoticed in the euphoria surrounding victory, and the end of the war in Europe.

Anti-submarine indicator loops were long lengths of heavy cable laid on the seabed in shipping channels of strategically important ports. They rely on the production of an induced current in a stationery loop of wire when a magnet (in this case, a submarine) moves overhead. Even if wiped or degaussed, submarines still have sufficient magnetism to produce a small current in a loop. The current is detected by galvanometers at a Loop Control Station on the shore. This technology was developed by the Royal Navy at HMS *Osprey* (Portland Naval Base) starting back in 1915, and first deployed at Scapa Flow, in the Orkney Islands. Loops were used extensively during the Second World War, but ceased in 1945 when more sophisticated methods (mainly sonar) were shown to be more useful.

Enid Richardson, born Enid Collins, in Harton Lane in South Shields, remembered: "On VE Day there was a street party with games and races. My dad hung bunting out attached to the upstairs bedroom window. I've still got it: red, white and blue stripes."

Ann Milne, in Aldwych Street, said: "There was a dance in the street and my step-father played the piano accordion. I remember going down, too, to a cul-de-sac off Osborne Avenue where the back lane was cement rather than cobbles, and the women had scrubbed it for their party."

Ron Drew would never forget VE Day. During the war, South Shields had lost more than 3000 merchant seamen, the highest proportion of any town in the country. Ron's brother, Stan, was a merchant seaman. "At home we were sitting eating our victory lunch, when my mother stiffened and rose from the table. She had seen my brother Stan walking down the path towards the front door, wearing a suit much too small for him. He had joined the *Avondale Park* as second engineer a few days earlier, knowing, as we did, that the war was almost over. The *Avondale Park* was torpedoed by a German submarine one mile south-east of May island in the Firth of Forth at 2300 hours on May 7, 1945, one hour before the end of hostilities. The chief engineer went down to the engine room after the torpedo struck to assess the damage. He and the donkeyman lost their lives. Stan had lost all his personal possessions and was kitted out by the local Mission to Seamen. We finished our meal, and as we thanked God for the end of hostilities, our thoughts were with Stan. He had only been able to celebrate VE Day by the skin of his teeth."

The general belief, certainly according to Norwegian sources, appears to be that Klusmeier deliberately ignored Dönitz's 4 May order; this being his first patrol as captain he wanted something to show for it, and knew that he would never get another chance. The Type XXIII was so crammed internally that she only carried two torpedoes and those had to be loaded externally in harbour. No reloads were carried.

U-2336 surrendered at Wilhelmshaven, Germany on 14 May 1945. She was taken to Lisahally on 21 June for Operation Deadlight, and was sunk on 3 January 1946 in position 56.06N, 09.00W by gunfire from the destroyer HMS *Offa*.

COLUMBA

Wreck No: 166		Date Sunk: 10 March 1918
Latitude: 56 09 31 N	**WGS84**	Longitude: 02 33 30 W
GPS Lat: 5609.516 N		GPS Long: 0233.508 W
Location: 1½ miles SSW of S tip of May		Area: May
Type: Trawler		Tonnage: 138 grt
Length: 100 ft	Beam: 20.1 ft	Draught: 10.1 ft
How Sunk: Mined		Depth: 46–51 metres

The iron steam trawler *Columba* was built in 1893 by Hawthorns of Leith. She was requisitioned by the Navy during the First World War, and was sunk by a mine on 10 March 1918, one and a half miles SSW of the south tip of the May Island. The position has also been recorded as 5609.525N, 0233.508W (WGS84). The wreck is substantially intact, and stands up 5 metres from the seabed.

BEN ATTOW

Wreck No: 167		Date Sunk: 27 February 1940
Latitude: 56 09 35 N		Longitude: 02 26 05 W
GPS Lat: 5609.583 N	**WGS84**	GPS Long: 0226.083 W
Location: 4 miles, 120° S Ness May Island		Area: May
Type: Trawler		Tonnage: 156 grt
Length: 115.5 ft	Beam: 22.1 ft	Draught: 11.9 ft
How Sunk: Mined or torpedoed?		Depth: 48 metres

The steam trawler *Ben Attow* was built in 1900 by Hall Russell of Aberdeen. She left Dundee on 27 February 1940 for the fishing grounds about 8 miles ESE of the May Island. She struck a mine seven miles east, and half a mile south of the Isle of May, and sank. Her crew of nine from Broughty Ferry, Monifeith and Tayport, were all killed. The explosion was witnessed by the trawler *Strathblane*. Wreckage from the *Ben Attow* was washed ashore near Berwick early in March. The wreck charted at 560935N, 022605W was first reported in 1945, and in 1979 a bad obstruction or wreck was reported at 560946N, 022520W (Kingfisher *Book of Tows Vol. 1*).

These positions are very close together, and are probably the same wreck. The *Ben Attow* was reportedly sunk by a mine seven miles east, half a mile south of the May Island. Seekrieg lists her as bombed and sunk by He111's of German KG26 (X Air Corps). As He111's were carrying torpedoes during anti-shipping missions, a torpedo hit might have been mistaken for a mine explosion. *Lloyd's* gave the position of the *Ben Attow* as 561130N, 022030W, with the descriptions 6 miles E by S of the May Island, or 7 miles E½S: Six miles E by S results in a position of approximately 561100N, 022218W. Seven miles E½S results in a position of approximately 561130N, 022042W. These positions lie in an area within which no wrecks were found during a search by the navy in 1977.

An unknown wreck was reported at 561000N, 022630W, which is 3½ miles, 120° from the May Island, and it was assumed that this wreck probably dated from the Second World War, but on 24 March 1919 an obstruction was reported at 561030N, 022400W. This tidy round figure is obviously only an approximation, and no obstruction could be found there in 1977. But in 1979 an obstruction, or wreck, was located less than half a mile away at 561008N, 022428W. Could one of these be the *Ben Attow* (1940)? *Thrive* (1946)? Or another wreck?

ARDGOUR II

Wreck No: 168		Date Sunk: 14 May 1985
Latitude: 56 11 30 N PA		Longitude: 02 11 30 W
GPS Lat: 5611.500 N	**WGS84 PA**	GPS Long: 0211.500 W
Location: 12 miles E of May Island		Area: May
Type: MFV		Tonnage: 25 grt
Length: 51.2 ft	Beam: ?	Draught:
How Sunk: Collision with *Silver Star*		Depth: 53 metres

On 14 May 1985 the Motor Fishing Vessel *Ardgour II* sank after a collision with the MFV *Silver Star* 18 miles east of Pittenweem, Fife. The position was given in *Lloyd's List* as about 561130N, 021130W.

DENMORE

Wreck No: 169		Date Sunk: 20 March 1879
Latitude: 56 08 36 N		Longitude: 02 38 19 W
GPS Lat: 5608.592 N	**WGS84**	GPS Long: 0238.398 W
Location: 5 miles SSE of Anstruther		Area: May
Type: Steamship		Tonnage: 328 grt
Length: 155.1 ft	Beam: 19.8 ft	Draught:
How Sunk: Foundered after running aground		Depth: 45–53 metres

The wreck here was located in 1984, but not investigated at that time. It was examined in 1994, when side-scan sonar indicated a height of 3 metres, length of 52 metres (170 feet) and beam of 7 metres (22 feet). The wreck is oriented 020/200° (stern 020°, bow 200°), and was thought to be lying on its side, embedded in the seabed. In fact the wreck is sitting upright, on an even keel. It is obviously a fairly old wreck, as the hull is of riveted construction, and many plates have become detached and are lying flat on the seabed, but the stern section of the ship is relatively intact. The ship has a single boiler with a two-cylinder engine and a donkey engine, and an old-style iron propeller with four narrow blades.

Heading forward, the wreck is very broken, as the sides of the ship have collapsed outwards. The bow is very confused, but recognisable although most of the riveted plates are on the seabed. There is a large amount of trawl net on the wreck – virtually everywhere. None of it is hanging, but large sections are clinging round the wreck with the "pips" drawn tight. All the wooden decking is long gone. There are still stacked plates in the galley, and a glass jar with a corroded metal bar holding it in position.

The iron steamship *Denmore* was built by A. Hall & Co. of Aberdeen in 1878. She left Leith shortly before midnight on 19 March 1879, bound for Aberdeen with a cargo of flour, and intended to pass north of the May Island. At 2.32 a.m. she was heading ENE at 8 knots, when a bright light was seen ahead. Captain Crombie wondered whether this might be the masthead light of a ship. He was afraid to turn to port, due to the proximity of the Fife coast, and turned instead to starboard, until he came close enough to see that the light was a ship at anchor. Two other lights were then seen on the starboard bow, and the *Denmore* steamed between them. Immediately after, at 3 a.m., an indistinct glare, or haze, was seen right ahead. *Denmore* turned to port, and her engine was put full astern. Before the ship could respond, however, her starboard bow struck the rocks at the north-west point of the May Island. The ship succeeded in backing off the rocks, but a large hole had been made in the starboard bow, and the forehold was rapidly filling with water. Captain Crombie then ordered the engines to be put full ahead, and the vessel was turned towards the land in an attempt to return to Leith or Granton. The crew used strenuous efforts to pump the water out, but it continued to fill the fore part of the steamer. By 4.15 a.m. there was nine inches of water in the hold, and she was so far down by the head that her rudder and propeller were partially out of the water, making it difficult to steer, or make further progress. By this time the vessel was about three miles off the May Island. The ship's boats were then launched, and seven of the men entered them in order to lie by the steamer, while five remained on board. The steamer *Princess Alice*, Captain Kerr from Liverpool to Dundee, came in sight at about 5 p.m., and at once proceeded to render assistance. After picking up the crew, Captain Kerr lay alongside for a few minutes, when the *Denmore* heeled over on her port side, and sank in about 29 fathoms of water. The remaining crew abandoned ship just before she sank. The *Princess Alice* took the rescued crew and their boats to Dundee.

UNKNOWN – PRE-1919

Wreck No: 170
Latitude: 56 10 10 N
GPS Lat: 5610.170 N
Location: 8 miles, 105° from May Island
Type:
Length: Beam:
How Sunk:

Date Sunk: Pre-1919
Longitude: 02 18 45 W
GPS Long: 0218.750 W
Area: May
Tonnage:
Draught:
Depth: 56 metres

A wreck was first reported in this position on 24 March 1919, but in 1977 the Navy found no trace of any wreck within a semi-circle of radius two and a half miles east through north to west of this position. The position given for the wreck in 1919 was perhaps slightly inaccurate, and it may lie outside the area searched in 1977.

ASTA

Wreck No: 171
Latitude: 56 10 06 N
GPS Lat: 5610.099 N   **WGS84**
Location: 6¼ miles, 105° from May Island
Type: Steamship
Length: 254 ft   Beam: 36.3 ft
How Sunk: Collision with *Breslau*

Date Sunk: 15 December 1927
Longitude: 02 21 38 W
GPS Long: 0221.637 W
Area: May
Tonnage: 1623 grt
Draught: 16.5 ft
Depth: 49–59 metres

The Swedish steamship Asta *(Author's collection)*

160

The Swedish collier *Asta* (ex-*Larnace*, ex-*Fingal*, ex-*Forest*, ex-*Allende*) was built in 1883 by Palmers Co. On 15 December 1927 she was en route from Methil to Copenhagen with a cargo of coal, when at 9.30 p.m., about eight miles east of the May Island, the steamship *Breslau* (1366 tons), belonging to James Currie & Co. of Leith, outward bound from Leith to Copenhagen with a general cargo, ran into her stern. The *Asta's* crew quickly realised their vessel was doomed and launched two of their boats. Within 20 minutes the *Asta* had sunk, and the crew of 19 were taken aboard the *Breslau*, which returned to Leith with damaged bows. Wreckage from the *Asta* was subsequently washed ashore at several places on the Fife coast.

The wreck is upright, but broken in two parts, almost in line. It is apparently about 75 metres long (vs 77 metres of the *Asta*), and stands up 9 metres from the seabed. The bows point NW, and the wreck is oriented 130/310°. Least depth is 49 metres, in a general depth of 59 metres.

THRIVE

Wreck No: 172		Date Sunk: 20 February 1946
Latitude: 56 10 23 N PA		Longitude: 02 20 06 W PA
GPS Lat: 5610.380 N		GPS Long: 0220.100 W
Location: 7 miles, 100° from May Island		Area: May
Type: Trawler		Tonnage: 9 grt
Length: 33.3 ft	Beam: 13.2 ft	Draught:
How Sunk: Trawled up a depthcharge		Depth: 58 metres

The Cockenzie motor fishing vessel *Thrive* had been fishing between the Bass Rock and May Island when her nets brought up a cylindrical object resembling an oil drum. Because of the weight, and damage to the nets, it was decided to cut them away. Immediately, there was a terrific explosion, which was heard on the Fife coast, over six miles away. Amazingly, none of the five crewmen was hurt, but their vessel was badly damaged, and was obviously going to sink. The crew had time to unbolt the mast and laid it across the deck before the *Thrive* sank below their feet, leaving them clinging to the floating mast.

The St Monance fishing vessel *Girl Christian*, just released from Admiralty service, rushed to the spot, but by the time it arrived, one of the men had disappeared, and another drowned before he could be taken on board the *Girl Christian*. In the heavy seas running at the time, the rescuers were unable to find the missing man. The three survivors were landed at St Monance. The exploding object is believed to have been a live depth charge. A wreck reported at 561023N, 022006W on 28 March 1949 was assumed to possibly be the *Thrive*, but a search in 1977 failed to find any wrecks within an area two and a half miles east through north to west from 561010N, 021845W.

EMLEY

Wreck No: 173		Date Sunk: 28 April 1918	
Latitude: 56 10 12 N		Longitude: 02 33 06 W	
GPS Lat: 5610.200 N	**WGS84**	GPS Long: 0233.102 W	
Location: ¾ miles SW of May Island		Area: May	
Type: Trawler		Tonnage: 223 grt	
Length: 112.1 ft	Beam: 22.5 ft	Draught: 12.5 ft	
How Sunk: Mined (mine laid by *UC-40*)		Depth: 50–52 metres	

The steel steam trawler *Emley* was built in 1911 by Cochrane & Sons of Selby. She was reported sunk by a mine on 28 April 1918 208°, three quarters of a mile from May Island light. The wreck is upright and intact, oriented 120/300°, and stands up 5 metres in a total depth of 52 metres.

UNKNOWN – "CHRIS"

Wreck No: 174		Date Sunk:	
Latitude: 56 10 06 N		Longitude: 02 33 08 W	
GPS Lat: 5610.108 N	**WGS84**	GPS Long: 0233.767 W	
Location: 1 mile S by W½W from May Island Lt		Area: May	
Type: Trawler		Tonnage:	
Length:	Beam:	Draught:	
How Sunk:		Depth: 42–55 metres	

This is an intact wreck of a trawler-type vessel on an even keel. The wheelhouse (with broken sink) is still in place. Directly behind the wheelhouse is a mast rising to 42 metres. From this mast a net is draped over the starboard side of the ship and wheelhouse. The keel is intact from the bow to the propeller shaft hub. One propeller blade is missing – sheared off. The hull plating above this part of the wreck is demolished, with the plating strewn about the sea-bed aft of the wreck. This damage to the stern seems to be consistent with a mine explosion. Going forward, the decking above the triple expansion engine is gone. Apparently there is a big stone in the centre of the wreck. The wreck has not been identified, but is known locally as the "Chris". The position has also been recorded as 5610.099N, 0233.861W (WGS84).

HOOSAC

Wreck No: 175		Date Sunk: 28 June 1926	
Latitude: 56 10 30 N PA		Longitude: 02 33 30 W PA	
GPS Lat: 5610.500 N		GPS Long: 0233.500 W	
Location: NE of Tarbet, May Island		Area: May	
Type: Steamship		Tonnage: 5226 grt	
Length: 400 ft	Beam: 52.2 ft	Draught: 21.5 ft	
How Sunk: Ran aground, but not sunk		Depth:	

Hoosac (ex-*Trojan Prince*, ex-*War Perch*) was built in 1918 by Bartram & Sons of Sunderland. She was registered in Liverpool, and operated by Furness Withy. In 1926 Furness Lines sold four of their vessels, including *Hoosac*. According to Les Pennington of East Coast Divers, whose information came from the May Island lighthouse keepers' logbook, the *Hoosac*, with a cargo of flour and grain, sank in 1926 north-east of Tarbet, May Island. No wreck is charted in that area, and there is no mention of the sinking of the *Hoosac* in *The Scotsman* newspaper in 1926. The dimensions and tonnage of the *Hoosac* would make it one of the largest wrecks in the Forth, and one would have thought that it should be well documented.

Unfortunately, the lighthouse keepers records for that period are no longer in existence, but a report in the *East Fife Observer* of 1 July 1926 tells how the *Hoosac*, belonging to the Warren Line of Liverpool, went aground on the May Island in fog while en route from Philadelphia to Leith with a cargo of grain. She was assisted by two salvage tugs, which succeeded in pulling her off the rocks after she had been lightened by the removal of some of her cargo. Later that year she was sold, and her new owners, a Yugoslavian shipping company, changed her name to *Nemanja*, and registered her in Dubrovnik. She had a long life as the *Nemanja* until she was torpedoed by the *U-84* (KL Horst Uphoff) at 4030N, 6450W at 0225 hours on 8 April 1942, and she sank at 0457 hours while carrying a cargo of 7207 tons of sugar on a voyage which left Macoris, in the Dominican Republic, on 30 March 1942 to Halifax, Nova Scotia and the UK. Thirteen of her 47 crew were lost.

UNKNOWN

Wreck No: 176	Date Sunk: Pre-March 1919
Latitude: 56 10 30 N PA	Longitude: 02 24 00 W PA
GPS Lat: 5610.500 N	GPS Long: 0224.000 W
Location: 5 miles, 100° from May Island	Area: May
Type:	Tonnage:
Length: Beam:	Draught:
How Sunk:	Depth: 52 metres

A wreck was first reported in this charted PA on 24 March 1919. I also have a note of the position as 5610.133N, 0224.470W. See also UNKNOWN – PRE-1919 at 561010N, 021845W. Could either of these be *UB-63*?

PRIMROSE

Wreck No: 177		Date Sunk: 16 November 1904
Latitude: 56 10 41 N		Longitude: 02 33 26 W
GPS Lat: 5610.688 N	**WGS84**	GPS Long: 0233.439 W
Location: ½ mile SW of May Island		Area: May
Type: Trawler		Tonnage: 91 grt
Length: 82.5 ft	Beam: 18 ft	Draught: 8 ft
How Sunk: Ran aground		Depth: 28–32 metres

In July 1992 divers were dropped on a wreck, which was initially assumed to be the trawler *Emley*. On recovering the bell, however, they discovered that the wreck they were on was actually the *Primrose* – a Peterhead steam trawler, which ran aground on the east side of the South Ness of May Island in the dark at 9 p.m. on 16 November 1904 in a force 6 westerly. *Primrose* had been built earlier that year by Mackie & Thomson of Glasgow, engine by W. V. V. Ligerwood.

Captain Seaton Hall and his crew of seven men went ashore to the island in their small boat. Over the following 12 days, salvage operations were carried out on behalf of her insurers. Four hundred and fifty new herring barrels were taken out to the wreck by the Leith tug *Earl of Powis*, and these, along with 350 other casks, were placed on board the trawler. It was hoped that when she was pulled off the rocks, the empty barrels would give the trawler sufficient buoyancy to keep her afloat with the aid of hand pumps. On 29 November the tug hauled her off the rocks, and then attempted to tow her to Leith. After only a short distance, however, she foundered to the west of the island. The salvage crew who were left aboard to work the pumps, made their escape in the small boat which was being towed astern, and were taken aboard the tug.

The wreck is quite broken up now, but the boiler and engine are still recognisable. In the middle of the wreck, the boiler stands up about 3 metres. It is the highest point of the wreck, which is home to a lot of life including soft corals, butterfish, prawns and small crabs hiding in the boiler tubes. Divers may also find themselves accompanied by seals. Underwater visibility on this wreck is variable, but typically around 7 metres, although it can be as much as 15 metres, when the whole wreck can be seen as you as descend the shot-line. There are very strong currents in this area near the South Ness, making it imperative to dive this wreck at slack water – one hour after high water at Leith. The wreck is normally buoyed during the summer months, but do not tie up to the buoy!

The wreck is charted at 5610.688N, 00233.439W (WGS84), or 5610.732N, 00233.457W (WGS84). The boiler is at 5610.698N, 0233.424W (WGS84). Another position given is 5610.650N, 0233.567W.

GARIBALDI

Wreck No: 178		Date Sunk: 11 May 1870
Latitude: 56 10 11 N	**WGS84**	Longitude: 02 32 22 W
GPS Lat: 5610.190 N		GPS Long: 0232.370 W
Location: Off May Island		Area: May
Type: Paddle Steamer		Tonnage: 73 grt
Length: 83.1 ft	Beam: 17.9 ft	Draught: 9.1 ft
How Sunk:		Depth: 8 metres

The wooden paddle steamer *Garibaldi* was built in 1864. According to Brodie's *Steamers of the Forth*, she was a tug sunk while towing off North Berwick on 17 June 1870, yet later in the same book, she is said to have sunk off the May Island on 11 May 1870.

The Norwegian steamship Scotland *(Courtesy of The Norwegian Maritime Museum, Oslo)*

SCOTLAND

Wreck No: 179		Date Sunk: 19 March 1916
Latitude: 56 11 01 N		Longitude: 02 32 46 W
GPS Lat: 5611.023 N	**WGS84**	GPS Long: 0232.773 W
Location: SE end, May Island		Area: May
Type: Steamship		Tonnage: 1490 grt
Length: 231.9 ft	Beam: 35.7 ft	Draught: 22.9 ft
How Sunk: Ran aground		Depth: 8 metres

The Norwegian steel steamship *Scotland* was built in 1912 by Nylands of Christiania (Oslo), for Fred Olsen Lines. She had a cargo of oak barrels, paper, and three motorboats at the time of running aground on the May Island, while en route from Oslo to Grangemouth. The wreck lies just out from the entrance to Kirkhaven, at the south-east end of the island. Strong currents surround the May Island, and nowhere are this more evident than at the south end of the island, where the water flowing over the reef is very disturbed. As the island lies roughly N/S, and the tidal flow is E/W, the northern and southern extremities of the island are where the currents are most noticeable. Off the west and the east of the island, the flow is almost imperceptible.

Many items salvaged from the wreck were auctioned at Anstruther harbour. Two of the three motorboats were sold for £9.50 and £10.50. Five hundredweights of copper (¼ ton) realised £25.50. (In 2006 ¼ ton of copper would be worth almost £1200). The ship's Walker patent log sold for £3.00, and the ship's wheel £1.75. Brass lanterns went for 62½d. each, while the remains of the wreck itself, lying off the east side of the May Island was sold for £26.

DUNBRITTON

Wreck No: 180		Date Sunk: 3 February 1906
Latitude: 56 11 00 N PA		Longitude: 02 33 00 W PA
GPS Lat: 5611.000 N		GPS Long: 0233.000 W
Location: Off May Island		Area: May
Type: Iron Barque		Tonnage: 1536 grt
Length: 234.3 ft	Beam: 39.6 ft	Draught: 23.1 ft
How Sunk: Foundered		Depth:

The Glasgow iron barque *Dunbritton* had left Hamburg for Honolulu with a general cargo, but sustained so much damage in stormy conditions in the North Sea that she had to run to Leith for repairs. She left Leith to resume her voyage on 25 January 1906, and by that afternoon had scarcely made the May Island when she again encountered SW gales and very heavy seas. Her foremast and mizzen topmast were carried away, and she was blown for 35 miles before her uncontrolled drift could be arrested. The wind veered to NW with snowstorms, then backed to SW then WSW.

The vessel was obviously in very serious difficulties by then, and was taken in tow by the Hull trawler *Mary Stuart*. For three days, during which the intensity of the storm increased, the trawler attempted to reach the Firth of Forth, but the tow finally had to be slipped when the *Dunbritton's* main mast was brought down by the force of the storm, and her deck was damaged, allowing water to enter the ship at a greater rate than her pumps could cope with. A second trawler, the *Loch Stenness*, appeared on the scene, and both trawlers took the gradually sinking *Dunbritton* in tow for a time until the tow had to be abandoned at about 5530N, 0020E. The crew of the barque used their own lifeboat to transfer to the *Loch Stenness*, and their own vessel was soon lost to sight, and is presumed to have foundered shortly after. The *Loch Stenness* landed the barque's crew at Aberdeen on Sunday, 4 February 1906.

ISLAND

Wreck No: 181		Date Sunk: 13 April 1937
Latitude: 56 11 02 N		Longitude: 02 32 52 W
GPS Lat: 5611.030 N		GPS Long: 0232.870 W
Location: ESE of May Island Tower		Area: May
Type: Steamship		Tonnage: 1774 grt
Length: 250 ft	Beam: 40 ft	Draught:
How Sunk: Ran aground		Depth: 13 metres

The steamship *Island*, formerly the Danish Royal Yacht, bound from Copenhagen to Leith, ran on to the east side of the May in dense fog on 13 April 1937. Because of the fog the light could not be seen, and the foghorn signal was heard only twice before the vessel struck the rocks. The engine room and after hold were quickly flooded, and radio calls for assistance

The Danish steamship Island *in happier times (Author's collection)*

The Danish steamship Island *aground on May Island (Author's collection)*

Another view of SS Island *aground on the May Island*
(Author's collection)

were transmitted. The 28 passengers were rescued by the Anstruther lifeboat. The ship could not be refloated, and salvage efforts were abandoned. Parts of the wreck are still visible on shore, well up the rocky slope on the east of the May Island, between Colms Hole and Foreigner's Point a quarter of a mile mile ESE from the low lighthouse. This stretch of the shore is now known as Island Rocks. An intact boiler can be found by diving a transit lining up the wreckage which can be seen half way up the shore, with the old lookout building adjacent to the island's helicopter landing pad. (This lookout building is visible from sea level to the right of the main lighthouse.) The seabed around this area towards Foreigner's Point is also littered with debris from other wrecks.

JASPER

Wreck No: 182		Date Sunk: 17 April 1894
Latitude: 56 11 12 N PA		Longitude: 02 33 03 W PA
GPS Lat: 5611.200 N		GPS Long: 0233.050 W
Location: 500yds SE by E May Island Lt		Area: May
Type: Steamship		Tonnage: 1256 grt
Length: 235 ft	Beam: 31.7 ft	Draught: 22.4 ft
How Sunk: Ran aground		Depth: 8 metres

The steamship *Jasper* was built in 1883 by W. B. Thompson, and owned by the Gem Line of Dundee. She ran on to rocks on the east side of May Island during a dense fog between two and three o'clock in the morning on 17 April 1894, while en route from Dundee to Burntisland in ballast. The fog was so dense that the May Island light could not be seen. Rockets were fired as soon as the *Jasper* grounded and the light keepers, along with several sailors working on the island, went to the assistance of the crew, who were all got ashore to safety. Their ship was lying in a very bad position, and making water. She was evidently badly holed in the engine room.

A member of the Salvage Association, who happened to be on holiday in Crail, and Lloyd's agent for the district, visited the wreck in the Northern Commissioner's launch. It was thought that it might be possible to raise the vessel by floating her at both ends if the weather kept moderately calm.

An inquiry into the stranding of the *Jasper* was held in Dundee. Compelling evidence was given by experienced Cellardyke fishermen about the thickness of the fog, and the relative inefficiency of the new electric light on the May, compared with the previous oil or gas light. In the opinion of the fishermen the heavy top current runing between the Carr Lightship and the May Island would certainly have an effect upon a vessel in ballast.

ANLABY

Wreck No: 183	Date Sunk: 23 August 1873
Latitude: 56 11 19 N	Longitude: 02 33 42 W
GPS Lat: 5611.317 N	GPS Long: 0233.700 W
Location: S of West Landing, May Island	Area: May
Type: Steamship	Tonnage: 1110 grt
Length: 231 ft Beam: 32.0 ft	Draught: 17 ft
How Sunk: Ran aground	Depth: 20 metres

Shortly after leaving Granton on 23 August 1873, bound for Danzig with a cargo of coal, the iron steamship *Anlaby* ran on to the rocks south of the West Landing, May Island. (The West Landing is at 5611.335N, 00233.774W.) *Anlaby* is at 561115N, 023352W (5611.250N, 0233.867W – OSGB36). She was proceeding dead slow in fog, when at about 6 p.m., she went on to the rocks on the west side of the May Island, and stuck fast with her forefoot on the rocks and her stern in 8 fathoms (15 metres) of water. Lighters and a tug were sent to her assistance, but failed to take her off.

A Board of Trade Enquiry into the loss of the *Anlaby* was held at Hull. Its findings were that despite the thick fog that prevailed at the time, Captain Thomas Martin did not take a cast of the lead for four hours, or even ascertain the vessel's speed for three hours. The court emphatically characterised such a proceeding as "blind navigation", and suspended the captain's certificate for six months. Several unsuccessful attempts were made to refloat the ship.

Anlaby *propeller and rudder (Courtesy of Mark Blyth)*

Just off the south of Altarstanes the wreck lies E/W on a rocky slope close to the cliffs, with the bows pointing towards the May Island in around 8 metres and her stern out to sea in about 18 metres. She is very broken up and flattened on the seabed. All that remains are iron ribs of the keel, with various pieces of machinery scattered around. The stern section, with the steering gear, and a large four-bladed iron propeller, stands up a couple of meters from the sand and shingle bottom.

The easiest way to find the wreck is to drop the divers in the West Landing Bay and let them swim south along the 12-metre contour to come across the ribs, and finally the stern section in 15–18 metres. There is often fish around the wreck, and seals frequently accompany divers.

CARMEN

Wreck No: 184		Date Sunk: 15 January 1923
Latitude: 56 11 18 N PA		Longitude: 02 33 15 W PA
GPS Lat: 5611.300 N		GPS Long: 0233.250 W
Location: 200yds W of May Island Light		Area: May
Type: Schooner		Tonnage: 1902 grt
Length: 251.3 ft	Beam: 43.7 ft	Draught: 17.9 ft
How Sunk: Ran aground		Depth: 22 metres

A report in the *Fife Free Press* of Saturday, 20 January 1923 says that the four-masted wooden schooner *Carmen*, belonging to Stockholm, ran ashore 800 yards west of Fife Ness Point, near Crail, early on Saturday morning of 13 January. The *Carmen* had left South Shields after discharging a cargo of pit props, and was proceeding light to Grangemouth to load a cargo of coal for Barcelona. A dense fog overhung the Forth during the night, and it appears the captain, who is part owner of the vessel, missed direction while attempting to enter the Forth. The vessel struck the rocks at 5.45 a.m., and at 5.50 a.m. fired a flare. The watchman at the Fife Ness Coastguard station had, however, already observed the schooner, and the life-saving apparatus was called out immediately, and saved the crew. The local lifeboat was also launched, and stood by the vessel.

During the day, a salvage tug from Leith arrived, and by midnight had succeeded in dragging the vessel from the rocks into a good position. A second tug was sent for, and the *Carmen* was towed towards Leith for repairs. That seemed to be the end of the matter, or so the reporter who submitted the above copy to his newspaper assumed. A reporter for the *East Fife Observer*, however, who was either more tenacious, or perhaps working to a differ-ent deadline for copy, continued the saga in the 18 January 1923 edition of his paper:

> A strong headwind retarded progress of the tow, and at dusk the vessel had only reached a position off North Berwick. The fear expressed by experienced sailors who witnessed the slow passage of the tugs up the Firth, that they would not man-age to tow the *Carmen* to safety, were fully confirmed later when the schooner broke

adrift from the tugs. Without a rudder, she was helpless, and drifted down the Firth and went ashore on the cliffs at the west side of the May. Anstruther lifeboat was called, and in a difficult operation lasting all night, took off the crew of the doomed vessel.

Later, a 40-foot section of the *Carmen*'s stern broke off when the tug *Earl of Powis* again attempted to pull the vessel from the rocks, and that section was successfully towed to Leith.

Carmen was built in 1917 in Astoria, Oregon, USA. Although she was primarily a sailing vessel, she did have two auxiliary eight-cylinder Bolinders oil engines, and twin screws. No wreckage from the *Carmen* has been found around the May Island. The stern section with the engines and propellers was taken to Leith. The rest of the ship, being wooden, will have long since been smashed to pieces and washed away.

GEORGE AUNGER

Wreck No: 185	Date Sunk: 25 April 1930
Latitude: 56 11 33 N PA	Longitude: 02 33 30 W PA
GPS Lat: 5611.550 N	GPS Long: 0233.500 W
Location: E Side of N.Ness, May Island	Area: May
Type: Trawler	Tonnage: 273 grt
Length: 125.4 ft Beam: 22.7 ft	Draught: 12.2 ft
How Sunk: Ran aground	Depth: 8 metres

The steam trawler *George Aunger*, built in 1918 by Cook, Welton & Gemmell of Beverley, and belonging to G.W. & J. Leiper of Aberdeen, went ashore in thick fog on the east side of North Ness, May Island at 11.10 p.m. on 25 April 1930. Although the fog signal had been heard, it was thought to be three or four miles distant. In the high seas running, her skipper and fireman were washed overboard and lost, D. Morrice the skipper being swept out through the wheelhouse window. The four other crew members were rescued by the lighthouse keepers who displayed great gallantry in climbing aboard the trawler by the anchor chain at low tide, some time after the vessel struck.

Anstruther and Broughty Ferry lifeboats were called to the scene, but owing to the heavy seas were unable to render assistance. One of the Anstruther lifeboat men expressed the opinion that no lifeboat ever built could have assisted in the prevailing conditions. The lighthouse keepers carried the four survivors across the island to the more sheltered west side, where they were transferred to the waiting lifeboat.

VICTORY

Wreck No: 186	Date Sunk: 6 March 1934
Latitude: 56 11 33 N PA	Longitude: 02 33 30 W PA
GPS Lat: 5611.550 N	GPS Long: 0233.500 W
Location: Norman Rock, N.Ness, May Island	Area: May

Type: Trawler   Tonnage: 164 grt
Length: 102 ft   Beam: 20.6 ft   Draught: 11 ft
How Sunk: Ran aground   Depth: 8 metres

The Aberdeen steam trawler *Victory* (A 692) was built by Earle's Shipbuilding and Engineering Company of Hull in 1898. The vessel sailed from Aberdeen on 5 March 1934
with a crew of nine, including the skipper, to fish off the North Carr Light. After fishing
in that area she proceeded to Methil, and took on board 60 tons of coal. Leaving there
at 6 p.m. on 6 March she proceeded towards proposed fishing grounds 17 miles E ¾ S
of May Island. It was intended to pass north of May Island, and at 7 p.m. Elie Light was
passed abeam at a distance of approximately three-quarters of a mile. Shortly after passing
Elie Light, the lights of numerous fishing vessels, estimated to be about 200–300, were
observed between the north end of May Island and the mainland. The same course and
speed were maintained until about 7.40 p.m. when the speed was reduced to "slow ahead",
about two knots, as the vessel was then in close proximity to the fishing craft, of which
a number were ring net boats fishing with steaming lights showing, (i.e. masthead and
sidelights), for which it was necessary frequently to alter course to negotiate a safe passage
through these vessels. The weather was fine, with a moderate W by S wind, smooth sea,
slight swell and good visibility, the lights being seen clearly, but a slight frost haze lay over
the low land.

Shortly after this, at about 7.45 p.m. or 8 p.m., the second hand observed the low land
of the May Island, and considering he was too close, gave the order to the skipper at the
wheel to "hard a port" and at the same time rang the engine telegraph to "stop", but before
the engines had stopped, the vessel took the ground, her head swinging to the NE. After
a short interval the second hand put the engine room telegraph to "full ahead," thinking
that the vessel had cleared the Norman Rock, but as soon as the engines moved, the vessel
commenced to grind heavily and the engines were stopped again. After it was thought
that the vessel had of her own accord cleared the rocks, an order to go full speed ahead
was given, but the ship bumped heavily and the order was given to stop the engines. When
attempting to move alternately slowly ahead and astern, the propeller was found to be
jammed.

Distress signals were then made. A small fishing vessel came alongside and was asked
to take out a kedge anchor, but the vessel was unable to do that on account of her size,
and she left with the ship's cook, who had become afraid. At about 9 p.m. the fishing
boat *Enterprise* came alongside and agreed to take an anchor out. The anchor, 15 fathoms
of chain and 120 fathoms of wire, were put on board, and two of the *Victory*'s crew also
went on board to assist in laying out the anchor. The anchor was laid out abeam and the
wire was being hove taut. But before any strain came on, one of the crew reported that
the vessel was making water aft, and it was then found that the water was nearly up to
the furnaces. At about 9.45 p.m., the furnaces being flooded and water found in the fish
room and cabin, it was decided to abandon the vessel, and at about 10 p.m. this was done.

Anstruther lifeboat had set out in response to *Victory*'s distress flares and siren sounding, but before the lifeboat arrived at the scene, the remaining crew had boarded the *Enterprise*, which landed them at St Monance. At high water the next morning, the *Victory* was lying at a steep angle, completely under water, except for a small portion of her stern, and was obviously a total loss.

Wreckage which may be part of the Thomas L Devlin *at May Island (Author's collection)*

THOMAS L DEVLIN

Wreck No: 187		Date Sunk: 20 December 1959
Latitude: 56 11 33 N		Longitude: 02 33 54 W
GPS Lat: 5611.550 N		GPS Long: 0233.900 W
Location: North Ness, May Island		Area: May
Type: Trawler		Tonnage: 211 grt
Length: 115.7 ft	Beam: 22.6 ft	Draught: 12.2 ft
How Sunk: Ran aground		Depth: 18 metres

The Granton trawler *Thomas L Devlin* (ex-*Phyllis Belman*) was built in 1915 by A. Hall & Co. of Aberdeen. She ran on to the North Ness of the May Island at 9.15 p.m. on 20 December 1959 in clear weather. Her 13 crew took to two life rafts, from which they were rescued by the Anstruther lifeboat. A large chunk of rusty steel wreckage lies above water, wedged in the inlet between North Ness and Mars Rock. Is this part of the *Thomas L Devlin*?

MARS

Wreck No: 188	Date Sunk: 19 May 1936
Latitude: 56 11 35 N	Longitude: 02 33 52 W
GPS Lat: 5611.580 N	GPS Long: 0233.870 W

Mars *breaking up on the May Island (Author's collection)*

Location: Mars Rock, North Ness, May Island   Area: May
Type: Steamship   Tonnage: 540 grt
Length: 170 ft   Beam: 26.7 ft   Draught: 12 ft
How Sunk: Ran aground   Depth: 18 metres

The Latvian steamship *Mars*, bound from Ballina, Ireland to Methil for coal, ran on to the North Ness of the May Island at 2.15 a.m. on 19 May 1936, while entering the Firth of Forth in fog. Although the fog signal was sounding, it was not heard. Her 13 crew were taken off by Anstruther lifeboat, leaving the *Mars* lying on her port side, facing south-east, three quarters of a mile from the lighthouse.

MALLARD

Wreck No: 189   Date Sunk: 13 July 1921
Latitude: 56 11 49 N   Longitude: 02 35 25 W
GPS Lat: 5611.820 N   GPS Long: 0235.420 W
Location: 1 mile WNW of May Island   Area: May
Type: Steamship   Tonnage: 213 grt
Length: 125.8 ft   Beam: 23.6 ft   Draught: 12.1 ft
How Sunk: Foundered   Depth: 42 metres

During an exercise in February 1989, HNLMS *Alkmaar* located a wreck one mile, 300° from the North Ness of the May Island (5611.792N, 00235.506W – WGS84). The wreck lies N/S with the bow pointing north, length 40 metres, beam 9 metres. She has a bridge aft, and a large single hold amidships. This description seems to suggest a small steamship with welldeck forward, and machinery aft – a very common configuration.

In 1990 divers reported an iron or steel ship similar to a puffer, sitting upright and apparently intact, with no obvious indication of the reason for sinking. The hold is full of coal, and the wreck appeared to have been on the sand and shingle bottom for some considerable time. Two portholes and the steam whistle were recovered, but no items to aid identification. The recovered items were lying loose, having become detached from their fastenings by long immersion. By 2000 most of her plating had fallen away leaving an almost skeletal structure. The boiler area and parts of the bows still retain their original form, but the rest of the wreck now provides a home to shoals of fish and large spiny spider crabs.

This wreck is probably the steamship *Mallard*, built in 1875 by Earles of Hull. She foundered en route from Dysart to Aberdeen with a cargo of coal on 13 July 1921. The vessel was caught in a heavy wind in the Firth of Forth while approaching the North Ness of the May Island, and the crew were helpless until the arrival of the motorboat *Snowdrop*, which took them off and landed them safely in Anstruther.

FOOTAH

Wreck No: 190	Date Sunk: 2 January 1902
Latitude: 56 12 00 N PA	Longitude: 02 37 00 W PA
GPS Lat: 5612.000 N	GPS Long: 0237.000 W
Location: 4 miles SE by E of Anstruther	Area: May
Type: Steamship	Tonnage: 100 grt
Length: 95.1 ft　　　　Beam: 14.2 ft	Draught: 8.7 ft
How Sunk: Struck wreckage	Depth: 25 metres

On Friday, 2 January 1902 the Alloa-registered iron steamship *Footah* – built in 1884 by Jones of Liverpool – foundered four miles SE by E of Anstruther, or 4 miles SE of Anstruther. With a crew of five, she left Leith at 8 p.m. on 1 January with a cargo of 120 tons of feeding stuffs and manure for Dundee. At about half past midnight on the 2nd, she struck some heavy floating wreckage with such force as to knock a large hole in her starboard side. In the dark it was impossible to see what the object was, and the crew were left no time to find out, as the water began to pour in. A small boat was launched, and the men had barely time to get in and cast off before their vessel foundered in 17 fathoms of water. Although the men had lost all their belongings, they reached Anstruther safely, and reported the disaster to the coastguards.

According to a report in *The Scotsman* newspaper, Pittenweem fishing boats, engaged in herring fishing, had their drift nets damaged by fouling what was supposed to be the wreck of the *Footah*. One of the crews whose nets had got entangled said he saw the top of the mast only about two fathoms below the surface of the water. The wreck located by the fishing crew lies in ten fathoms of water, half a mile from the shore, bearing south-east from Anstruther lights. As this is such a very different position from "four miles SE by E of Anstruther", it must have been a different wreck.

UNKNOWN – PRE-1919

Wreck No: 191
Latitude: 56 12 20 N PA
GPS Lat: 5612.333 N
Location: 1 mile NE of May Island
Type:
Length: Beam:
How Sunk:

Date Sunk: Pre-March 1919
Longitude: 02 33 10 W PA
GPS Long: 0233.167 W
Area: May
Tonnage:
Draught:
Depth: 40 metres

The wreck charted one mile north-east of the May Island at 561220N, 023310W PA with at least 28 metres over it in 45 metres, was reported on 24 March 1919. The *Northumbria* sank a mile from this location in 1917, and this may be a slightly incorrect estimate of the position of the wreck of the *Northumbria*. Many vessels are known to have been lost near the May Island over the years, and this may be the position of one of the vessels named elsewhere in this book for which no accurate position has yet been established. It is, of course, also possible that this may be another wreck altogether. One possibility is that this may be the bows of the *K-14*, which were sheared off in collision with the *K-22* during the Battle of May Island on 31 January 1918. Another possibility is that this may be the sloop *Packet* with a cargo of coal. She was reported sunk half a mile north-east of the May Island in 1817.

NORTHUMBRIA

Wreck No: 192
Latitude: 56 12 26 N
GPS Lat: 5612.239 N
Location: 1 mile N of May Island
Type: Trawler
Length: 115.5 ft
How Sunk: Mined

WGS84

Beam: 19.8 ft

Date Sunk: 3 March 1917
Longitude: 02 34 43 W
GPS Long: 0234.633 W
Area: May
Tonnage: 211 grt
Draught: 9.9 ft
Depth: 33 metres

The steam trawler *Northumbria* was built in 1906 by Cook Welton & Gemmell of Beverley. She was hired by the Admiralty in 1914 for use as an armed patrol sweeper, and struck a mine one mile north of the May Island on 3 March 1917. One naval officer and eight ratings were killed.

The bow points east, but is smashed and twisted, possibly as a result of the mine explosion. The rudder still stands vertically, but stern plates on the starboard side have fallen away, and are lying flat on the seabed, giving the impression that the vessel was wider than she really was. The boiler stands four metres high, and the triple-expansion steam engine and winches on the deck are still recognisable. The remainder of the wreckage is no more than one metre high in a general depth of 34 metres. Slack water is one and a half hours before high water at Leith. (See the wreck charted at 561220N, 023313W PA, first reported on 24 March 1919.)

UNKNOWN – WWII ?

Wreck No: 193		Date Sunk: WWII	
Latitude: 56 12 30 N PA		Longitude: 02 27 00 W PA	
GPS Lat: 5612.500 N		GPS Long: 0227.000 W	
Location: 3¾ miles E of May Island		Area: May	
Type:		Tonnage:	
Length:	Beam:	Draught:	
How Sunk:		Depth: 52 metres	

The wreck charted as Wk PA at 561230N, 022700W, 3.75 miles east of the May Island was reported in 1945, and is thought to be an unknown Second World War loss. The accurate position for this wreck might be as given below.

UNKNOWN – BEN ATTOW

Wreck No: 194		Date Sunk:	
Latitude: 56 12 49 N		Longitude: 02 24 58 W	
GPS Lat: 5612.820 N		GPS Long: 0224.970 W	
Location: 5 miles E of May Island		Area: May	
Type:		Tonnage:	
Length: 100 ft	Beam:	Draught:	
How Sunk:		Depth: 52 metres	

The wreck charted at 561249N, 022458W in a depth of 52 metres, 5 miles east of the May Island is apparently 100 feet long. The wreck is orientated 010/190°. This might possibly be the *Ben Attow*, although the position of the *Ben Attow* was described in 1940 as 7 miles E ½ S of the Isle of May. Another possibility is that this wreck might be the Granton steam trawler *Ethel Nutten* (GN59), which foundered while under tow near the May Island in a severe NW force 12 storm on 7 January 1923. The position has been variously described as two miles east, or S by W of May Island. *Ethel Nutten* was built by Hall Russell of Aberdeen in 1906 (Yard No. 417). She was 182 grt and measured 110 ft × 22 ft × 13 ft.

BALLOCHBUIE

Wreck No: 195		Date Sunk: 20 April 1917	
Latitude: 56 13 40 N		Longitude: 02 14 04 W	
GPS Lat: 5613.670 N		GPS Long: 0214.070 W	
Location: 11 miles E of May Island		Area: May	
Type: Steamship		Tonnage: 921 grt	
Length: 200 ft	Beam: 31.3 ft	Draught: 12.7 ft	
How Sunk: Torpedoed by *UC-41*		Depth: 53 metres	

The steamship Ballochbuie
(Courtesy of Aberdeen Art Gallery & Museums)

The wreck charted at 561340N, 021404W, 11 miles east of the May Island, was first located in 1962 by HMS *Scott*. The least depth was reported as 45 metres, and the wreck was standing up some 8½ metres from the sand and gravel seabed, which is at 54 metres. The wreck appears to be upright and intact, and is apparently 200 feet long, which coincides with the length of the steamship *Ballochbuie*, built in 1905 by John Duthie S. B. Co., Aberdeen, engine by J. Abernethy, Aberdeen. She was owned by the Aberdeen Lime Co. Ltd.

While on passage from Aberdeen to Sunderland in ballast on 20 April 1917, she was torpedoed by *UC-41* (KL Kurt Bernis). The master and two of the crew were lost. The Hydrographic Department gave the position as 561300N, 021800W, nine miles east of the May Island. *Lloyd's* described the position as seven miles east of May Island. The wreck has a four-bladed propeller, and two holds forward. The stern is damaged, and this is the apparent reason for her sinking.

K-17

Wreck No: 196		Date Sunk: 31 January 1918
Latitude: 56 15 32 N		Longitude: 02 11 24 W
GPS Lat: 5615.510 N	**OSGB36**	GPS Long: 0211.468 W
GPS Lat: 5615.528 N	**WGS84 Main**	GPS Long: 0211.494 W
GPS Lat: 5615.345 N	**WGS84 Bow**	GPS Long: 0211.778 W
Location: 13 miles E of Fife Ness		Area: May
Type: Submarine		Tonnage: 2565 grt
Length: 338 ft	Beam: 26.6 ft	Draught: 16 ft
How Sunk: Collision with HMS *Fearless*		Depth: 46–52 metres

K-17 was sunk in collision with HMS *Fearless*. The wreck was first located by HMS *Scott* in 1962. Least depth 46 metres and standing up some 6 metres from the seabed at 52 metres.

Two British K-class submarines lie fairly close to May Island. They were lost in 1918 during a massive naval exercise that went tragically wrong. Both submarines lie very close together – only 100 metres apart – in around 55 metres on a mud and gravel bottom, 13 miles east of Fife Ness.

K-17 is broken in two. The larger stern section lies upright and largely proud of the seabed of mud, sand, shells and gravel. The conning tower lies on the seabed close to the starboard side, with a gun lying aft of this. The funnels and hatches also lie on the seabed, leaning against the starboard side of the hull. Through an open hole in the hull, where the conning tower had originally been, a ladder reaches down into the control room which is partially filled with silt, although a control panel, cups and stacked dinner plates are still visible. Forward of this a few holes in the hull reveal more valves and gauges, and further forward still, is a disarray of bent metal and non-ferrous pipes and conduits remaining of the connection to the sliced off bow. The bow section is missing. It lies some distance SW of the main section of the submarine.

There is generally a south-going tidal flow over the wreck, which is lies with her stern east and "bow" west, but the currents here are not too strong. As the wreck is deep and dark, however, it should only be dived with proper planning and safety precautions. Another two positions given for *K-17* are 5615.456N, 0211.594W and 5615.446N, 0211.570W.

K-6 *(Courtesy of the Imperial War Museum)*

THE BATTLE OF MAY ISLAND
The sinking of HM Submarines *K-4* and *K-17*

THE SUBMARINES

The K-class submarines were monsters in their day, being twice as long and three times as heavy as other submarines of that era, and had no fewer than seven power sources – two steam turbines of 10500 shp gave a maximum speed of 24 knots on the surface, four electric motors of 1400 hp, which produced a maximum speed underwater of 9 knots, and an auxiliary diesel engine of 1800 hp for manoeuvring on the surface while building up steam. Their normal complement was 53 men, and the maximum diving depth was 150 feet. The armament consisted of ten 18-inch torpedo tubes, two of which were mounted in the funnel superstructure for surface use at night, two 4-inch guns, (except *K-17* which had 5.5-inch guns), and one 3-inch anti-aircraft gun.

Because of their technical complexity, a time-consuming procedure had to be carried out before diving. This included extinguishing the boiler furnaces for steam production, retracting the two funnels and covering their 3-feet diameter holes with watertight plates, closing four mushroom-shaped air intake vents, and about 30 other openings in the hull. These submarines had to be trimmed with great care. The large flat foredeck lacked buoyancy and produced a tendency to dive, as a result of which most of the class had at some time unintentionally nose-dived to the bottom.

Occasionally, sea water entered through the air intakes and down the funnels, extinguishing the boiler fires, causing explosions, shorting out the electrical circuits and converting the boiler room into a flooded sauna. In an attempt to correct some of the faults inherent in the original design, these submarines were all modified by lengthening the funnels and fitting bulbous swan bows, within which extra buoyancy tanks were installed. The forward gun was also removed as it proved impossible to man even in calm water at speeds over 12 knots.

K-13 sank on trials in the Gareloch in 1917 when she dived with the air intake vents still open. Of the 80 crew and dockyard men aboard, only 47 were saved after a rescue operation taking three days. She was raised and renumbered *K-22*.

THE EXERCISE

In a massive naval exercise, code named EC1, involving a large number of battleships and cruisers, nine K-boats two flotillas of Royal Navy ships and numerous destroyers, left Rosyth after dark on the night of 31 January 1918, and steamed down the Forth at 19 knots in line astern, strung out over 20 miles, each following the shaded blue stern light of the vessel ahead. Radio silence was observed, and the navigation lights were switched off. The first flotilla was led by the cruiser *Ithuriel*, followed by the *K-11*, *K-17*, *K-14*, *K-12* and *K-22*, then the cruisers *Australia*, *New Zealand*, *Indomitable* and *Inflexible*. A few miles astern, the cruiser *Fearless* led the next flotilla consisting of the *K-4*, *K-3*, *K-6* and *K-7* followed by the battleships and destroyers.

*K-boat at speed, illustrating the problem of manning
the forward gun (which has been removed)*

THE CAUSE

Ahead of them in the darkness and mist, a small group of minesweepers was patrolling across their path, unaware of the fleet exercise in progress. On seeing them, *K-11* reduced speed and turned to port, as did *K-17*. Approaching May Island, Cdr. Thomas Harbottle, in *K-14*, was suddenly aware that the *K-17* (Lt. Cdr. H. J.Hearn) immediately ahead of him, had swerved to port, and at the same time saw two small vessels emerging from the mist to cross his bow. On taking avoiding action with full right rudder, the helm jammed in that position, causing the boat to continue in a circle clear of the *K-12*, but broadside into the path of the *K-22*, which was still running at 19 knots. Unable to avoid her, *K-22* rammed into *K-14*'s port side, damaging her own bows, and slicing off *K-14*'s bows aft of the forward torpedo room. By closing watertight doors, immediate disaster was averted, but both submarines were now lying stopped in the water with flooded compartments in the path of the cruisers bearing down on them at 19 knots. Lights were switched on, flares fired and radio silence was broken as calls for assistance went out.

Three of the battle-cruisers swept past safely, their wash rolling the crippled submarines violently, but the fourth, the *Inflexible*, smashed into the *K-22*, bending 30 feet of the submarine's already-damaged bows at right angles to the hull and shearing off a ballast tank as she rode over her, forcing *K-22* under the surface. As the cruiser continued on her way in the dark, apparently unaware that she had run down the submarine, *K-22* popped up again behind her and resumed calling for help.

THE ABORTIVE RESCUE

The *Ithuriel* (Captain Ernest Leir) picked up the distress calls from the submarines astern, but due to a decoding error, the erroneous impression gained in the *Ithuriel* was that a vessel named *Nova Scotia* had collided with *K-12*. Twenty minutes later, the correct message was received, and *Ithuriel* – by this time some 18 miles east of the May – turned back with her remaining submarines to assist. Realising the danger of running headlong into the second flotilla of warships still steaming down river towards them, the navigation lights

1. Ships involved in Exercise EC1, which resulted in the Battle of May Island

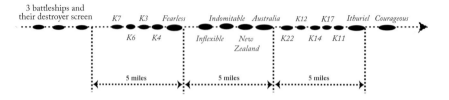

2. The original collision between *K14* and *K22* at 7.15 p.m.

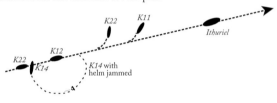

26 minutes later, at 7.41 p.m., the *Inflexible* struck the *K22*

3. Turnback of *Ithuriel* and her submarines, and the collision between *Fearless* and *K17*

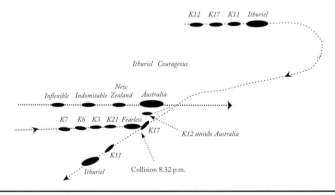

4. The collision between *Fearless* and *K17*, then the collision between *K6* and *K4*

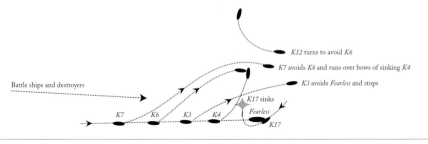

were turned on, but no radio message was sent out to warn the oncoming ships that she had turned back. *K-12* suddenly found the cruiser *Australia* bearing down on her. By luck they just missed each other, but were so close that the officers on *Australia* were able to look down *K-12*'s funnels and see the glow of her furnaces!

Fearless, leading the second wave of ships, had also picked up the distress calls and had switched her navigation lights on. At 7.45 p.m. she passed clear to the east of the May Island. According to the radio reports of the original collision, the danger area, a mile and a half north of the May, should have been safely astern, and speed was increased to 21 knots. Unfortunately, her commander, Captain Charles Little, was unaware that the *Ithuriel* and her submarines had turned back towards them, and very shortly, both groups of ships met head on in the darkness and mists, 13 miles east of the May Island.

THE FATAL CIRCUMSTANCES

At 8.32 p.m. the *Fearless* rammed into *K-17* just forward of her conning tower, but all 56 crew managed to escape from the submarine in the eight minutes before she went down. The group swimming in the water stayed together, imagining that with the number of ships in the area, they would soon be picked up. Immediately behind the *Fearless*, the *K-4*, (Lt. Cdr. David de B. Stocks), turned to port and stopped. *K-3* behind her did likewise, but overshot *K-4*, closely scraping past to stop some distance away. *K-6* then met *K-12* coming back upriver on a collision course straight towards her, having only just narrowly avoided colliding with the Australia, and in taking avoiding action, *K-6* rammed *K-4*, almost slicing her in half. Entangled with each other, both submarines began to sink, and it was only by going full astern that *K-6* managed to break free from *K-4* to avoid being dragged to the bottom with her.

Seconds after *K-4* turned over and sank *K-7* passed overhead, gently brushing her keel, and stopped to look for survivors. Her deck party were stripped off, ready to enter the water to help their fellow submariners, but there were no survivors from *K-4*. Another of the shortcomings of the K-boats was that they were not equipped with any form of underwater escape apparatus.

THE FINAL DEBACLE

By this time the battleships and destroyers following behind *Fearless* and her submarines arrived on the scene at 21 knots, and ploughed through the cluster of damaged and confused ships. Two of them missed *K-3* by the thickness of her hull plating, and washed *K-7*'s deck party off the casing, so that they too had to be rescued. In seconds they passed the spot where *K-17* had gone down, chopping up or sucking under and drowning the men still swimming in the water. By the time they passed by, only nine remained alive, one of whom died shortly after being picked up by *K-7*. News of this disastrous episode was suppressed at the time. It had cost almost 100 lives, the loss of two submarines, damage to three others and two surface ships, and later became known as the Battle of May Island.

The damage to the bows of HMS Fearless

K-14 was taken to Rosyth for examination, but the steering fault could not be reproduced. But, of course, her 19-knot speed at the critical time could not be replicated in the dock. The rudder has no bottom support to eliminate bending effect on the shaft. Applying full rudder at 19 knots would exert considerable force on the rudder shaft, causing it to act as a lever, with the shaft bearing in the hull as the fulcrum.

K-14 *in drydock at Rosyth*

K-4 *aground on Walney Island (Courtesy of Mirrorpic)*

K-4

Wreck No: 197		Date Sunk: 31 January 1918
Latitude: 56 15 27 N		Longitude: 02 11 30 W
GPS Lat: 5615.453 N	**OSGB36**	GPS Long: 0211.507 W
GPS Lat: 5615.456 N	**WGS84**	GPS Long: 0211.594 W
Location: 13 miles E of Fife Ness		Area: May
Type: Submarine		Tonnage: 2565 grt
Length: 338 ft	Beam: 26.6 ft	Draught: 16 ft
How Sunk: Collision with *K-6*		Depth: 52–57 metres

The *K-4* was sunk in collision with HM submarine *K-6*. This wreck was first located by HMS *Scott* in 1962. Least astronomical depth is 46 metres, with the wreck standing up some 7 metres from the seabed at 53 metres. A more normal condition would be to find the wreck at 50 metres, and the seabed at 57 metres. *K-4* is the more complete of these two submarines, and is lying E/W upright, but with a bow-up attitude. The stern is almost level with the seabed, and the propellers are partially buried, whereas the bows project above the seabed. A deep gash across the hull, aft of the rear gun, and about 30–35 metres aft of the conning tower, appears to be where *K-6* rode over the *K-4*. It is not clear whether this split in the external housing also penetrates the pressure hull, but in any case the conning tower was displaced, and forced over to starboard, still attached to the hull, but lying horizontally on the deck. The forward periscope is damaged, and a fishing net covers the gun and the conning tower. One diver described the 4-inch gun as a long-barrelled bruiser pointing forward, and standing aft of a large recessed hatch between the funnel hatches, which are still in place. He was able to distinguish the side torpedo tubes, and expressed the opinion that the propellers seemed small for a boat of this size.

TO COMMEMORATE THOSE MEMBERS
OF THE SHIPS' COMPANIES OF
HIS MAJESTY'S SUBMARINES K4 AND K17
WHO GAVE THEIR LIVES
IN THE SERVICE OF THEIR COUNTRY
OFF THE ISLE OF MAY
ON 31ST JANUARY 1918
ERECTED IN THEIR MEMORY DURING THE SUBMARINE CENTENARY YEAR 2001

The memorial plaque at Anstruther (Author's collection)

Eighty-four years later, on 31 January 2002, a cairn with a memorial plaque was erected at Anstruther harbour, on the Forth shore opposite May Island, in memory of the men who lost their lives in the submarines *K-4* and *K-17*. Over 100 men were lost that night. Two submarines had been sunk, and four damaged, along with a light cruiser. The plaque was unveiled by members of Fife Council and representatives of the Royal Navy Submarine Service.

CAUTION
Protected Wrecks in the UK

WRECKS DESIGNATED UNDER THE PROTECTION OF MILITARY REMAINS ACT 1986:
This Act makes it an offence to interfere with the wreckage of any crashed, sunken or stranded military aircraft or designated vessel without a licence. This is irrespective of loss of life or whether the loss occurred during peacetime or wartime. All crashed military aircraft receive automatic protection, but vessels must be individually designated. Currently, there are 21 vessels protected under this Act, both in UK waters and abroad, and it is likely that the Ministry of Defence will designate more vessels in the future.

There are two levels of protection offered by this Act, designation as a **Protected Place** or as a **Controlled Site**.

Protected Places include the remains of any aircraft which crashed while in military service or any vessel designated (by name not location) which sank or stranded in military service after 4 August 1914. Although crashed military aircraft receive automatic status as a Protected Place, vessels need to be specifically designated by name. The location of the vessel does not need to be known for it to be designated as a Protected Place.

Diving is not prohibited on an aircraft or vessel designated as a **Protected Place**. However, it is an offence to conduct unlicensed diving or salvage operations to tamper with, damage, remove or unearth any remains or enter any hatch or other opening. Essentially, diving is permitted on a 'look but don't touch' basis only. *K-4* and *K-17* are both included in the list of **Protected Places**.

Controlled Sites are specifically designated areas which encompass the remains of a military aircraft or a vessel sunk or stranded in military service within the last two hundred years. Within the controlled site it is an offence to tamper with, damage, move or unearth any remains, enter any hatch or opening or conduct diving, salvage or excavation operations for the purposes of investigating or recording the remains, unless authorised by licence. This effectively makes diving operations prohibited on these sites without a specific licence.

For further information on this Act and its administration, contact the Ministry of Defence, or, in the first instance, see the Maritime and Coast Guard Agency's website: http://www.mcga.gov.uk/c4mca/mcga-environmental/mcga-dops_row_receiver_of_wreck/mcga-dops-row-protected-wrecks.htm

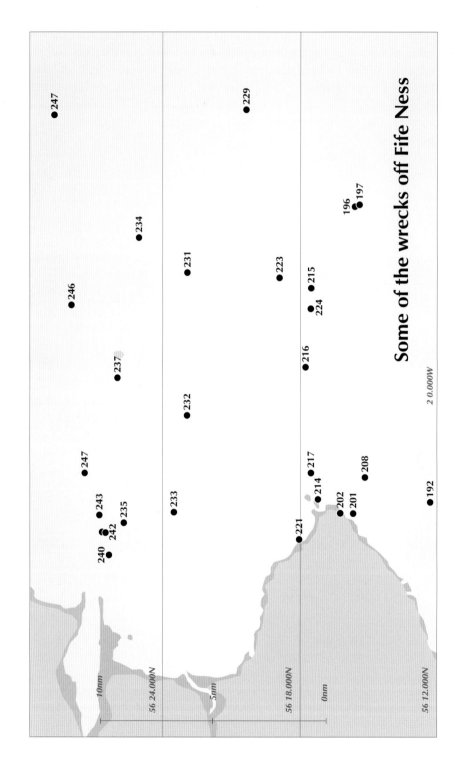

Some of the wrecks off Fife Ness

7

Fife Ness

ROSEBERY

Wreck No: 198		Date Sunk: 19 January 1934
Latitude: 56 16 00 N PA		Longitude: 02 36 00 W PA
GPS Lat: 5616.000 N		GPS Long: 0236.000 W
Location: Near Crail		Area: Fife Ness
Type: Trawler		Tonnage: 200 grt
Length:	Beam:	Draught:
How Sunk: Ran aground		Depth:

The steam trawler *Rosebery* was heading for Aberdeen after a 16-day fishing trip when she ran ashore near Crail. The weather was calm, and for several hours the crew tried to free their vessel from the rocks, but without success. At low tide the trawler was high and dry on the rocks, with her bow pointing inshore. She lay only 200 yards from the shore, and it was possible to walk out to her. Three of her propeller blades had been broken in the attempts to free her. It had been hoped that she might be refloated on the next high tide, but that attempt also failed. The Leith tug *Bullger* arrived to assist, but despite her efforts, the *Rosebery* remained firmly stuck on the rocks. The receeding tide finally forced the *Bullger* to leave the scene.

BULLGER

Wreck No: 199		Date Sunk: 20 January 1934
Latitude: 56 13 00 N		Longitude: 02 41 30 W
GPS Lat: 5613.000 N		GPS Long: 0241.500 W
Location: Outside Anstruther harbour		Area: Fife Ness
Type: Tug		Tonnage: 364 grt
Length:	Beam:	Draught:
How Sunk: Ran aground		Depth: 10 metres

After her unsuccessful attempts to free the *Rosebery* from the rocks near Crail, the *Bullger* (ex-*Traveller*, ex-*Storm Cock*, built in 1883) left to reach Anstruther before the tide receded too far to allow her to enter the harbour. (She was named *Bullger* after the chairman of Leith Salvage & Towing Company's dog.) Because of the neap tides, the water was much shallower than usual, and at full speed the *Bullger* struck rocks near the harbour entrance, and was holed near the bow. She got off again immediately, however, and the crew made frantic efforts to reach the harbour while she filled rapidly. She was just about to turn into the harbour when she settled down – within ten minutes of striking the rocks. The members of her crew reached the pier safely in their small boat. At high tide, the *Bullger*'s masts and funnel were all that could be seen, and as she lay in the fairway to the harbour, the drifters had to make a slight detour to avoid the wreck. Over the following two months the Leith salvage vessel *Reclaimer*, with divers and pumps, made considerable efforts to move the wreck into the harbour, but little progress was achieved, the wreck having been moved only about four feet. During that time the hull of one drifter had to be repaired after striking the wreck. In April the superstructure of the tug was swept away in a terrific storm with huge waves which washed wreckage into the harbour, as a result of which it had to be closed to all vessels for a time until the loose wreckage had been removed. After the storm it was found that although the hull was still in the same position where she sank, it no longer interfered with the movement of vessels into and out of the harbour.

The smashed remains of the tug will probably still be lying just outside the harbour in 5–6 metres of water, posing no more danger to vessels than the rocks at either side of the entrance.

ROBERT SCOTT

Wreck No: 200	Date Sunk: 4 July 1864
Latitude: 56 13 00 N PA	Longitude: 02 41 15 W PA
GPS Lat: 5613.000 N	GPS Long: 0241.250 W
Location: Off Anstruther harbour	Area: Fife Ness
Type: Tug	Tonnage: 77 grt
Length: 82.3 ft Beam:	Draught:
How Sunk: Foundered – but refloated	Depth:

The steam tug *Robert Scott* was built in 1862. She obviously had a dual role, as one contemporary newspaper described her as a fine, powerful double-engined steamer, well known on the Aberdour service. This would seem to imply she was used as a ferry, probably carrying passengers to Leith, or perhaps also as an excursion steamer.

In 1864, when she was still only two years old, she was sold to Russia, and left Leith on 4 July for the long delivery voyage to Cronstadt, near St Petersburg, on the Baltic Sea, where she was to be employed in towing. In order to steam such a distance, the vessel was very heavily laden with coal, and shortly after setting out, she began making water, but the voyage was continued until the May Island had been reached. By that time, the leaks had been partially stopped, but the state of the vessel induced the master to make for the shore. She was anchored off Anstruther about 10 a.m., and the master landed in a small boat to send a telegram to Leith, asking for assistance. He then returned to his vessel, and a group of local fishermen offered to take the vessel to a place of greater safety, but their offer was firmly refused. Meantime, those on board continued their struggle to keep the *Robert Scott* afloat, but had to abandon the vessel at 1.30 p.m., and a few minutes later she sank by the bow. The position of sinking was described as about quarter of a mile east of the harbour in three fathoms at low water. Her mast and funnel were still visible above the surface. The same newspaper report went on to say it was imperative that the wreck should be removed as quickly as possible from that position, as it lay directly in the fairway of the harbour.

She must have been successfully refloated, as *Lloyd's List* of 20 September 1864 reported that the steamer *Robert Scott* of and from Leith for Cronstadt, which had sprung a leak and sunk in the Firth of Forth, off Cellardyke on 4 July, drove on shore in Ward Bay, six miles south of Peterhead on 18 September 1864. The village of Ward was renamed Port Errol, and the adjoining village of Invercruden was renamed Cruden Bay in 1924. The wreck must therefore lie in Cruden Bay, somewhere around 5724.500N, 0151.000W PA. Any remains near there will long ago have been smashed to pieces, and buried in the sand.

RIVER AVON

Wreck No: 201		Date Sunk: 7 February 1937	
Latitude: 56 15 38 N		Longitude: 02 35 30 W	
GPS Lat: 5615.630 N		GPS Long: 0235.500 W	
Location: Kilminning Rock, Fife Ness		Area: Fife Ness	
Type: Trawler		Tonnage: 202 grt	
Length: 115.4 ft	Beam: 22.5 ft	Draught: 12.1 ft	
How Sunk: Ran aground		Depth: 10 metres	

The Granton steam trawler *River Avon* ran on to Kilminning Rock, about three quarters of a mile south-west of Fife Ness, at 11.30 p.m. on 7 February 1937. She was of steel construction, built by Rennie, Forrest of Wivenhoe in 1919.

Crail LSA took off the youngest member of the crew by breeches buoy, but the others remained aboard to take off some of the cargo of 200 boxes of fish, which were landed by their small boat. The Fishery Protection cruiser *Brenda* illuminated the operation with her searchlight.

Kilminning Rock is not marked on the chart, but it is the very prominent rock on the shore to the east of Sauchope caravan site. On the ordnance survey map, this rock is named Kilminning Castle, and it is sometimes called Kilminning Craig. The *River Avon* struck the rock which dries at low water, about 150 metres off the shore, directly off the larger of two old sewer pipes which are visible on the shore about 150 metres east of Kilminning Craig. Just off the north side of this rock is a propeller shaft with a four-bladed iron propeller. A few yards off the west of the rock, there is a boiler, about 10 feet in diameter and 10 feet long. A 'D'-shaped rudder about 6 feet tall also lies nearby. There are also iron or steel ribs or hull frames, but no sign of any hull plating. These may all be part of the remains of the *River Avon*, but some of the wreckage in the area may be from the *Pladda*. As

The very prominent Kilminning Rock, with the sea breaking over the drying rock to the east, on which the River Avon *and the* Pladda *came to grief (Author's collection)*

the *Pladda*'s boiler was salvaged, however, the boiler must be from the *River Avon*. There must be more wreckage scattered amongst the kelp-covered rocky gullies and boulders.

PLADDA

Wreck No: 202		Date Sunk: 14 December 1890
Latitude: 56 16 12 N		Longitude: 02 35 30 W
GPS Lat: 5616.200 N		GPS Long: 0235.500 W
Location: 120 mtrs E of Kilminning Rock		Area: Fife Ness
Type: Steamship		Tonnage: 421 grt
Length: 181.5 ft	Beam: 23.1 ft	Draught: 13.2 ft
How Sunk: Ran aground		Depth: 9 metres

The Dundee iron steamship *Pladda* went ashore in thick fog, on rocks about one mile east of Crail while en route from Newcastle to Dundee on 14 December 1890. The wreckage is very broken up and covered in kelp, in an area of boulders and crevices, 120 metres east of Kilminning rock, about 150 metres off the shore. When she went ashore at 1 a.m., her distress signals were heard by the local Lloyd's Receiver who alerted the coastguard. A fishing boat in the Forth also heard her signals and succeeded in going alongside the Pladda taking off her passengers and landing them at Crail. The lifesaving brigade stood by with their rocket apparatus to take off the crew who had remained aboard in the hope of being able to refloat their vessel. This proved to be impossible, however, as with the incoming tide, she filled with water and swung broadside on to the shore. Gales over the

SS Pladda *(Author's collection)*

following two days prevented any salvage attempt, and the vessel was gradually battered to pieces. Her cargo included bleaching powder, soda ash, coils of lead pipe, marble and sheet iron. Some of the cargo was subsequently salvaged, and her boiler was refloated and towed to Leith. Among the cargo recovered were 40 coils of lead pipe, two cases of marble, a quantity of petroleum, and other goods.

Her remains can be dived from the shore at slack water, but as the tidal stream can run at up to two knots, it would be better to dive by boat from the slipway at Crail or from Anstruther. From the land, take the Crail to Fife Ness road, and turn right down a road leading to a picnic area at the eastern edge of the old airfield. From the south west corner of the picnic area, a path leads down the cliff. A short distance to the east of the bottom of the path are two old sewer pipes. The wreck lies directly out from the larger of these pipes.

CHINGFORD

Wreck No: 203		Date Sunk: 23 December 1924
Latitude: 56 15 58 N		Longitude: 02 35 46 W
GPS Lat: 5615.970 N		GPS Long: 0235.770 W
Location: Sauchope, near Crail		Area: Fife Ness
Type: Steamship		Tonnage: 1517 grt
Length: 264.5 ft	Beam: 37 ft	Draught: 17.8 ft
How Sunk: Ran aground		Depth: 6 metres

Chingford *aground on Kilminning Sands (Author's collection)*

The Dundee steamship *Chingford*, built in 1889, was driven ashore on Kilminning Sands, Crail, during a severe southwesterly storm. She had been en route from Transgund and Dundee to Grangemouth with a cargo of timber. Anstruther and Brought Ferry lifeboats went to her assistance, but when they arrived, great rollers were sweeping over the vessel and sending up huge clouds of spray. Crail LSA rushed to the scene and made efforts to get a line to the stricken ship, which had a crew of 22, commanded by Captain Chapman. Six of the crew were saved by breeches buoy, but the sixth man was nearly drowned. The 16 others were rescued by the Anstruther boat.

Some salvage was carried out, but efforts to continue the salvage were aborted when the vessel broke up in storms.

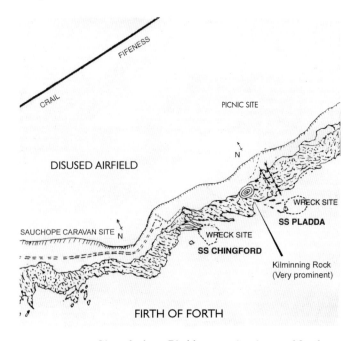

Locations of Chingford *and* Pladda, *immediately east of Crail*

The keel, propeller shaft and four-bladed propeller with squared-off blade ends lie close to the shore off the Sauchope static caravan site at Crail. Find the only piece of sandy beach, near the eastermost end of the caravan site, then dive out to sea between the two rock spines. Part of the keel is just visible above water at low tide. The bow section lies slightly further out in six metres.

JANE ROSS

Wreck No: 204	Date Sunk: 14 September 1934
Latitude: 56 16 08 N	Longitude: 02 35 36 W
GPS Lat: 5616.130 N	GPS Long: 0235.600 W
Location: Kilminning Point	Area: Fife Ness
Type: Trawler	Tonnage: 184 grt
Length: 110.1 ft Beam: 21.2 ft	Draught: 11.6 ft
How Sunk: Ran aground	Depth:

The Aberdeen steam trawler *Jane Ross*, built in 1901 by Hall & Co., was making for Methil to replenish her coal bunkers when she ran aground in thick fog at Kilminning Point, two miles from Crail. The crew launched their small boat, but the painter snapped, and the boat drifted away to shore without them. It was later secured and anchored by a Crail fisherman. The Crail fishing boat *Maple Leaf* managed to get alongside the *Jane Ross* and took off the nine crew who were landed safely at Crail.

STORJEN

Wreck No: 205	Date Sunk: 2 July 1978
Latitude: 56 14 51 N	Longitude: 02 27 12 W
GPS Lat: 5614.800 N	GPS Long: 0227.200 W
Location: 5 miles ESE of Fife Ness	Area: Fife Ness
Type: MFV	Tonnage:
Length: Beam:	Draught:
How Sunk: Fire	Depth: 51 metres

The Oban-registered MFV *Storjen* (OB 71) sank after a fire. Her two crew were rescued. Charted as a wreck with at least 40 metres over it in 51 metres.

OTHONNA

Wreck No: 206	Date Sunk: 20 April 1917
Latitude: 56 15 00 N PA	Longitude: 02 30 00 W PA
GPS Lat: 5615.000 N	GPS Long: 0230.000 W
Location: Off Fife Ness	Area: Fife Ness
Type: Trawler	Tonnage: 180 grt
Length: 110.8 ft Beam: 20.8 ft	Draught: 11.1 ft
How Sunk: Mined	Depth: 36 metres

The steel-hulled steam trawler *Othonna* was built in 1899 by J. Duthie & Son, Aberdeen, engine by Whyte & Mair, Dundee. She struck a mine laid by *UC-41* and sank on 20 April 1917. The approximate position 561500N, 023000W dates from 24 March 1919. The depth at this position in 36 metres, but varies 30–50 metres within a radius of one mile. Asdic searches in this position in 1955, 1960 and 1977 failed to find any trace of her. Another, apparently more accurate position very close by at 561455N, 022950W, also dates from 1919. These positions are so close to each other – only 240 metres apart – that it seems unlikely that an asdic search around the first position would fail to detect a wreck in the second position.

SPEY

Wreck No: 207		Date Sunk: 22 December 1880
Latitude: 56 16 50 N		Longitude: 02 35 00 W
GPS Lat: 5616.830 N		GPS Long: 0235.000 W
Location: Craighead, Fife Ness		Area: Fife Ness
Type: Steamship		Tonnage: 659 grt
Length:	Beam:	Draught:
How Sunk: Ran aground		Depth:

The steamship *Spey* ran aground below Craighead quarries, Fife Ness on 22 December 1880 while en route, in ballast, from Dundee to Burntisland. She stranded just inside the North Carr Beacon, and a short time after striking the water was up to the beams in the forward hold, with sea breaking over the vessel. Captain Donald and his crew were saved.

LINGBANK

Wreck No: 208		Date Sunk: 26 April 1927
Latitude: 56 15 10 N PA		Longitude: 02 32 50 W PA
GPS Lat: 5615.170 N		GPS Long: 0232.830 W
Location: Off Fife Ness		Area: Fife Ness
Type: Trawler		Tonnage: 257 grt
Length: 132 ft	Beam: 22 ft	Draught: 10.8 ft
How Sunk: Foundered		Depth: 17 metres

The German steam trawler *Lingbank* was seen flying distress signals off Fife Ness at about 5 a.m. on 26 April 1927. The morning was bright and clear, with a flat calm sea. Before the lifeboat could be launched, another trawler went alongside and took off the crew. The *Lingbank* had sprung a leak, and sank at about 7.15 a.m. In 1927 the position was given as 561510N, 023250W, two miles, 141.5° from Fife Ness, and charted as Wk PA, but the wreck was not located by HMS *Scott* in 1960.

UNKNOWN

Wreck No: 209

Latitude: 56 15 27 N

GPS Lat: 5615.450 N

Location: 7 miles ESE of Fife Ness

Type:

Length: 112 ft   Beam:

How Sunk:

Date Sunk:

Longitude: 02 22 54 W

GPS Long: 0222.900 W

Area: Fife Ness

Tonnage:

Draught:

Depth: 51 metres

This wreck is in two parts, which might provide a clue to the reason for her sinking – possibly mined or torpedoed? The wreck appears to be about 112 feet long, and stands up 10 feet from the bottom. Possibly the *Othonna*?

VILDFUGL

Wreck No: 210

Latitude: 56 16 45 N

GPS Lat: 5616.750 N

Location: Ashore at Fife Ness

Type: Tanker

Length: 157 ft   Beam: 25.6 ft

How Sunk: Ran aground

Date Sunk: 28 May 1951

Longitude: 02 35 00 W

GPS Long: 0235.000 W

Area: Fife Ness

Tonnage: 477 grt

Draught: 10.9 ft

Depth: 12 metres

The small Norwegian tanker *Vildfugl* was built in Fredrikstad, Norway in 1941. She was seized by the Germans and renamed *Feiestein* (of Kiel). This ship was found at the U-boat pen *Dora I* in Trondheim after the war, and was reclaimed by the Norwegians in 1945. At 1.55 a.m. on 28 May 1951 she ran ashore on Fife Ness Point, 200 yards from the Coastguard Station. She was en route in ballast from Inverness to Grangemouth. She was wedged tight on a flat rock, having narrowly missed the jagged reef that runs out from the Fife Ness. Fife Ness LSA fired a rocket with a light line to the stranded vessel, and this was used by the Crail LSA to transfer a heavier line to carry the breeches buoy which took off the 14 crew. Within a few hours, the heavy seas battered the deck structure from the wreck, which broke into three parts, and became a total loss.

DOWNIEHILLS

Wreck No: 211

Latitude: 56 16 59 N PA

GPS Lat: 5616.983 N

Location: PA ¼ mile NE of Fife Ness

Type: Trawler

Length: 117.1 ft   Beam: 22.1 ft

How Sunk: Ran aground

Date Sunk: 18 January 1926

Longitude: 02 35 13 W PA

GPS Long: 0235.208 W

Area: Fife Ness

Tonnage: 227 grt

Draught: 12.6 ft

Depth: 10 metres

The steel-hulled Peterhead trawler *Downiehills* was built by Hawthorns of Leith in 1917. En route from Aberdeen to Methil on 18 January 1926, she stranded at Fife Ness during the night, having failed to see the North Carr lightship in thick fog. In a thrilling rescue which took only ten minutes, but which was witnessed by a crowd of over 300, the skipper and crew of four were rescued by the Crail life-saving apparatus, which had to be brought three miles to the scene. Five minutes after the rocket line was shot across the ship, which lay 300 yards out, the first man was hauled safely ashore.

KNOT

Wreck No: 212	Date Sunk: 5 November 1916
Latitude: 56 17 00 N	Longitude: 02 34 30 W
GPS Lat: 5617.000 N	GPS Long: 0234.500 W
Location: On North Carr Rock, Fife Ness	Area: Fife Ness
Type: Trawler	Tonnage: 168 grt
Length: 110.3 ft Beam: 20.9 ft	Draught: 11.1 ft
How Sunk: Ran aground	Depth: 12 metres

The steel steam trawler *Knot* was built in 1903 by Goole S.B.& Rprg. Co., and engined by C. D. Holmes of Hull. She ran on to North Carr Rock on 5 November 1916. The position given was reported on 24 March 1919, but no wreck was located here by HMS *Scott* in 1959. This is hardly surprising, as it will be well broken up and scattered, making it impossible to distinguish from the rocky bottom by echo sounder.

The steam trawler Knot *(Courtesy of W.E. Butland collection)*

BJORNHAUG

Wreck No: 213	Date Sunk: 5 April 1940
Latitude: 56 17 12 N	Longitude: 02 34 30 W
GPS Lat: 5617.200 N	GPS Long: 0234.500 W
Location: Balcomie Briggs, Fife Ness	Area: Fife Ness
Type: Steamship	Tonnage: 443 grt
Length: 143.4 ft Beam: 28.4 ft	Draught: 11.4 ft
How Sunk: Ran aground	Depth: 8 metres

The Norwegian steamship *Bjornhaug* (ex-*Kauko*, ex-*Torborg*, ex-*Torborg I*) was built at Nystads Skip, Uusikaupunki, Finland in 1921. She ran ashore in darkness on Balcomie Briggs near Fife Ness, while en route from Copenhagen to London with a cargo of paper on 5 April 1940. Three of the crew, including the ship's cat, came ashore in the ship's boat, while seven were rescued by Anstruther lifeboat. The wreck will be well broken up and scattered, making it impossible to distinguish from the rocky bottom by echo sounder.

Shipwreck Index of the British Isles lists her as steamer *Torborg I* at the time of loss on Balcomie Briggs, Fife Ness on 5 April 1940, with a cargo of paper. According to this source she was a wooden steamer built at Nystads Skip & M.V. Co, Nystad, registered in Bergen. Det Norske Veritas' *Norges, Sveriges og Danmarks Handelsflåter* lists her as *Bjørnhaug*, ex-*Torborg I*, and says she was a motor vessel which ran aground in the Firth of Forth on the date given above, on a voyage from Copenhagen to London with general cargo.

MUSKETIER

Wreck No: 214	Date Sunk: 2 November 1962
Latitude: 56 17 12 N	Longitude: 02 34 30 W
GPS Lat: 5617.200 N	GPS Long: 0234.500 W
Location: Balcomie Briggs, Fife Ness	Area: Fife Ness
Type: Motor vessel	Tonnage: 384 grt
Length: 152 ft Beam: 24.7 ft	Draught: 10.5 ft
How Sunk: Ran aground	Depth: 10 metres

The Dutch coaster *Musketier* (ex-*John V*, ex-*Lena*) ran on to Balcomie Briggs at 9.28 a.m. on 2 November 1962, while en route from Dunkirk to Perth with a cargo of slag. She was perched on a reef of jagged rock about a mile and a half north of the golf course at Crail,

Musketier *(Courtesy of World Ship Society)*

and her engine room was badly holed. Her seven crew abandoned ship in the life rafts at 11 a.m., and were picked up by Anstruther lifeboat, which landed them at 11.50 a.m. By next morning her decks were awash, and two days later she broke in two. The forward section sank, and the stern section was barely visible. She is now smashed to pieces in 6–10 metres of water.

EINAR JARL

Wreck No: 215		Date Sunk: 17 March 1941	
Latitude: 56 17 30 N PA		Longitude: 02 18 00 W PA	
GPS Lat: 5617.500 N		GPS Long: 0218.000 W	
Location: 9 ¾ miles E of Fife Ness		Area: Fife Ness	
Type: Steamship		Tonnage: 1858 grt	
Length: 265.3 ft	Beam: 42.1 ft	Draught: 17.9 ft	
How Sunk: Mined		Depth: 53 metres	

The Norwegian steamship *Einar Jarl*, Captain J. Herfjord, was en route in ballast from Hull via Methil to Loch Ewe. At Loch Ewe she was to join a westbound Atlantic convoy for Halifax, Nova Scotia. After leaving Methil in convoy EN86A, however, she struck a mine 9¾ miles east of Fife Ness at 2050 hours on 17 March 1941. At first it was thought an air attack was to blame (torpedo), but neither the escorting destroyer HMS Westminster, nor other ships in the convoy agreed with this theory. It was therefore assumed the cause of the explosion was a drifting mine. The ship was abandoned ten minutes later, and

The Norwegian steamship Einar Jarl *(Courtesy of World Ship Society)*

sank south-east of the Bell Rock, around three miles from the Isle of May. One Greek fireman was lost when he returned to his cabin to collect some of his belongings. There were 23 survivors, 17 of whom were landed at Aberdeen by SS *Medway Coast*.

Einar Jarl was built in Fredrikstad in 1921 for Det Nordenfjeldske Dampskipsselskap, Trondheim.

Lloyd's gave the position as 561730N, 021800W, hence the wreck charted as PA in this position. The Norwegian Maritime Directorate gives 561800N, 021800W PA. The nearest accurately charted wreck is at 561736N, 021930W, but this is reported to be only 40 metres long (132 feet). The next nearest charted wreck is at 561858N, 021712W, and this wreck is reported to be 95 metres long (313.5 feet). Neither of these matches the 265-foot (80 metres) length of the *Einar Jarl*.

JU88 AIRCRAFT ?

Wreck No: 216		Date Sunk: 16 October 1939 ?
Latitude: 56 17 48 N		Longitude: 02 24 05W
GPS Lat: 5617.857 N	**WGS84**	GPS Long: 0224.167 W
Location: 6 miles E of Fife Ness		Area: Fife Ness
Type: Aircraft		Tonnage:
Length: 100 ft	Beam:	Draught:
How Sunk:		Depth: 46–52 metres

The wreck charted six miles east of Fife Ness was located in 1977. It is apparently 100 feet long, but broken in two pieces about 15 feet apart. It had been suggested that this might be the *UB-63*, but when dived in 1980 it was found to be a twin-engine aircraft broken in two pieces about five metres apart. The remains stand up more than three meters from the seabed, festooned with fishing nets. The main body of the aircraft lies 110/290°. The position has also been given as 5617.800N, 0224.080W (WGS84).

Ju-88A aircraft (Author's collection)

In attempting to identify this two-engine aircraft, three possibilities emerged:

i) Handley Page Hampden L4107 of RAF 61 Squadron stalled and crashed into the sea five miles east of Leuchars on 6 June 1939. That would place it over ten miles away from this aircraft wreck.

ii) Bristol Beaufighter 1 N1075 of RAF 489 Squadron crashed into the sea off Leuchars on 2 October 1941. (How far off Leuchars, and in what direction?)

iii) The Forth has the unenviable distinction of having been the scene of the first enemy attack on the British mainland during the Second World War.

The first German aircraft to be shot down over the UK during the Second World War were two Ju-88s on a bombing raid on Royal Navy ships anchored off Rosyth, including the battleship HMS *Repulse* and the cruisers HMS *Southampton* and HMS *Edinburgh*. The ships attacked were moored just downstream from the Forth Bridge. The Ju-88s were shot down by Spitfires piloted by Flt.Lt. Pat Gifford of 603 (City of Edinburgh) Squadron and Flt.Lt. George Pinkerton of 602 (City of Glasgow) Squadron on 16 October 1939.

One of the German bombers fell into the sea four miles north-east of Port Seton, and the other about three miles east of Crail. Helmut Pohle, the pilot of that Ju-88, had sustained a fractured skull and facial injuries, and was taken for treatment to the naval hospital at Port Edgar, where he was later visited by George Pinkerton, who had shot him down. Helmut and George had quite a lot in common. In civilian life they were both farmers, and in later life both had hip replacement operations. They were engaged in friendly correspondence with each other for many years, often criticising the Common Agricultural Policy, until George Pinkerton died in 1994.

The Ju-88 off Port Seton was raised about two weeks after being shot down, and taken to Leith, but as far as I know, the other was never recovered, and will still be there. Perhaps this is the remains of Pohle's aircraft.

ISLANDMAGEE

Wreck No: 217		Date Sunk: 26 October 1953
Latitude: 56 17 30 N		Longitude: 02 32 18 W
GPS Lat: 5617.500 N		GPS Long: 0232.300 W
Location: Off Fife Ness		Area: Fife Ness
Type: Steamship		Tonnage: 227 grt
Length: 117 ft	Beam: 22 ft	Draught: 10 ft
How Sunk: Foundered		Depth: 29 metres

The steam dredger *Islandmagee* sank during a severe force 9 gale on 26 October 1953. Six of the crew were lost, as were six of the crew of the Arbroath lifeboat *Robert Lindsay* which was attempting to assist. The wreck was positively identified as the *Islandmagee* by the builders' plate and bell which were recovered in 1986. The wreck is intact and upright, standing six metres high. Depth to the top of the wreck is 34 metres and to the seabed of rock and sand, 40 metres. There is one forward hold, and the engine is aft. A large grab used for collecting sand from the seabed, lies on the starboard side of the deck.

There are fairly strong tidal streams in this area, and the slack water period is of very short duration. The 1990 chart shows the wreck at 561745N, 023224W, but several WGS84 positions for the *Islandmagee* have been recorded as: (5617.535N, 00232.440W) / (5617.520N, 00232.490W) / (5617.548N, 00232.484W) / (5617.480N, 00232.446W) / (5617.481N, 00232.447W) and (5617.528N, 0232.424W). These positions are all so close together that the wreck should be found by using any one of them.

UNKNOWN

Wreck No: 218		Date Sunk:
Latitude: 56 17 36 N		Longitude: 02 19 29 W
GPS Lat: 5617.587 N	**WGS84**	GPS Long: 0219.584 W
Location: 8½ miles E of Fife Ness		Area: Fife Ness
Type:		Tonnage:
Length: 150 ft	Beam:	Draught:
How Sunk:		Depth: 47 metres

The wreck charted at 561736N, 021930W is reported to be 45 metres long (150 feet) by 10 metres wide and standing up 7 metres from the seabed. The bows point NE, and the wreck appears to be intact, other than a small detached piece lying close to the port side amidships.

FESTING GRINDALL

Wreck No: 219		Date Sunk: 4 October 1928
Latitude: 56 17 45 N		Longitude: 02 34 30 W
GPS Lat: 5617.750 N		GPS Long: 0234.500 W
Location: Ashore 1 mile N of Fife Ness		Area: Fife Ness
Type: Trawler		Tonnage: 236 grt
Length: 117 ft	Beam: 23 ft	Draught: 13 ft
How Sunk: Ran aground		Depth: 10 metres

The steam trawler *Festing Grindall* was built in 1917 by Smiths Dock at Middlesbrough. She ran ashore in fog one mile north (True) from Fife Ness Point on a voyage from Aberdeen to Granton for coal. The crew of nine landed in their own boat. The vessel was very badly damaged and became a total wreck. The position given above is not immediately adjacent to the shore, but on the outlying Tullybothy Craigs, which uncover at low water.

KATE THOMPSON

Wreck No: 220	Date Sunk: 9 January 1895
Latitude: 56 17 50 N	Longitude: 02 37 24 W
GPS Lat: 5617.830 N	GPS Long: 0237.400 W
Location: On rocks 2¼ miles N of Crail	Area: Fife Ness

Type: Steamship   Tonnage: 259 grt
Length: Beam: Draught:
How Sunk: Ran aground   Depth: 5 metres

The Newcastle-registered steel steamship *Kate Thompson* was built by Edwards of North Shields in 1894. She became a total loss after stranding on rocks, variously given as two and a quarter miles north of Crail, or two miles east of Anstruther, while en route from Dundee to Leith in ballast on 9 January 1895. She was 154 tons net.

If the description "2¼ miles north of Crail" is correct, that would suggest she ran on to Carr Brigs, near the North Carr Beacon – the position given above. On the other hand, if the description "two miles east of Anstruther" is correct, that would imply she ran ashore somewhere near The Pans, at about 561500N, 023800W, approximately one mile west of Crail. Given that her voyage was from Dundee to Leith, however, the former position seems by far the more likely.

SUCCESS

Wreck No: 221   Date Sunk: 27 December 1914
Latitude: 56 18 00 N   Longitude: 02 37 36 W
GPS Lat: 5618.000 N   GPS Long: 0237.600 W
Location: Cambo Sands, Kingsbarns   Area: Fife Ness
Type: Destroyer   Tonnage: 385 grt
Length: 214.5 ft   Beam: 21 ft   Draught: 10.8 ft
How Sunk: Ran aground   Depth: 1 metre

HMS Success *docked (Author's collection)*

The destroyer HMS *Success* was built in 1901 by W. Doxford & Sons. After a 17-day refit, she left Aberdeen at 10.05 p.m. on 26 December 1914, and proceeded towards Rosyth. At 0200 hours speed was reduced to nine knots. At 0320 hours the position of the ship was considered to be 6½ miles S45E of the Bell Rock, and her course was altered to S76W. At 0400 hours speed was reduced to eight knots.

Because her port propeller shaft was defective in some way, which had been noted by the unusual noise it made, it was decided to run the port engine at 120 rpm and the starboard at 180. Later, at 11 p.m., the port engine was eased to 80 rpm. The revolutions per knot of *Success* were 12.5 and her CO, Lt. William Pennefather, considered that this would give a speed of 10 knots. As an additional safeguard to knowing the speed through the water, he had the patent log streamed, and this confirmed his belief. At 4.30 a.m. the course was altered to SW and the patent log was hauled in to enable the sounding machine to be started. The log showed 51.9 miles run since 11 p.m. At approximately 4.40 a.m. land was sighted ahead. This was presumed to be the May Island, and the course was altered to SE, to pass round the south of the Island. Ten minutes later breakers were sighted ahead. The engines were put full astern, and the rudder turned hard to port, but the ship grounded, and remained firmly fixed on rocks. It was intensely dark in the early morning, and the vessel had struck on the submerged reef known as Cambo Briggs. Water was coming into the ship forward and aft, and the pumps were unable to prevent the water level continuing to rise. The seas were too heavy to launch boats from the starboard side of the ship, but the port boats and rafts were made ready in case it became necessary to abandon ship. Signals of distress were at once sent out, reporting that she had run aground, and the destroyer HMS *Mallard* was sent to stand by. Later, another torpedo boat destroyer, HMS *Cheerful*, and two minesweepers also appeared on the scene in response to the call for help.

At about 6 a.m. Andrew Cunningham, the coxswain of the Crail lifeboat, received a message from the Coastguards at Fife Ness, informing him of the wreck, and requesting that the lifeboat should immediately proceed to the scene of the disaster. Steps were immediately taken to summon the crew, but a full hour elapsed before the boat was launched. The voyage of three miles to the wrecked destroyer was accomplished, despite the heavy seas, in little over an hour. As she hove in sight the crew of the destroyer raised a cheer, and shouts of "Happy Christmas" were extended to the rescuers. The men were lined up as best could be, considering that the greater part of the vessel was already under water.

The shore at this point is a confusion of jagged rocks, some visible, and others hidden. At first it was thought that an effort to get into touch with the destroyer from the windward side could be made, but a closer view led coxswain Cunningham to the conclusion that he would be dashed against the destroyer's side if he approached at close quarters. Standing off some distance, the rocket apparatus was resorted to, the crew hoping that with the aid of the wind they would be able to cast a rope over the deck. This, however, failed. Despite the breakers, the crew decided to take their chance closer in, and though there was the prospect of the lifeboat being caught by a wave and cast upon the rocks, it was cleverly manoeuvred, and, aided by the lee of the helpless warship, the rescuers got a rope aboard.

On being told that there were 67 men on board, coxswain Cunningham replied that he could only take about 20 at a time. In landing the third party of sailors on the beach, the lifeboat was dashed against the rocks, and was badly stove in, putting it out of action. There were thirteen men still on the wreck, and fears began to be entertained for their safety.

At approximately 8 a.m. the inhabitants of the east side of St Andrews were somewhat alarmed by the firing of the rocket signals for the lifeboat to turn out. With the possibility of a German raid being in the minds of the people living on the east coast of Scotland, many citizens naturally thought, when they heard the first rocket fired, that the Germans had started to bombard the city, or that a sea fight had commenced in the Bay. The firing of further rockets, however, revealed the true cause of the noise. A considerable number of people rushed to the Lifeboat house to learn what kind of craft was in distress, and they were greatly surprised to learn that the British torpedo boat destroyer HMS *Success* had been driven on to the rocks at Kingsbarns by the force of the hurricane.

Coxswain Chisholm and his men turned out very promptly. During the night a full gale had been blowing from the south-east and there was a heavy sea running along the shore. Despite the heavy seas, the boat was launched on the East Sands. After clearing the breakers, the lifeboat then set sail for Kingsbarns. News was received in St Andrews that the Crail lifeboat was also proceeding to the rescue, and as it had less than half the distance the St Andrews boat had to go in the teeth of the wind, it arrived on the scene first, at 9 a.m. and succeeded in taking off all the crew except thirteen.

Just then the St Andrews lifeboat appeared on the scene and succeeded in taking off the remaining thirteen men, but coxswain Chisholm, seeing what had happened to the Crail lifeboat, refused to land the men on the beach.

HMS *Cheerful*, one of the destroyers which had appeared on the scene in answer to the wrecked vessel's wireless message for help, took the St Andrews lifeboat in tow to within half a mile of the harbour. A great crowd had appeared to watch the return of the lifeboat. The rescued men in the lifeboat included the Captain, two or three officers, and men who, from their appearance, looked as if they had just left the engine room.

In reply to anxious enquiries, the lifeboat men were able to tell the waiting crowd that all the sailors had been rescued from the destroyer, but that the vessel itself was lying a wreck almost submerged, two of its funnels being out of sight.

When it was learned that every man had been saved, the sailors on the beach at Cambo Sands gave three rousing cheers for the lifeboat men. The sailors were driven to Kingsbarns, awakening the village with their singing of *It's a long way to Tipperary*. Every villager turned out to greet them, and the school was thrown open as a temporary hostel. Supplies of food and warm drinks were soon forthcoming, along with dry clothes, and everything possible was done to make the sailors comfortable. Three of the men were rather the worse for their immersion and severe buffeting, and they were quite overwhelmed by the ministrations of the women folk. After a brief rest the sailors returned to the shore. They found that the destroyer was badly holed, and that water had flooded the engine room. Large crowds flocked from the surrounding district to witness the wrecked ship.

By the afternoon of the 27th, the vessel had turned round, and lay with her bows pointing seawards. The bows were firmly on the rocks but the stern was swaying greatly. At that stage the full extent of the damage was not realised, and hopes were still being entertained that the ship could be refloated after some repairs. These hopes were soon proved to be forlorn. For the next four days, all her guns, torpedo tubes, copper piping, dynamo and engine were stripped out. Her two polished torpedoes, which had been re-covered, lay on the shore, and steamers were alongside the wreck to receive her guns and other moveable gear. HMS *Success* eventually broke up and slid under the surface. Only the keel remains, buried in the sand.

HMS *Success* was the Royal Navy's first destroyer loss of the First World War. A notice on the beach at Kingsbarns, and the photograph hanging in the village hall are reminders of the wrecking of the ship. The photograph of HMS *Success* was presented by the ship's company as a token of appreciation for the willing assistance they had received. The caption reads: "With our most grateful thanks to the Crew of the lifeboats of St Andrews and Crail for rescuing our lives on Dec 27th 1914, and to the inhabitants of Crail and Kingsbarns for their great kindness to us after the wreck."

HARLEY

Wreck No: 222		Date Sunk: 14 November 1944
Latitude: 56 18 54 N		Longitude: 02 09 12 W
GPS Lat: 5618.895 N	**WGS 84**	GPS Long: 0209.295 W
Location: 15 miles E of Fife Ness		Area: Fife Ness
Type: Steamship		Tonnage: 410 grt
Length: 133.3 ft	Beam: 24.1 ft	Draught: 11.2 ft
How Sunk: Foundered		Depth: 58 metres

The steamship *Harley* (ex-*Condor*, ex-*Hondene*) was built in 1919 by A. de Jong of Vlaardingen, Belgium. She was overwhelmed by stress of weather, and foundered off Fife Ness on 14 November 1944 while en route from Sunderland to Aberdeen with a cargo of coal. Seven of the crew were lost. Charted as a wreck with at least 27 metres over it in about 56 metres.

UNKNOWN – EINAR JARL

Wreck No: 223		Date Sunk: ?
Latitude: 56 18 58 N		Longitude: 02 17 12 W
GPS Lat: 5618.953 N	**WGS 84**	GPS Long: 0217.297 W
Location: 10 miles E of Fife Ness		Area: Fife Ness
Type: Steamship		Tonnage:
Length: 313.5 ft	Beam:	Draught:
How Sunk:		Depth: 49 metres

The wreck charted at 561858N, 021712W, 10 miles east of Fife Ness is reported to be 95 metres long (313.5 feet), with a minimum depth of 41 metres in about 50 metres. This is obviously a fairly substantial ship and as an aid to establishing her identity, it would be helpful to know when the wreck was first discovered.

The wreck has been dived, and found to be a fairly large, but rather broken up steamship, with one propeller and a single big boiler. No cargo was noted, and although coal is evident in the wreck, this may be bunker coal, rather than part of the cargo. The position of this wreck is only one and a half miles from the approximate position given for the sinking of the *Einar Jarl*, which had only one boiler. The fact that there is only one boiler suggests the ship is not British. Lloyds would have insisted on two boilers for a ship of this size.

At the time of writing this book nothing has been recovered from the wreck to confirm its identity, but it is strongly suspected that this is the *Einar Jarl*. As *Einar Jarl* was 80 metres long, however, it is also suspected that the 95 metres reported length of this wreck must have been over-estimated (see Wreck No. 215).

BLACKWHALE

Wreck No: 224		Date Sunk: 3 January 1918
Latitude: 56 20 00 N PA		Longitude: 02 30 00 W PA
GPS Lat: 5620.000 N		GPS Long: 0230.000 W
Location: Off Fife Ness		Area: Fife Ness
Type: Whaler		Tonnage: 237 grt
Length: 125 ft	Beam: 25 ft	Draught: 8.5 ft
How Sunk: Mined		Depth:

HM Whaler *Blackwhale* was built by Smiths Dock in 1915, for use as an anti-submarine escort vessel. She was armed with one 12-pounder gun, and was mined off Fife Ness on 31 January 1918.

UNKNOWN – ABERDON ?

Wreck No: 225		Date Sunk:
Latitude: 56 21 28 N		Longitude: 01 54 24 W
GPS Lat: 5621.467 N	**WGS84**	GPS Long: 0154.403 W
Location: 23 miles E by N from Fife Ness		Area: Fife Ness
Type: Steamship		Tonnage: grt
Length: 244 ft	Beam: 46 ft	Draught: 9.2 ft
How Sunk: Torpedoed?		Depth: 35–38 metres

This wreck was found in 2007. It appears to be a cargo steamship sitting upright on a sea-bed of sand and gravel. There seems to be torpedo damage to both port and starboard sides close to the stern, but the ship is otherwise intact. The wreck is oriented 105/285°, with the bow pointing a little north of west. She has a raised fo'c'sle and two forward holds. Her bridge, accommodation and machinery occupy the after half of the ship.

This may be the 1005-grt steel screw steamship *Aberdon*, which was built by Hall Russell of Aberdeen in 1911 (Yard No. 500) for Adam Brothers of Aberdeen. The *Aberdon* disappeared after leaving Seaham Harbour, south of Sunderland, on 9 March 1915 with a cargo of coal for Aberdeen. She was apparently never seen or heard of again, and her registry was closed on 20 April 1915 – vessel missing since leaving Seaham Harbour for Aberdeen on 9 March 1915.

Her voyage took her through the patrol area of *U-12*, which sank her later on the same day she sailed from Seaham – the day before *U-12* was herself sunk by HMS *Ariel*, and the position of this wreck is consistent with her voyage to Aberdeen. It had been thought that *Aberdon* had been sunk further south, off St Abbs Head, but the wreck has not been found in that area.

Aberdon had a triple expansion steam engine and two boilers. She was capable of 11 knots. Steurmann Rath, one of the survivors from *U-12* was not able to identify the name of the ship that *U-12* sank on 9 March, but he did say that the ship sank in four minutes after being hit in the stern by a torpedo. He also said that the sinking took place between Todd Head and St Abbs Head, and that after the sinking, *U-12* had spent the night running east and west. However, there is a slight problem with the theory that this wreck might be the *Aberdon*. The wreck apparently measures 73.8 metres by 14 metres by 2.8 metres (i.e. 243.5 ft × 46.2 ft × 9.2 ft), whereas the *Aberdon* measured 210.5 ft × 32.1 ft × 16 ft. The discrepancies in the dimensions might be due to the torpedo damage creating a debris field at the stern, together with scouring of the seabed at both bow and stern, and possible collapsing of the wreck during 93 years of immersion?

So far I have been unable to identify any other obvious candidate for this ship, and must therefore wait until it has been dived for further information.

U-12

Wreck No: 226	Date Sunk: 10 March 1915
Latitude: 56 14 37 N	Longitude: 01 51 25 W
GPS Lat: 5614.618 N	GPS Long: 0151.422 W
Location: 24 miles E of Fife Ness	Area: Fife Ness
Type: Submarine	Tonnage: 493/611 tons
Length: 188.3 ft Beam: 18.7 ft	Draught: 10.2 ft
How Sunk: Rammed by HMS *Ariel*	Depth: 49–53 metres

U-11 – *a sister to* U-12 *(Author's collection)*

U-12 was powered by two Körting petrol engines and two electric motors. She had two bow torpedo tubes, and two stern tubes, and carried six 45-centimetre (18-inch) torpedoes. No gun was fitted when she was built. She was 493 tons surfaced, 611 tons submerged. The position of her sinking has been consistently recorded as 560712N, 022000W, which is 8 miles SE of the May Island, but no authority has been stated for that position, and there is no wreck there. Clive Cussler claimed to have found *U-12* in 2000 at 5604.500N, 0218.00W, but that position, and the area around it has been thoroughly searched, and there is no wreck there either.

Diver and wreck researcher Kevin Heath found an interesting account of the sinking of *U-12* in the American book *Verschollen: World War I U-boat Losses* by Dwight R. Messimer, published by the Library of Congress in 1937. Messimer's description of the event is corroborated by his fellow American Robert M. Grant, in *U-boats Destroyed*, originally published in 1964. Their accounts give good reason to think that neither of the above positions is correct, and that the *U-12* lies some 11–12 miles further north, off Fife Ness.

Under the command of KL Hans Kratzsch *U-12* left Heligoland on 4 March 1915 to operate off the east coast of Scotland. On 6 March the trawler *Duster* spotted *U-12* off Aberdeen, but was unable to send a message to report the sighting because she had no radio. It was not until the next day, when *Duster* met a yacht equipped with a radio set, that word of the sighting could be passed on. On 8 March trawlers of the Auxiliary Patrol reported sighting *U-12* in the morning and again in the evening. The Royal Navy's 1st destroyer Flotilla was sent to intecept *U-12* as she moved south. The U-boat succeeded in slipping through the search line on 9 March however, and made an unsuccessful torpedo attack on HMS *Leviathan*. That attack alerted the 1st Destroyer Flotilla that their quarry had eluded them, and that the U-boat was south of them. At 0900 hours on 10 March the trawler *May Island* reported a U-boat at about 5615N, 0156W – 21 miles east of Fife Ness. The 1st Flotilla headed for that position, and at 1010 hours the destroyers *Acheron*, *Attack* and *Ariel* were steaming on a north-east course in line abreast at one-nautical-mile intervals. The wind was force 2, the sea calm, weather hazy. At 1010 hours HMS *Attack* spotted the *U-12* two points to port steering north-west at almost a right angle to the destroyer's course. The destroyer opened fire and went to full speed to attack. Two minutes later HMS *Ariel* (Lt. Cdr. J.V. Creagh) saw the *U-12* two and a half points to starboard at a distance of two nautical miles. All three destroyers turned to attack, and the U-boat dived. The *Ariel* saw the periscope four points to starboard, 200 yards away. *Ariel* turned towards the periscope, saw the conning tower just below the surface, and rammed *U-12* at an angle of 70 degrees. Two minutes later the badly damaged U-boat surfaced, encountering gunfire from the destroyers which hit the conning tower again, killing the captain, Kratsch. Explosive charges were set off as the crew tried to escape, and *U-12* sank so rapidly at 1030 hours that only two officers and eight men could be rescued. The Admiralty immediately announced that *U-12* had been sunk by *Ariel* and that 10 prisoners had been taken. The other 19 of the U-boat's crew were lost. The *Ariel* was so badly damaged that she had to be towed to port.

Steurmann Rath, one of the survivors captured from *U-12* said: "We sighted destroyers to the south approaching at high speed. Dived, quickly reached trim at nine metres, and manoeuvred to attack. A destroyer was five to ten metres off our port beam. The boat was just starting to dive deeper when a colossal explosion shook the entire boat and immediately the boat was rammed in the area of the conning tower. The blow rolled the boat 90° to starboard, blew out three rivets near the compass and destroyed the port breaker panel. Water poured through the periscope gland, the lights went out and the batteries shorted. The captain ordered the tanks blown with compressed air and the boat quickly gained the surface. The conning tower hatch could be opened only half way. The crew abandoned ship while three British destroyers fired into the boat."

Oberleutnant zur See Max Seeburg said: "I was asleep in my bunk when I was suddenly awakened by an alarm. I went immediately to the control room and met War Pilot Völker whose face was very pale. He said that destroyers had surprised us, and that the crew had been ordered forward to speed the dive. Visibility on the surface was from five hundred to one thousand metres. We were then at twenty-five metres and I heard Käpitänleutnant Kratsch order the boat to rise to eleven metres and make two torpedoes ready for firing. As we approached eleven metres, Käpitänleutnant Kratsch extended the periscope and immediately ordered the boat to dive quickly to twenty-five metres. Just as the periscope motor started running to retract the periscope I heard an ear-splitting noise of tearing metal. The boat rolled hard to starboard and dropped sharply by the bow. Immediately a tremendous explosion shook the boat."

The treatment of the survivors created a diplomatic incident. During the First World War the British attitude towards U-boat men was that they were regarded as pirates, nothing else, and the best thing would be to hang them. A contemporary postcard, illustrating *Ariel* ramming *U-12* is captioned "Ramming and Sinking of German Pirate Submarine 'U 12' by H.M. Ships 'Ariel' and 'Attack'." This, along with letters published in *The Times*, reveals the prevailing state of mind in Britain in those days.

The British imprisoned the crew in solitary confinement. The German government got news of this – it was reported in *The Times* and newspapers in neutral countries – and

Contemporary postcard (Courtesy of Jim Macleod)

reacted by applying the same measures to British prisoners of war. It was only through United States pressure on the British government, and the assistance of Swiss diplomats, that the episode was resolved. An interesting sequel is that one of the ten U-boat prisoners, the war pilot Völker, escaped from prison in Britain and made his way to Hull, where he signed aboard the Swedish barque *Jonstorp* as an able bodied seaman. (A war pilot was a merchant marine officer taken on board to help identify landmarks and merchant ships while on patrol.) On 1 October 1915 the barque was stopped off the Firth of Forth by the homeward-bound *U-16*, which took Völker off and brought him home to Germany. Völker did not survive the war, however, as he was posted as war pilot on *U-44*, and was lost when that U-boat was sunk off the south of Norway on 12 August 1917.

An analysis of the logs of the destroyers HMS *Ariel*, *Acheron* and *Fearless* resulted in three different positions for the sinking of *U-12*. The mid-point of the triangle formed by these three positions was calculated, but there were no charted wrecks anywhere nearby. However, a newly-discovered wreck lay only half a mile from that point, and from a sonar image it looked like a submarine! A perfect match was obtained when the sonar image was compared with photographs and a drawing of *U-12*. We had found our wreck!

This was confirmed by a dive on 12 January 2008. The wreck is sitting upright on a hard sandy seabed at 48 metres at mid-tide. Both propellers are clear of the sand, so the wreck is hardly embedded in the seabed. It had been expected that signs of the ramming by HMS *Ariel* would be very obvious on the port side, but in fact there is only a slight dent visible on the port side of the U-boat. There is a large rock on the seabed off the starboard side, just aft of the conning tower, and a corresponding gap in the outer hull with an impression on the pressure hull in the same area. This must be the ramming damage – otherwise *U-12* must have hit this rock when she sank. There are lots of old fishing nets, and one new nylon net, over the forward deck. The forward hatch is missing – probably trawled off.

There are six portholes with wiper blades on the conning tower, in pairs facing forward, and to each side. The conning tower hatch is also missing – again probably trawled off. Lots of brass can be seen inside, but many external fittings are apparently missing – most likely the result of trawling. Parts of the wreck look as if they have been polished by the nets moving due to tidal action. The outer casing is corroded and holed, but the pressure hull seems to be more intact.

The masts seem to have been trawled off, and so has the periscope – a velvet crab is stuck well down the brass tube. A piece of the bow is missing forward of the two torpedo tubes. It is lying nearby, just off the starboard side. The doors on both forward torpedo tubes are closed. There is some collapsing around the bow, which looks as if it has suffered an explosion – probably one of *Ariel*'s towed charges that exploded in contact with the U-boat. (Remember Steurmann Rath and OL Max Seeburg both mentioned a tremendous explosion.)

The induction and exhaust pipes are still there, hinged down in the recess in the after deck, but the rear hatch is missing. The port side rear torpedo tube door is open, and there is a torpedo in the tube. A lobster has taken up residence in the tube, beside the torpedo. The starboard rear torpedo tube door missing, and the tube is empty. The hydroplanes have been mangled by trawl nets.

U-12 has a unique claim to fame. She was the world's first submarine aircraft carrier. In 1915 the German submarine *U-12* carried a Friedrichshafen FF-29 seaplane on its fore-casing, which it launched by partially submerging the bow. The first flight was carried out on 6 January 1915 when one of these aircraft, piloted by Leutnant Freidrich von Arnauld de la Perrière, a brother of the famous First World War U-boat ace Lothar von Arnauld de la Perrière[1], flew the aircraft from *U-12* during tests at Zeebrugge. Although the submarine was unable to submerge while carrying the aircraft, by this means the range of the aircraft could be effectively increased, and an aircraft could be delivered within closer striking range of England. [2]

The FF-29 was placed across the deck of the *U-12* and lashed down. When the U-boat left the shelter of the harbour, however, KL Walter Forstmann, *U-12*'s commander at the time, realised that the heavy swell might endanger the operation by either damaging the aircraft, or washing it away. After less than an hour it was decided to launch the seaplane. *U-12*'s forward tanks were flooded, and despite the pitching of the submarine, von Arnauld's FF-29 floated off the deck and took off without difficulty. Von Arnauld then flew along the Kent coast, apparently without being detected. He had intended to rendezvous with the U-boat, but decided against it, and flew directly back to Zeebrugge.

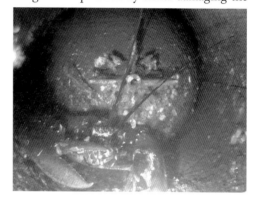

Although the experiment had demonstrated that an aircraft could be carried and launched by floating off, it was realised that calmer seas and more secure fastening of the aircraft were required. Von Arnauld and Forstmann were keen to try the experiment again but the German High Command vetoed it.

---

1   Lothar von Arnauld de la Perrière was the top-scoring U-boat ace of all time. He is credited with sinking 194 ships totalling 454,000 tons while in command of *U-35* and *U-139* during WWI.

By comparison, Wolfgang Lüth, one of the top-scoring U-boat aces of WWII, is credited with sinking 46 ships totalling 225,000 tons, while Otto Kretschmer sank 44 ships totalling 266,000 tons.

2   On 21 Dec 1914 a German FF-29 seaplane from Zeebrugge conducted the first air raid against Britain, dropping bombs in the sea near Dover. On 24 Dec 1914 the first bombs were dropped on Britain during a second raid on Dover by the same German aircraft. There were no casualties and little damage. (These were only 12 kg [26.5 lb] bombs.) A third raid by the same aircraft on the 25th resulted in two bombs being dropped near Cliffe railway station, Kent.

RUDOLF

Wreck No: 227
Latitude: 56 14 56 N
GPS Lat: 5614.928 N   **WGS84**
Location: 41 miles E of Fife Ness
Type: Steamship
Length: 289.7 ft   Beam: 42 ft
How Sunk: Torpedoed by *U-56*

Date Sunk: 2 December 1939
Longitude: 01 23 32 W
GPS Long: 0123.525 W
Area: Fife Ness
Tonnage: 2119 grt
Draught: 17.7 ft
Depth: 55 metres

The Swedish steamship *Rudolf* was built by Blyth SB & DD Co. in 1922. Under the command of her Master, Bertil Persson, she left West Hartlepool on 2 December 1939 bound for Malmö with a crew of 23 and a cargo of 2760 tons of coal. She headed north in good visibility, but with a WNW wind, and high seas from the west. At 2315 hours she was torpedoed by *U-56* (KL Wilhelm Zahn) in AN5134, which equates to about 561500N, 012500W. The torpedo struck *Rudolf* in the stern, and her whole after end was blown away taking with it nine of her crew who were off watch and asleep. Two lifeboats were launched. Six of the crew boarded the starboard boat, and eight took to the port boat. The boats stayed with the sinking vessel until it sank at around 0015 hours on the 3rd, after which they lost sight of each other in the darkness.

Broughty Ferry Lifeboat *Mona* was launched to search for survivors. All crewmembers in the starboard lifeboat were picked up by the trawler *Cardew* of West Hartlepool at around 2300 hours on the 3rd, and the port lifeboat was sighted by the Swedish steamer *Gunlög* at around 0600 hours on the 4th. The steamer and trawler landed their charges in Newcastle. Eight of the nine casualties were Swedes, the ninth (a stoker) was Norwegian.

At the time of her loss on 2 December 1939, *Rudolf* was thought to have been sunk by striking a mine at about 5615N, 0125W, but the survivors confirmed that she was in fact torpedoed and gunned. The Hydrographic Department has recorded the *Rudolf* at 561500N, 012330W. Could this vessel have been the source of the food washed up around the mouth of the Tay?

Less than an hour before torpedoing the *Rudolf*, Zahn had also torpedoed the 3289-grt British steamship *Eskdene* (Capt E.J. Niblett), but she did not sink. *Eskdene* had become detached from convoy HN3 in a gale, and was torpedoed by Zahn in 5630N 0140W. *Eskdene* was carrying a cargo of timber which kept her afloat. A tug was sent out on the 4th to bring her in, but could not find her – the weather very bad and there was little daylight. A Danish steamer *Grenra* found her on the 6th. A photograph taken of *Eskdene* showed her to be wearing Danish colours, although Captain Niblett alleged that these were not carried. She was taken in tow for the Forth at 0700 hours on 7 December, escorted initially by the destroyer HMS *Stork*, and later by aircraft. The tow was taken over by two tugs and she was taken to Shields, where she was beached on the Herd Sands. Refloated on 25 December 1939, she was taken to the Albert Edward Dock at Shields for repair. *Eskdene* was eventually torpedoed and sunk by *U-107* on 8 April 1941 in 3443N 2421W, south-east of the Azores.

UNKNOWN

Wreck No: 228
Latitude: 56 19 36 N
GPS Lat: 5619.600 N
Location: 12 miles ENE of Fife Ness
Type:
Length:
How Sunk:

OSGB 36

Beam:

Date Sunk:
Longitude: 02 13 48 W
GPS Long: 0213.800 W
Area: Fife Ness
Tonnage:
Draught:
Depth: 44 metres

This wreck is oriented about 035/215° in 44 metres. In 1964 it was reported that the east side of this wreck gave a better sonar echo than the west side. Perhaps this indicates the wreck is lying with a list to one side?

The wreck was not found during a search in 2008.

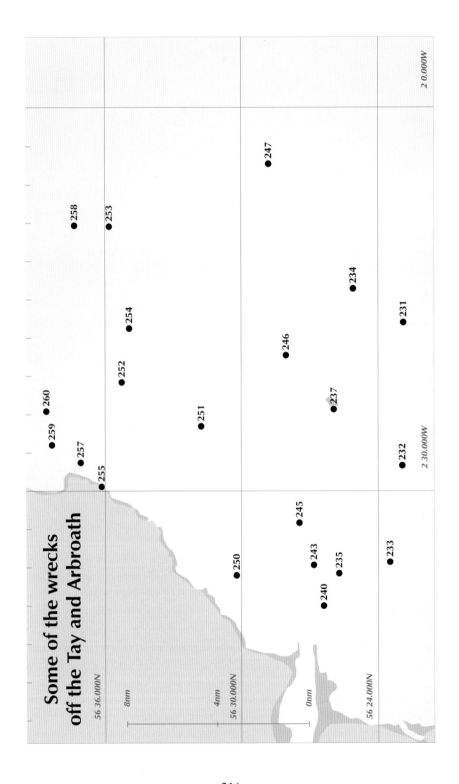

Some of the wrecks
off the Tay and Arbroath

8

The Tay and Arbroath

UNKNOWN

Wreck No: 229		Date Sunk:
Latitude: 56 22 05 N		Longitude: 02 12 41 W
GPS Lat: 5622.077 N	**WGS84**	GPS Long: 0212.676 W
Location: 7½ miles SE of Bell Rock		Area: Arbroath
Type:		Tonnage:
Length:	Beam: 44.5 ft	Draught:
How Sunk:		Depth: 49–55 metres

The wreck found here in 1962 is 26 metres long (86 feet) by 8 metres wide, and stands up 4 metres from the seabed. These dimensions suggest this is possibly a fishing boat.

UNKNOWN

Wreck No: 230		Date Sunk:
Latitude: 56 20 25 N		Longitude: 02 04 03 W
GPS Lat: 5620.399 N	**WGS84**	GPS Long: 0204.217 W
Location: 19 miles E of Fife Ness		Area: Tay
Type: Steamship or fishing vessel		Tonnage:
Length: 115.5 ft	Beam: 15 ft	Draught:
How Sunk:		Depth: 49–53 metres

The unidentified wreck found in 1962 at 5620.417N, 0204.050W, 19 miles east of Fife Ness, looked an exceptionally good candidate for the *U-12*. This is 7 miles NW of the position in which *U-12* was first spotted, heading north-west, and she was sunk about one hour after the sighting.

Taking advantage of an appropriate window of opportunity as regards weather, sea state, tidal conditions and daylight, diver Martin Sinclair led a team of hand-picked divers to examine this wreck on 20 December 2007. This involved a 5 a.m. start for the long trip from Eyemouth aboard Marine Quest's fast Offshore 105 vessel *North Star*. At that time, everyone was fully expecting to find the *U-12*, but were surprised to find they were instead on a very old steamship sitting upright on a seabed of fine sand. Underwater visibility was 15 metres. No dimensions had been recorded for this wreck, but the least depth to the wreck is 49 metres in a general depth of 53 metres. There is also another wreck extremely close by. On 4 May 2005 the unmanned ex-MFV *Northards* sank under tow from Montrose to Bridlington at 5620.217N, 0203.757W.

The old steamship has the classic characteristics of a fishing vessel, about 35 metres long and 4.5 metres wide. She has a large fo'c'sle with portholes. An anchor, which had evidently been lying on top of the fo'c'sle, has dropped inside, after the deck had rotted away. The fact that the anchor was on top of the fo'c'sle, rather than in the hawse-holes, may indicate that she was not in the habit of anchoring, and might therefore be a further indication that she was a fishing vessel. There are a couple of good-sized winches, and a galley near the front of the bridge. A large rectangular window glass from the bridge was noted. The compass was the size and shape of half a large basketball. The glass was intact but the bowl was perforated.

The stern was described as scallop-shaped, with a shallow curve, and the vessel has a two-cylinder steam engine at the stern, and a small three-bladed propeller about 1.2 metres in diameter. The hull has collapsed both inwards and outwards. Some of the debris has fallen across the bridge area, and underneath the wreckage, window glass and crockery, plus some brass items are visible. The bell was not seen, but it probably lies amongst the debris within the hull. The hull seemed quite thick and the plates were heavy but very corroded and perforated. The rust was a reddish-brown colour, but although none of them could recall seeing any black rust, the consensus of opinion amongst the divers was that the hull was iron, rather than steel. The forward hold contained debris and a small amount of coal.

Diver Jim Macleod lifted a dinner plate from the galley. There was no name or crest on it to aid identification of the ship, or its owner, but there was a makers' mark on the underside of the plate. This enabled the manufacturer of the plate to be identified as the Bellevue Pottery of Hull, which was in business from 1802–1841. That makes it a very old plate.

We have a vessel with a two-cylinder steam engine driving a three-bladed screw propeller. The screw propeller was invented by Robert Wilson of Dunbar in 1828. The fact that the ship is carrying pottery made in Hull might suggest the vessel came from there. No obvious candidate for its identity has been found in a search through the records of vessels known to have been lost in this area. This might have been a vessel that sailed from Hull, or some other port, and was never seen again. Based on what we know so far, however, it is supposed that she possibly sank some time in the period 1840–1880 or thereabouts. Perhaps she was one of the victims of the Great Storm of 1881.

FYLGIA

Wreck No: 231		Date Sunk: 24 January 1918
Latitude: 56 22 58 N		Longitude: 02 16 36 W
GPS Lat: 5622.966 N	**WGS84**	GPS Long: 0216.763 W
Location: 5 miles SE of Bell Rock		Area: Arbroath

Type: Steamship   Tonnage: 1741 grt
Length: 266 ft   Beam: 37 ft   Draught: 16 ft
How Sunk: Torpedoed by *UC-49*   Depth: 49 metres

Charted as Wreck 40 metres in 51 metres, 5 miles south-east of the Bell Rock. The Swedish steamship *Fylgia* (ex-*Talavera*) built by W. Dobson of Newcastle in 1889, was torpedoed by *UC-49* on 24 January 1918. The wreck is reported to be about 76 metres (251 feet) long, lying 085/265°, and rising up 7.5 metres from the seabed. The wreck is apparently upright, but collapsed at the bow and stern. Swedish National Archives gives the position of the *Fylgia* as 5623N, 0215W, and a small wreck, about 19 metres long has been located at 5622.61N, 0215. 894W (WGS84), but it is not known whether this has anything to do with the *Fylgia*. The *Fylgia* had been en route from Gothenburg to Rouen with a cargo of iron, steel and wood pulp.

UGIE ?

Wreck No: 232   Date Sunk: 16 March 1900
Latitude: 56 22 59 N   Longitude: 02 27 40 W
GPS Lat: 5622.980 N   GPS Long: 0227.670 W
Location: St.Andrews Bay   Area: Tay
Type: Steamship   Tonnage: 236 grt
Length: 130 ft   Beam: 21.1 ft   Draught: 10 ft
How Sunk: Collision with *Taymouth*   Depth: 34 metres

The position has also been given as 5622.992N, 0227.782W. A wreck about 42 metres long (138.6 feet) was first reported in this position in 1976, lying 109/289°. The wreck has one hold and one boiler, and lies with a slight list to port on a white sand/shell seabed at 34 metres. The midships section has disintegrated, but the rest of the wreck is reasonably intact. Various old bottles and clay jars have been recovered, and a large cranberry lamp globe found in the forward house. It may be the *Ugie* (ex-*Reine des Belges*, ex-*Piscator*), an iron screw steamship of 236 grt, 130 ft × 21.1 ft × 10 ft, built in 1886 by McKnight of Ayr, two-cylinder engine by Muir & Houston of Glasgow. She sank after a collision with the Dundee trawler *Taymouth*, while en route from Peterhead to Leith.

SOPHRON

Wreck No: 233   Date Sunk: 22 August 1917
Latitude: 56 23 30 N   Longitude: 02 35 45 W
GPS Lat: 5623.500 N   GPS Long: 0235.750 W
Location: Off St.Andrews   Area: Tay
Type: Trawler   Tonnage: 195 grt
Length: 113.6 ft   Beam: 21 ft   Draught: 11.2 ft
How Sunk: Mined (mine laid by *UC-41*)   Depth: 28 metres

The steel steam trawler *Sophron* was built in 1903 by Cook, Welton & Gemmell of Hull, and registered in Grimsby. While in Admiralty service she struck a mine and sank at about 562335N, 023530W PA on 22 August 1917. The mine had been laid by *UC-41*. In 1970 Alex Crawford located a wreck at 562330N, 023545W, very close to the approximate position given for the *Sophron* in 1919. The wreck lies in about 28 metres, with lots of net over bow and stern, making identification very difficult. The wheelhouse lies on the sand off the starboard side.

JONKOPING II

Wreck No: 234		Date Sunk: 24 January 1918
Latitude: 56 25 04 N		Longitude: 02 14 03 W
GPS Lat: 5625.084 N		GPS Long: 0214.489 W
Location: 5 miles E of Bell Rock		Area: Arbroath
Type: Steamship	Beam: 34.2 ft	Tonnage: 1294 grt
Length: 245.5 ft		Draught: 16.1 ft
How Sunk: Torpedoed by *UC-49*		Depth: 62 metres

The Swedish steamship *Jonkoping II* (ex-*Ardle*, ex-*Stella*) was built by Gourlay Bros., Dundee in 1888 (Yard No.134). According to one report she was sunk by the German submarine *UC-49* three miles east of the Bell Rock on 24 January 1918, while en route from Gothenburg to Hull with a general cargo. The Swedish authorities describe the position of loss as 3.3 miles ESE ½E from the Bell Rock. Strictly speaking, this is invalid terminology for the position. The correct description should be E by S ½S. (i.e. 106.875° from the Bell Rock). The nearest charted wreck is at 5625.070N, 0214.050W, five miles 100° from the Bell Rock, and this is probably the *Jonkoping II*.

The charted position seems to be slightly inaccurate, however, as I have been reliably informed that the correct position is 5625.084N, 0214.489W. This is considered to be a very large wreck, about 500 feet long. I can find no record of any vessel even approaching that length, which might have sunk in this area, and assume the length dimension must have been derived from a side-scan sonar image. Dimensions estimated from these images are notoriously unreliable – especially if they were obtained with the relatively early equipment available about 40 or more years ago.

Jonkoping II was a fairly substantial vessel, but at 245 feet long, she is only half the estimated length of this wreck. This wreck has been dived twice – once at the bows and once at the stern. The ship has a square stern and her four-bladed steel propeller is clear of the hard sandy seabed. The aft hold appears to be full of tank tracks or something very similar.

UC-41

Wreck No: 235	Date Sunk: 21 August 1917
Latitude: 56 25 44 N	Longitude: 02 36 27 W
GPS Lat: 5625.740 N	GPS Long: 0236.460 W

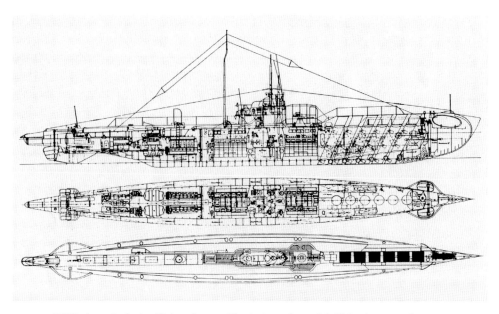

UCII-class minelaying U-boat layout. The 6 mine tubes each held 3 mines – total 18 mines

Location: 4.7 miles SE of Buddon Ness			Area: Tay
Type: Submarine			Tonnage: 417 grt
Length: 163 ft		Beam: 17.2 ft	Draught: 12.2 ft
How Sunk: Depth-charged			Depth: 27 metres

This wreck was first recorded on 31 January 1934 at 562548N, 023622W. It is in two parts, one about 100 feet long [1], lying 037/217°, the other not more than 50 feet long, close north of the centre of the larger part (5625.786N, 00236.484W – WGS84). It was dived in 1989 at 562544N, 023628W, and recognised as a UCII-class minelaying U-boat in two sections, 20 metres apart, in a depth of 27 metres. *UC-41* displaced 417 tons on the surface, 493 tons submerged.

These U-boats were powered by two Körting diesel engines and two electric motors, which drove twin bronze propellers. They were armed with two bow and one stern torpedo tubes, and one 88-mm forward deck gun. They also carried 18 × UC200 mines in six tubes in the forward section of the boat (see drawing). The mines exited from the bottom of the tubes.

UC-41 (Oblt.z.S Hans Förste), was said to have been sunk in an accident with its own mines on 21 August 1917, in or off the Tay estuary, and there are two slightly different versions of how she met her fate. One version claims she was caught in the act of laying mines by trawlers engaged in minesweeping in the approaches to the Tay. A lookout on

---

[1]   The length of this longer part was actually recorded as about 200 ft, but I assume this must be a transcription error, as *UC-41* was only 163 ft long.

the trawler *Jacinth* spotted a periscope on her starboard beam, while at the same time, a German mine came to the surface, its mooring wire having been cut by the trawler's sweep. The trawler turned to starboard to pass over the spot where the periscope had been seen, and the sweep wire parted when it fouled the submarine, causing small bubbles of air to rise to the surface. A depth charge was dropped, causing the water to boil, and big air bubbles came to the surface. In a second run over the submarine, another depth-charge was dropped, and this caused a tremendous secondary explosion which almost lifted the *Jacinth* out of the water, damaging her wireless, and bringing a mass of brown oil to the surface. The mine which had previously been brought to the surface was sunk by the trawler *Thomas Young*.

I am indebted to historian Pamela Armstrong for this very detailed second version of events:

> Oblt.z.S. Hans Förste assumed command of the boat on 5th August 1917.
>
> On the boat's last patrol, and the new skipper's first, SM *UC-41* departed Germany on 18 August 1917. Förste had instructions to sink allied ships off the Scottish east coast and to lay mines between Dundee and Aberdeen.
>
> On 21 August 1917, three Royal Navy trawlers, *Jacinth*, *Thomas Young* and *Chikara* were carrying out routine minesweeping duties in the Tay estuary, when an almighty underwater explosion took place on *Jacinth's* starboard beam, shortly before 1700 hrs. The trawlers, which were on a SSW heading, made full haste to the location, about one mile southeast of the River Tay buoy. As *Jacinth* altered course and swept towards the position, an obstruction fouled her sweeping gear and caused her to lose some of it, while *Thomas Young* narrowly avoided doing exactly the same thing. Suddenly a German mine bobbed to the surface and a sharpshooter on *Thomas Young* used his .303-rifle to detonate it. Meanwhile the trawler's hydrophones had picked up the sound of electric motors running. *Jacinth* moved in and dropped two depth charges over the site. A massive explosion then lifted the surface of the sea and large quantities of oil and bubbles came up. *Jacinth* dropped a third depth charge and *Chikara* also closed in and dropped four more. The result was another colossal explosion and a deep thumping sound, then the surface of the sea boiled up, after which pieces of woodwork, oil, debris and human remains floated up amongst the bubbles.

The following day another mine was swept up and for three days, oil came to the surface. Trawlers operating in auxiliary patrol sectors V, VI and VII were equipped with Mk 2 portable hydrophones, and it has been said that for two hours after the last explosions, the boat's electric motors could be heard running non-stop. In view of the damage found when divers examined the wreck nine days later, this seems most unlikely. Perhaps other noises were mistaken for motors on the poor-quality equipment of the day. It may be possible that the mine explosions could have started *UC-41*'s torpedo motors running, but it is unlikely that they would have had an endurance of two hours.

On 30 August 1917 divers under Salvage Officer Lt. McGuffie surveyed the wreck and found an 8-foot-long break on the starboard side, plus a second fracture on the superstructure further aft. However, by the end of that week, they had discovered a massive 40-foot tear, abaft the conning tower. The first three mine-chutes still contained mines and there was also one in number five-chute. The mines in number six had already been laid. There is no evidence that divers actually entered the U-boat, but divers inspecting the wreck a month later, recovered a number of articles and raised the U-boat's gun, before salvage activities were abandoned.

It was believed that SM *UC-41* was in the process of laying her mines in the estuary and became aware of the trawlers, either through her periscope or via her hydrophones and, in an attempt to escape, detonated one of her own mines.

The U-boat was actually cut almost in two about 12 metres aft of the conning tower, near to the stern section. It may be possible that some of the damage came from one of *UC-41*'s own mines. The explanation as to the way UCII boats could sink on their own mines is simple enough – they would drop a mine, which deployed immediately, then it could come up and hit the stern of the boat. The mines were fitted with a timer – a soluble plug that was supposed to dissolve through in about half an hour, or up to an hour, to give the U-boat time to get clear before the mine activated itself. The timers were brittle, however, and occasionally they failed to prevent immediate activation of the weapon. This is what is assumed to have happened to the *U-74* off Dunbar, and it may also have been what happened with *UC-41*. If a mine had exploded in a tube, the boat would have been blown to pieces. The fact that divers could count mines in the adjacent tubes strongly indicates that this did not happen. Presumably, the damage to the superstructure and fore-ends was caused by depth charges, and they may have set off the other mines that *UC-41* had already deployed, but mines still on board were definitely not detonated. As can be seen in the above drawing of the layout of UCII-class U-boats, the mine tubes were forward, and the forward part of the boat was largely intact. If a mine had exploded in a tube, the wreck would have been smashed to smithereens, not merely cut in two, but no one will ever know for certain what happened.

The wreck lies on a seabed of mud and sand, in a general depth of 22 metres (72 feet), being the lowest astronomical depth. She is upright, partially buried and well broken up, with her conning tower removed. Tidal streams are fairly weak, but it should be borne in mind that the wreck is also a war grave.

The latest description of the wreckage is as follows: Lying in 28 metres of scour, in two parts 15 metres apart. The bow section has been blasted by divers, and now has a very mangled front end opening to a myriad of pipe work within the hull. The forward hydroplanes are evident, 5 metres from the battery area at which point the wreck is severed. Both parts rise 3–4 metres from the seabed. The stern section is almost intact, apart from the break at the battery compartment, and the stern is blown off. The hull lies with a slight list to port (about 20°). The starboard propeller is visible, but with only one blade still attached. There is an access area about 5 metres from the battery compartment, possibly where the conning tower was, or an access hatch. The telegraph came out of this area, plus there are other "treasured items" around this opening. The three torpedo tubes have become detached from the wreck, and one of them is flattened. The outer hull has corroded away in many places from much of the submarine, but the internal hull is still sound. Apparently the hatches were still operable a few years ago. There is some structure leading out from the main body of both sections of the wreck, but these go into the silt.

The wreck now lies deep in scour, and the seabed is about level with the top of the wreck. At least one rope with a few lobster pots is snagged on the bow. Both sections can be dived on the one outing as there are cable and rope connections between the sections.

UNKNOWN – DALHOUSIE ?

Wreck No: 236		Date Sunk:	
Latitude: 56 25 52 N		Longitude: 02 44 22 W	
GPS Lat: 5625.870 N		GPS Long: 0244.370 W	
Location: Mouth of the Tay		Area: Tay	
Type:		Tonnage:	
Length:	Beam:	Draught:	
How Sunk: Ran aground		Depth: 1 metre	

A wreck visible at low water is charted at 562552N, 024422W, and was in this position near the south-east edge of Abertay sands in 1943. I had originally thought this might be the 956-grt steamship *Stancourt* (ex-*Oder*), which was built in 1909 by Ramage & Ferguson of Leith. She sustained serious bomb damage in an attack by aircraft on 30 January 1940, and was run ashore on Abertay sands, but was refloated with the assistance of HM Danlayer *Willow* and HM Drifter *Suilven* on 23 February, and taken to Dundee for repair. She was obviously successfully repaired fairly quickly, as she went through a survey at Dundee in March 1940, then sailed to Methil and Shields.

In January 1942 she was sold to a Panamanian company who changed her name to *Inaki*, and she was finally sunk off Finisterre in September of that year.

The wreck charted on Abertay sands may be the remains of the steamship *Dalhousie*, which was wrecked at the mouth of the Tay, near Abertay Sands on 23 November 1864. When the London–Dundee steamer *London* arrived at Dundee about midnight on 23 November 1864, her master reported having seen a distress rocket and a series of blue lights which appeared to have come from a vessel on the Abertay Sands. The *London* herself had been damaged by mountainous seas.

In the ESE gale, two Dundee tugs, the *Sampson* and the *Hercules*, and the Broughty Ferry lifeboat *Mary Hartley* set out to search the area, but found no trace of the source of the lights seen by the master of the *London*, although the lifeboat took off the crew of a Montrose schooner which was in distress in the Tay estuary. Next morning, two bodies and a large quantity of wreckage, including lifebelts bearing the name *Dalhousie* were found washed ashore on Kinshaldy Sands. The *Dalhousie* had left Newcastle on the 22nd with 20 passengers and a crew of 14, and had been due to arrive in Dundee at about the same time as the *London*. The 156 ton iron screw steamer *Dalhousie* was built by Gourlay Bros. of Dundee in 1861.

Going back to the night of 30 January 1940, historian Dr. Andrew Jeffrey tells a wonderful story about the events of that night:

> The *City of Bath, Lady Shirley* and *Stancourt* were attacked by enemy aircraft off the entrance to the Tay. 609 Squadron scrambled but did not intercept. The first attack was made on the Hull trawler *Lady Shirley*. Her radio messages were heard then, ten minutes later, the bomber attacked the *City of Bath*, which put up AA fire. *Stancourt* was attacked thereafter. Captain Griffiths ordered his crew below as four bombs dropped around his ship and the bomber made repeated strafing passes. One of her crew, a young lad from St Ives on his first trip to sea, told reporters, 'When it power-dived over us and dropped a bomb, we just scrammed for cover.' *Stancourt*, formerly the Dundee–Hamburg trader *Oder*, attempted to run up the Tay for safety at low water, but without a pilot and in a snowstorm, she went ashore on the north side of Abertay Sands. Broughty Ferry Lifeboat *Mona* dropped anchor and attempted to veer down on *Stancourt*, but the anchor dragged. Then *Stancourt* shifted on the sands and Coxswain Jim Coull found a lee and was able to go alongside. *Stancourt*'s captain was at first reluctant to leave his ship, but relented when the vulnerability of his ship, both to further attack and the weather, was pointed out to him. The first man to jump for the lifeboat missed and had to be pulled, freezing, from the water. The crew of 21 officers and men were landed safely.
>
> *Stancourt* was refloated on 23 February 1940 by HM trawler *Willow* and HM drifter *Suilven*, and repaired in Dundee's East Graving Dock.
>
> As the rescue was completed, tins of ham, boxes of eggs and barrels of butter drifted ashore on both sides of the Tay. Rationing of bacon and butter had started on 8 January 1940, and the beaches became like fairyland with the twinkling of small torches as locals began to salvage the cargo. The Lifeboat crew had six big tins of ham in the shed. Searching the beach, they found a large cask clearly marked 'butter' near Broughty Ferry Castle. It was too heavy (1 cwt) for one of them to carry and rolling it back to the shed would have caused a considerable racket. Just then, they saw a shaded torch and heard, 'Hello, what's going on here then?' It was a hefty policeman and Coull recalled that they told him what it was and what their problem was. Saying, 'Well, see's a heave up wi'it', he heaved the butter onto his shoulders and carried carried

it back to the shed. He got his share. Another crew member found some eggs and it was ham and egg breakfasts all round - something of a rarity in wartime.

War Reserve Constable John Jamieson Blair was patrolling at the Barnhill end of the Esplanade. There was snow on the ground when he spotted what he thought were sheep on the beach. The moon burst through the clouds as he passed the Chalet Ballroom, and he saw it was barrels. He phoned Broughty Police Office from the box at the Chalet at about 2100 and by the time he got back along to the Ferry end, the beach was crowded with people recovering the booty.

Boats were out the following morning and women were to be seen hoisting up their skirts and wading out into the freezing water. Prams, barrows and sledges pulled by children were being used to carry away lumps of butter and hams. Many of the butter barrels had burst and lumps of butter were found covered with sand. These were cleaned off and salvaged. One sledge loaded with four barrels of butter was seen being pulled away by several children. A Dundee Courier reporter put the size of the crowd at Broughty Beach at 1,000. Some recall bottles of gin and rum drifting ashore. Police kept an eye on proceedings but did nothing at first. Many people also loaded cars and carts at Easthaven. On the Fife side, the RAF from Leuchars surrounded the area of the wreckage with red flags denoting mines. Then they helped themselves to the rest of the cargo. This unexpected bounty, coming at a time of austerity, was referred to in the press as the 'Sea Harvest'.

The Receiver of Wrecks, Mr. B.W. Cannon, warned that all goods recovered should be handed over, otherwise those keeping booty would be prosecuted. He instructed police to recover food, and some was taken away by lorry - by no means all of it though. Some people sent anonymous letters informing on their neighbours.

ARGYLL

Wreck No: 237		Date Sunk: 28 October 1915
Latitude: 56 26 00 N		Longitude: 02 23 30 W
GPS Lat: 5626.000 N		GPS Long: 0223.500 W
Location: W side of Bell Rock		Area: Arbroath
Type: Cruiser		Tonnage: 10850 grt
Length: 450 ft	Beam: 68.5 ft	Draught: 25.5 ft
How Sunk: Ran aground		Depth: 15 metres

The cruiser HMS *Argyll* was heading south towards Rosyth during the night of 27/28 October 1915. She was steaming at reduced speed because of stormy seas, and before turning in

HMS Argyll *(Courtesy of Glasgow University Archives)*

for the night, her commanding officer, Captain James Tancred, had radioed ahead to Rosyth, asking for the Bell Rock light to be lit to guide him past the danger about 12 miles off Arbroath. The midnight to 0400 hours watch passed uneventfully, but just after 04.00 hrs in the pitch darkness, the Argyll ran on to the Bell Rock and stopped dead in her tracks.

During wartime the lighthouses remained blacked out, and were only lit by special request. Argyll's request had never reached the Bell Rock. The lighthouse had neither telephone nor radio, and all messages had to be delivered by boat. Captain Tancred's request had been transmitted to Inchkeith, and a torpedo boat had been despatched with the message.

Unfortunately, the torpedo boat had only got as far as the mouth of the Forth when she was forced back by the storm, and her commander had asked that a bigger ship should be sent to take the message. The vital instruction was then radioed to the battleship *Queen Mary* which was patrolling off the Forth, but at 0217 hours, the battleship radioed to Rosyth that because of the heavy seas, she was unable to communicate with the lighthouse. Apparently no-one thought to warn HMS *Argyll* that the lighthouse remained unlit. At 0425 hours the first message from HMS *Argyll* was transmitted to say that she was aground on the Bell Rock. As dawn broke, those on board the *Argyll* saw the lighthouse only 100 yards away.

While six destroyers, several tugs, the Broughty ferry and St Andrews lifeboats were battling their way against the southerly gale to reach the Bell Rock, the lighthouse keepers managed to float a light line attached to an empty barrel across to the cruiser. A thick hawser was attached to that line by the crew of the *Argyll*, but before the keepers could haul it in, the first two destroyers *Hornet* and *Jackal* arrived on the scene. Half of *Argyll*'s crew had taken to the boats, and were picked up by the two destroyers. HMS *Argyll* was then lifted up by a huge wave and swung round to face the other way. *Jackal* closed with the stranded *Argyll*, and despite being battered against the cruiser's side, took off the remainder of her 655 crew. The rescue was completed five hours after the *Argyll* ran aground, and not one man had been lost. The *Argyll* broke up in the heavy seas, and a few weeks later, the lighthouse was equipped with a radio.

The Bell Rock is an almost submerged red sandstone reef situated approximately 12 miles from Arbroath. The conical granite and sandstone tower was finished in 1811. It was designed and built for Trinity House by Robert Stevenson. The lighthouse has been unmanned since 1988 and is now controlled remotely.

Extensive salvage has been carried out, and the remains of HMS *Argyll* are now well broken up and scattered in fairly shallow water on the west side of the reef, about 420 feet west of the lighthouse. Despite the salvage work, there are still worthwhile non-ferrous goodies to be found, including portholes, but beware of shells for the large-calibre guns. The propellers have gone, but the huge shafts are still there. As there are fairly strong currents running N/S around the reef, it would be better to dive at slack water.

Ironically, steel hull plates recovered from the *Argyll* were reputedly sent to Germany, to be used in the manufacture of X-ray equipment. The steel from these plates was, apparently, particularly useful for that purpose because it was free of radioactive contamination. Radioactivity in the atmosphere has increased over time with the continual testing of atomic bombs of all types. Steel makers need vast amounts of air to make steel so it would follow that steel made nowadays contains certain amounts of radioactivity. Prior to dropping the first A-bomb in 1945, steel was radioactive free, and the only remaining source of this 'clean' steel is pre-1945 wrecks that lie on the seabed.

QUIXOTIC

Wreck No: 238		Date Sunk: 5 December 1939
Latitude: 56 26 00 N		Longitude: 02 23 00 W
GPS Lat: 5626.000 N		GPS Long: 0223.000 W
Location: Bell Rock		Area: Arbroath
Type: Trawler		Tonnage: 197 grt
Length:	Beam:	Draught:
How Sunk: Ran aground		Depth:

The steam trawler *Quixotic*, built in 1898, ran on to the Bell Rock in darkness, immediately under the lighthouse, which was not lit because of the blackout imposed during the war. The lighthouse keepers threw ropes which the crew of the *Quixotic* were unable to reach. The crew then set fire to their bedding to act as flares which were seen on the mainland, and the Arbroath and Broughty ferry lifeboats went out. Despite the proximity of the dangerous rocks, the Broughty Ferry boat was able to approach close enough for the nine crew to jump aboard. A Silver Medal was awarded to Coxswain James Coull and Bronze Medals to Acting Second Coxswain George B. Smith and Motor Mechanic John Grieve for this daring rescue.

FERTILE VALE

Wreck No: 239		Date Sunk: 17 July 1941
Latitude: 56 26 10 N		Longitude: 02 39 18 W
GPS Lat: 5626.170 N		GPS Long: 0239.300 W
Location: Off the Tay		Area: Tay
Type: Drifter		Tonnage: 91 grt
Length: 90 ft	Beam: 20 ft	Draught:
How Sunk: Collision with *Empire Isle*		Depth:

The drifter *Fertile Vale* (ex-*Fogbow*), was built in 1917 and requisitioned for Admiralty use as an examination vessel in December 1939. She sank in a collision with the *Empire Isle* off the Tay on 17 July 1941.

CLAN SHAW

Wreck No: 240		Date Sunk: 23 January 1917
Latitude: 56 26 28 N		Longitude: 02 38 43 W
GPS Lat: 5626.470 N	**OSGB36**	GPS Long: 0238.720 W
GPS Lat: 5626.513 N	**WGS84**	GPS Long: 0238.924 W
Location: Mouth of the Tay		Area: Tay
Type: Steamship		Tonnage: 3943 grt
Length: 360 ft	Beam: 48.1 ft	Draught: 24.5 ft
How Sunk: Mined		Depth: 8 metres

The steel steamship *Clan Shaw* was built in 1902 by W. Doxford & Sons Ltd., Sunderland, and registered in Glasgow. While inward bound from Chittagong to Dundee with a cargo of jute on 23 January 1917, she struck a mine laid in the mouth of the Tay by the *UC-29*. Two of her crew were lost. One was a lascar seaman who was thought to have been blown up by the mine explosion, and the second was a crewman who was lost when a lifeboat filled and sank. The remainder of the crew got away from the ship and were landed at Dundee by a drifter.

Because of the size of the vessel and the shallow depth, part of her hull and superstructure remained visible above the surface for a time after she settled on the bottom, making her position relatively easy to establish with accuracy, and she was charted at 562632N, 023846W. Several vessels were damaged by striking the wreck in 1919, including the *Circassia*, HMS *Hearty*, the *City of Naples*, the *Glentaise* and the *Kintoye*. Dispersal work was carried out by a Sunderland firm early in 1920, and the Admiralty paid one third of the cost of this work.

Either the shifting sands have moved the wreck slightly over the years, or her position was not recorded quite as accurately as it might have been, as she was relocated close by at 562628N, 023843W in 1955.

The wreck was reported to be approximately 200 feet long in a general depth of 10 metres to a muddy seabed. The stern stood up three metres from the bottom, but the forward part of the vessel was apparently missing. This could explain why the length of the wreck was reported as 200 feet, while the original length of the *Clan Shaw* was 360 feet.

LEONARD

Wreck No: 241		Date Sunk: 12 February 1920
Latitude: 56 26 28 N		Longitude: 02 38 43 W
GPS Lat: 5626.470 N		GPS Long: 0238.720 W
Location: Mouth of the Tay		Area: Tay
Type: Drifter		Tonnage: 89 grt
Length: 80 ft	Beam: 18.5 ft	Draught: 8.5 ft
How Sunk: Foundered		Depth: 10 metres

The drifter *Leonard* started life in June 1900 as the Yarmouth drifter *Two* (YH473) in the fleet of the Smith's Dock Trust Company, all of whose ships were numbered in words up to *Thirty Eight*. All were steel built. *Two* was sold to Macduff in May 1907, being renamed *Leonard* with the registration BF632. She was requisitioned for Admiralty use during the First World War. After the war requisitioned vessels were gradually released back to civilian use. Still as HM drifter *Leonard*, she sailed from Inverkeithing on Thursday, 12 February 1920 bound for Dundee, but never arrived, and was lost with all hands. She was reported in distress off the mouth of the Tay. The crew of nine according to some accounts, and six according to others, had been employed for some time in delivering vessels to be reconditioned by the Admiralty from port to port. Vessels surplus to Admiralty requirements after the end of the First World War (and, indeed, the Second World War) were reconditioned before being returned to civilian use.

None of the bodies of her crew were found, but while dispersal work was being carried out on the wreck of the *Clan Shaw* on 16 February 1920, the wreck of the *Leonard* was found lying partly foul of that wreck. This would seem to suggest that the *Leonard* sank as a result of running into the *Clan Shaw*, but this was considered impossible, as the *Clan Shaw* had by that time already been dispersed to give a clearance of 18 feet at low water. The *Leonard* must either have drifted in a sinking condition, until she finally foundered almost directly on top of the *Clan Shaw*, or perhaps more likely, the sea state was such that the clearance over the wreck in the troughs in the waves was reduced to a dangerously low level.

The wreck of the *Leonard* is easy to find. Just swim along the exposed propeller shaft of the *Clan Shaw* to the propeller, which is sitting 1.5 metres high off the sand. Directly off the end of the propeller, less than 20 feet away, lies the small wreck of the *Leonard*.

ANU

Wreck No: 242		Date Sunk: 6 February 1940
Latitude: 56 26 44 N		Longitude: 02 36 59 W
GPS Lat: 5626.727 N	**WGS84**	GPS Long: 0236.978 W

Location: Mouth of the Tay   Area: Tay
Type: Steamship   Tonnage: 1421 grt
Length: 250 ft   Beam: 36.2 ft   Draught: 17.6 ft
How Sunk: Mined   Depth: 20-24 metres

The Estonian coaster *Anu* was built by J. Redhead & Co. in 1883. On 6 August 1940, while inward-bound from Gothenburg and Aberdeen to Dundee with a cargo of paper, she struck a mine and sank between Nos. 1 and 2 buoys at the entrance to the River Tay. The mine she hit had been laid almost eight months earlier on 12 December 1939 by *U-13* (Scheringer). When the *Anu* struck the mine at 6.15 p.m., her engine room was shattered, and the ship immediately broke in two and sank. Six of the crew were killed, including Captain Johannes Raudsoo and his wife Liis. Thirteen survivors drifted ashore at Carnoustie on a raft, and were found wandering around on the golf course. One of them, Elma Jorgensen (or Elna Jürisson?), a Finnish cook, had been scalded by escaping steam and later died in Dundee hospital. Flotsam was spread over five miles of the Angus coastline.

The wreck was located in 1969, embedded in a sand and mud seabed, and oriented 045/225°. Underwater visibility here is rather variable – typically 3–4 metres, but it can be a lot less, sometimes with a lot of litter from Dundee stuck on the wreck. There are no nets on the wreck. The engine stands three meters high with a huge wheel on the side, with brass pipes running vertically near the aft of the wreck. This can have a stunning appearance in good visibility. There are two large winches aft, with other winches around the wreck. The main wreckage – about three quarters of the wreck – stands only two metres high off seabed. Her large propeller is partially embedded in the sand, but three quarters of it is still visible. The bow section, which must comprise about one quarter of the ship, is missing, although it has been located by echo-sounder quite close by at 5626.915N, 0237.656W.

The steamship Anu *(Author's collection)*

UNKNOWN ARMED TRAWLER – FERTILE VALE ?

Wreck No: 243		Date Sunk: Pre-1918	
Latitude: 56 27 54 N		Longitude: 02 35 41 W	
GPS Lat: 5626.900 N	**OSGB36**	GPS Long: 0235.680 W	
GPS Lat: 5626.848 N	**WGS84**	GPS Long: 0235.725 W	
Location: Off Elbow Light Buoy		Area: Tay	
Type: Drifter		Tonnage:	
Length:	Beam:	Draught:	
How Sunk:		Depth: 25–28 metres	

The wreck of an armed trawler or drifter on an even keel, standing about 3 metres above the sand has been found at 562706N, 023548W. Possibly the *Fertile Vale*? Depth to the top of the wreck is 25 metres, while depth to the sandy seabed is 28 metres.

PROTECTOR

Wreck No: 244		Date Sunk: 29 August 1889
Latitude: 56 27 25 N		Longitude: 02 41 34 W
GPS Lat: 5627.420 N		GPS Long: 0241.570 W
Location: Gaa Sand, 1 mile E of Buddon		Area: Tay
Type: Paddle Tug		Tonnage: 89 grt
Length: 89.3 ft	Beam: 18 ft	Draught: 9.5 ft
How Sunk: Collision with *Duncan*		Depth: 8 metres

The wreck of the paddle tug *Protector* is charted four and a half miles east of Tentsmuir Point, and one and a half miles from Old Low Lighthouse which is on Buddon Ness, between Carnoustie and Monifieth. She was sunk in a collision with the steam tug *Duncan* near Abertay light vessel on 29 August 1889.

BURNSTONE

Wreck No: 245		Date Sunk: 19 March 1918
Latitude: 56 28 00 N		Longitude: 01 44 39 W
GPS Lat: 5628.180 N	**WGS84**	GPS Long: 0144.657 W
Location: 28 miles E of Arbroath		Area : Arbroath
Type: Steamship		Tonnage: 2412 grt
Length: 307.2 ft	Beam: 44.5 ft	Draught: 20 ft
How Sunk: Torpedoed by *UB-62*		Depth: 46-53 metres

The 2412-grt British steamship *Burnstone* (ex-*Kilsyth*) was built by Craig Taylor of Stockton in 1903 (Yard No. 96). She was torpedoed by the *UB-62* (KL Bernhard Putzier) on 19 March 1918. The bow is intact and upright but her bridge has collapsed. Her four holds are still full of coal. The torpedo apparently struck the stern, as it is very broken up and lying to the starboard.

BAY FISHER

Wreck No: 246		Date Sunk: 7 February 1941	
Latitude: 56 28 09 N		Longitude: 02 19 12 W	
GPS Lat: 5628.178 N	**WGS84**	GPS Long: 0219.350 W	
Location: 3½ miles NE of Bell Rock		Area: Arbroath	
Type: Steamship		Tonnage: 575 grt	
Length: 164.8 ft	Beam: 27 ft	Draught: 11.1 ft	
How Sunk: Bombed		Depth: 51 metres	

The 575-ton steamship *Bay Fisher* (ex-*Tarnwater*) was built in 1919 by J. Lewis & Son, Aberdeen. She was bombed and sunk three and a half miles NE of the Bell Rock at 1100 hours on 7 February 1941, while en route from Scapa Flow to Rosyth on government charter, with 200 tons of government stores. She had a crew of eleven and one gunner. Seven crew and the gunner were lost. Four survivors were picked up by the armed trawler HMS *Heliopolis*, and taken to Dundee.

The wreck of the *Bay Fisher* lies in a total depth of 51 metres. Least depth to the bow is 45 metres. The wreck is oriented 315/225°, lying with a list of about 30° to port. The fo'c'sle is intact, and still contains storm lamps, a toilet etc., although they are fairly broken up. The wreck is clear of silt due to the tidal streams in the area, and the bow is covered in life. Aft of the fo'c'sle the wreck changes somewhat. The area of what is probably the forward hold is littered with large gas cylinders and large sections of wreckage. Aft of this is uncharted, although the wreck could possibly be in two parts due to only a 'short' reading on the sounder. A bell with the name TARNWATER 1919 inscribed on it was recovered some years ago.

Bay Fisher *(Courtesy of John Griffith Jones collection)*

GRENMAR

Wreck No: 247
Latitude: 56 28 54 N
GPS Lat: 5628.900 N
Location: 10 miles ENE of Bell Rock
Type: Steamship
Length: 261.5 ft   Beam: 36.5 ft
How Sunk: By submarine (*UC-77*)

Date Sunk: 24 March 1917
Longitude: 02 04 24 W
GPS Long: 0204.400 W
Area: Arbroath
Tonnage: 1438 grt
Draught: 16.3 ft
Depth: 50 metres

This wreck, found in 1969, is apparently about 150 feet long, sitting upright, and projecting 10 feet up from the bottom. It is possibly part of the Norwegian steamship *Grenmar*, which was captured by *UC-77* and sunk on 24 March 1917, while en route from Blyth to Christiania with a cargo of coal. *Lloyd's World War One Losses* describes the position of attack as 34 miles N by E ½E of St Abbs Head. The *Grenmar* (ex-*Wynnstay*, ex-*Nora*) was built by Palmers Co., Newcastle in 1884.

ROCKINGHAM

Wreck No: 248
Latitude: 56 29 00 N PA
GPS Lat: 5629.000 N
Location: 53 miles SE ½E of Stonehaven
Type: Destroyer
Length: 310 ft   Beam: 31 ft
How Sunk: Mined

Date Sunk: 27 September 1944
Longitude: 00 57 00 W PA
GPS Long: 0057.000 W
Area: Arbroath
Tonnage: 1190 grt
Draught: 9.3 ft
Depth:

HMS *Rockingham* (ex-USS *Swasey*, DD-273) was one of the 50 First World War four-stack flush-decked American destroyers acquired under the Lend-Lease Act in 1940. She was a Clemson-class destroyer built in 1919 by Bethlehem S.B. Co., and had four 4-inch guns and 12 torpedo tubes. USS *Swasey* was assigned to the Pacific Fleet, and arrived at Pearl Harbour in the fall of 1919. She served there until the summer of 1922 when she returned to San Diego, where she was decommissioned on 10 June 1922 and assigned to the reserve fleet for the next 17 years.

On 2 September 1940, in response to two requests by British Prime Minister Winston Churchill in May and June of that year, the Congress of the United States approved a deal brokered by President Franklin D. Roosevelt to transfer 50 old destroyers to bolster British escort forces in the face of heavy destroyer losses suffered by the Royal Navy due to Dunkirk and other costly operations. By the date the deal was approved, the RN had lost 33 destroyers of all types, the majority being modern, capable units. As a result of this agreement, the US gained basing rights at such locations as Argentia, Newfoundland, Bermuda and various Caribbean locations. Following the German occupation of

HMS Rockingham *(Courtesy of Robert Hirst)*

Denmark on 9 April 1940, the ability of the Danish government to conduct any kind of independent foreign policy was curtailed. This was realised by the Danish ambassador in Washington, Mr Kaufmann, who immediately declared himself independent from the Danish government. In accordance with US wishes, he therefore took it upon himself to conclude an agreement in April 1941, by which the US agreed to defend Greenland and Iceland, thereby gaining bases in those places to support the convoy lanes to Britain.

Between 9 September and 5 December 1940 the USN transferred 3 Shaw-, 23 Wickes- and 18 Clemson-class destroyers to the Royal Navy and 4 Wickes- and 2 Clemson-class destroyers to the Royal Canadian Navy. In 1941 an additional ten 250-foot Coast Guard Cutters were also transferred to Britain. The RN ships were given town names common to both Britain and the United States. The other five ships transferred directly to the RCN were given the names of Canadian rivers. The destroyers in British service were known as the *Town Class* and broken into the *Belmont, Lewes, Campbeltown,* and *Bath* groups. The former Coast Guard Cutters were known as the *Banff* class and were designated as Escort Sloops.

Whilst sorely needed at the time they were offered, they needed extensive modernisation and refits to bring them up to Royal Navy operational standards, and the quality can only be described as poor overall. It became apparent that they also had inherent design faults. They could not stand up to the weather in the North Atlantic, the steering system was poor – the turning circle was enormous – and the very narrow stern was a cause of damage to propellers when manoevering alongside. Because of the time taken to complete the refits they were not really in full service until mid-to-late 1941, although most were commissioned between September and December 1940, when the emergency under which they were acquired had largely abated. The building programme in Britain was producing new and far superior ships by this time to fill the gaps which these old destroyers of First World War vintage had been intended to fill.

USS *Swasey* was transferred to Britain on 26 November 1940, and renamed HMS *Rockingham*. HMS *Rockingham* initially joined the 1st Escort Group at Londonderry, Northern Ireland, later transferring to Escort Group B.1. She seems to have been continuously employed between October 1941 and late 1943 in escorting Atlantic convoys from the UK to North America and back again. In January 1944 she was retired from active service and converted to an "air target", basically acting as a 'clockwork mouse' to allow aircrew to train in attacking a moving ship at sea, and also acting as a safety ship on the range, being based at Rosyth.

At 0446 hours on 27 September 1944 HMS *Rockingham* struck a mine 30 miles southeast of Aberdeen at 5647N, 0130W. The mine detonated under her stern, and one member of her crew was killed. She did not sink immediately and was taken in tow, but this had to be abandoned at 2026 hours, when she sank stern first at 562900N, 005700W PA, which is 58 miles ENE of Fife Ness. The postion has also been recorded as 562600N 002100W. It was found that she had strayed into a British defensive minefield, due to navigational difficulties caused by the poor weather.

EXMOUTH

Wreck No: 249		Date Sunk: 31 July 1944	
Latitude: 56 28 33 N		Longitude: 01 38 28 W	
GPS Lat: 5628.554 N		GPS Long: 0138.466 W	
Location: 31½ miles E of Arbroath		Area: Arbroath	
Type: Steamship		Tonnage: 4979 grt	
Length: 392.3 ft	Beam: 54.3 ft	Draught: 28.2 ft	
How Sunk: Mined		Depth: 39–56 metres	

The American steamship *Exmouth* (ex-*Blue Triangle*) was built in 1919. On 29 July 1944 she left Hull, in ballast (1500 tons of slag ballast), bound for New York via Loch Ewe. She joined a north-bound convoy for a while, before proceeding independently. At 0715 hours on 31 July in dense fog the ship struck two mines. Her position at that time was estimated to be about 60 miles off the Scottish coast. The first mine hit No. 1 hold on the starboard side, and a minute later a second mine struck No. 2 hold on the port side. The No. 1 hold filled quickly, and the ship began to settle by the head. The second explosion broke the ship in two, forward of the bridge. Her 43 crew and 27 armed guards abandoned ship in four lifeboats as the foredeck settled beneath the water. *Exmouth* sank at 0820 hours. The lifeboats stayed together in the vicinity, and the fog lifted at 1030 hours. At 2120 hours RAF rescue launch 2731 saved all hands and landed them at Dundee at 2300 hours.

Exmouth was was reported to have been mined in a British minefield at about 5630N, 0212W on 31 July 1944. I imagine that report must have been made by the crew of the rescue launch, based on the position in which she found the lifeboats. It is only 25 miles from 5630N, 0212W to Dundee – remember the RAF rescue launch took only about an hour and a half to make the trip to Dundee from the position of the lifeboats.

According to the Official Chronology of the US Navy, the *Exmouth* was mined and sunk at about 56°33'N, 01°38'W. The nearest charted wreck is at 5628.554N, 0138.466W. This is a large wreck, originally thought to possibly be the tanker *Desabla*. In August 2008 Marine Quest of Eyemouth took a party of divers 38 miles out to this wreck. In superb visibility the divers could see a large, intact wreck below them from about 25 metres depth. The wreck has collapsed on its starboard side so the port side bridge area is at 39–40 metres lying at an angle of about 40°. Thinking they were descending on the *Desabla*, the divers were surprised to see open holds when they were expecting tanks, and on the seabed, noticed a gun tub with what looked like an Oerlikon or 20-mm cannon. The port gun tub is still intact on the bridge, complete with a gun, and in the wheelhouse the compass binnacle, steering pedestal and tele-graphs are still there. There are also many portholes on the wreck. Crockery marked "American Export Lines" was also found, and there are three guns at the bow and two at the stern. The gun tubs looked very like those seen on American Liberty ships. The wreck was obviously not the tanker *Desabla*, but the American four-hold cargo steam-ship *Exmouth*. Slabs of concrete or asphalt lying about must be some of the 1500 tons of slag ballast.

HOCHE

Wreck No: 250		Date Sunk: 29 October 1915
Latitude: 56 30 16 N		Longitude: 02 36 30 W
GPS Lat: 5630.248 N		GPS Long: 0236.591 W
Location: Off Arbroath		Area: Arbroath
Type: Sailing ship		Tonnage: 2211 grt
Length: 276.6 ft	Beam: 40.3 ft	Draught: 22.5 ft
How Sunk: Foundered		Depth: 20 metres

The wreck charted as 19.2 metres at 563016N, 023630W was first located in 1969. It is about 300 feet long, lying NE/SW, and stands up 15 feet in a general depth of 21 metres. The WGS84 position has also been given as 5630.193N, 00236.685W. The French steel sailing ship *Hoche* was built at Nantes in 1901. She was being towed by a tug from Ipswich to Leith when bad weather forced them past the mouth of the Forth. The tow was slipped, and the *Hoche* foundered. The complete wreck is there. The bows are intact, lying over to starboard, and the after section is partly buried in mud. Depth to the bow is 20 metres, while the muddy seabed is at 24 metres.

PRIMROSE ? or DAYSPRING ?

Wreck No: 251		Date Sunk: 5 February 1917
Latitude: 56 31 47 N		Longitude: 02 24 54 W
GPS Lat: 5631.780 N	**WGS84**	GPS Long: 0224.902 W
Location: 6.7 miles E of Arbroath		Area: Arbroath
Type: Trawler		Tonnage: 136 grt
Length: 100 ft	Beam: 20 ft	Draught: 10.9 ft
How Sunk: Mined		Depth: 55 metres

The steel-hulled Granton trawler *Primrose* was built in 1891 by J. T. Eltringham of South Shields. She was mined and sunk on 5 February 1917, 17 miles SSW of Tod Head. Nine crewmen were lost, including the skipper. The wreck charted 6.7 miles east of Arbroath might be the *Primrose*. On the other hand, the MFV *Dayspring* took on water and sank at about this position on 10 August 1992. *Dayspring* was only 33 feet long.

CANGANIAN

Wreck No: 252		Date Sunk: 17 November 1916
Latitude: 56 35 24 N		Longitude: 02 21 30 W
GPS Lat: 5635.280 N	**WGS84**	GPS Long: 0221.527 W
Location: 5 miles NE of Arbroath		Area: Arbroath
Type: Steamship		Tonnage: 1142 grt
Length: 227.7 ft	Beam: 33 ft	Draught: 13.2 ft
How Sunk: Foundered		Depth: 55–64 metres

On 24 November 1916 a nameboard marked "Canganian" washed ashore in Montrose Bay, along with other wreckage, evidently from the Cardiff steamship *Canganian*. She was reported to have foundered 8–10 miles from Montrose on 17 November 1916 while en route from Methil to Scapa Flow with a cargo of coal. The position given in 1919 was 563650N, 022515W. The wreck charted at 563524N, 022130W was located on 15 September 1930 when the trawler *Camelia* fouled her gear. The position has also been recorded as 563520N, 022130W.

HMS *Beagle* reported in 1969 that it is apparently a large wreck, about 280 feet long, and standing up some eight or nine metres from the bottom. The least depth by echo sounder was 55 metres in a total depth of 64 metres. The wreck is oriented 337/157°. This wreck is in the right position for the *Canganian*, but the length of the wreck seems to have been over-estimated, as the *Canganian* was 227.7 feet long. The position has also been given as 5635.210N, 0221.646W (WGS84).

BRACONBURN

Wreck No: 253	Date Sunk: 30 July 1944
Latitude: 56 35 00 N PA	Longitude: 02 10 00 W PA

GPS Lat: 5635.000 N		GPS Long: 0210.000 W
Location: Near the Bell Rock		Area: Arbroath
Type: Trawler		Tonnage: 203 grt
Length: 115.4 ft	Beam: 22.1 ft	Draught: 12.1 ft
How Sunk: Collision *Le Baron Russell Briggs*		Depth: 48 metres

The Fleetwood steam trawler *Braconburn* (A768, ex-*Richard Briscoll*) was built in 1918 by Hall Russell of Aberdeen (Yard No. 645). In 1944 she was requisitioned for use as a blockship, and was en route to Scapa Flow on 30 July 1944 when she was sunk near the Bell Rock in collision with the liberty ship *Le Baron Russell Briggs*. Six crewmembers were lost. The position was recorded as 563500N, 021000W PA. The nearest charted wreck is at 5635.849N, 0209.273W, but this is the very much larger *Nailsea River.*

In 1945 a wreck lying 180/360°, estimated to be about 180 feet long and standing up 24 feet, was reported to have been located at 563430N, 020530W. The length of that wreck might easily have been over-estimated in 1945, but the wreck was not found in 1969. *Le Baron Russell Briggs* was scuttled in 16000 feet of water 283 miles off Cape Kennedy, Florida on 18 August 1970, with a cargo of lethal nerve gas.

NAILSEA RIVER

Wreck No: 254		Date Sunk: 15 September 1940
Latitude: 56 35 55		Longitude: 02 09 22 W
GPS Lat: 5635.922 N	**WGS84**	GPS Long: 0209.370 W
Location: 10 ¾ miles east of Red Head		Area: Arbroath
Type: Steamship		Tonnage: 5548 grt
Length: 410.2 ft	Beam: 52.2 ft	Draught: 30.2 ft
How Sunk: By aircraft – torpedo		Depth: 52–65 metres

The British steamship *Nailsea River* (ex-*Actor*) was built in 1917 by D. & W. Henderson of Glasgow, and operated by Manchester Lines. At 2230 hours on 15 September 1940, while en route from Buenos Aires to the Tyne with a cargo of 7000 tons of wheat, she was reported to have been attacked four miles east of Montrose by a torpedo-carrying aircraft of the same enemy formation that had sunk the *Halland* shortly before. *Nailsea River* sank three hours later, at 1.30 a.m. on the 16th. Six of her crew were lost and the survivors were taken to Methil in the minesweeper trawler *Fandango*.

According to *Lloyd's War Losses* she sank in 5641N, 0205W. That position is 11.6 miles east of Scurdy Ness, but HMS *Beagle* did not find the *Nailsea River* in this position after an extensive search. It seems strange that a ship of her size could apparently remain unlocated for over 60 years. In 1969 HMS *Beagle* found a very large wreck oriented 022/202° at 563554N, 020911W. The wreck was apparently 500 feet long, and stood up 40 feet from the seabed. The minimum depth was 46 metres in a total depth of 58 metres.

I can find no evidence to suggest that any vessel of 500 feet long may have sunk near here.

Dimensions recorded by side-scan sonar are, however, notoriously unreliable, and it is therefore entirely possible that the length dimension recorded was inaccurate. If we can assume the length to be about 400 feet, two possible candidates emerge – *Nailsea River* and *Exmouth*. *Exmouth* can be eliminated, however, as she broke in two before sinking, and has been found at 5628.544 N, 0138.466 W. *Nailsea River* is by far the more likely, as this wreck is only 5.6 miles SSW of the sinking position recorded by Lloyd's. Perhaps because of the excessively over-estimated length of the wreck, no-one seems to have realised that this is the wreck of the *Nailsea River*. *Nailsea River* lies in 65 metres. The shallowest part is the top of the bows at 52 metres. As far as I am aware the only part of the wreck that has been dived so far is the bow section to about amidships.

LORD BEACONSFIELD

Wreck No: 255	Date Sunk: 17 October 1945
Latitude: 56 36 22 N	Longitude: 02 29 30 W
GPS Lat: 5636.370 N	GPS Long: 0229.500 W
Location: Off Prail Castle, Auchmithie	Area: Arbroath
Type: Trawler	Tonnage: 302 grt
Length: 135 ft Beam: 23.5 ft	Draught: 12.3 ft
How Sunk: Ran aground	Depth: 10 metres

The Grimsby trawler *Lord Beaconsfield* (ex-*Tribune*) was built in 1915 by Cochranes of Selby. She was hired by the Admiralty in 1939 as an armed patrol trawler then converted to a minesweeper in 1941. On 17 October 1945, while en route to a potential buyer, she ran aground almost under Prail Castle and sank. The ship's Walker log, engine room guages and a Seibe Gorman diving knife with brass sheath were recovered some years ago. The

Lord Beaconsfield *(Author's collection)*

wreck has been well smashed up over the years, and there is not much left now, other than boiler plates and broken pieces of rusted steel.

FOUNTAINS ABBEY

Wreck No: 256
Latitude: 56 37 00 N PA
GPS Lat: 5637.000 N
Location: Near Red Head
Type: Steamship
Length: 243 ft   Beam: 32.2 ft
How Sunk: Ran aground

Date Sunk: 15 November 1921
Longitude: 02 38 00 W PA
GPS Long: 0238.000 W
Area: Arbroath
Tonnage: 1285 grt
Draught: 18 ft
Depth:

The iron steamship *Fountains Abbey* was built in 1879 by Palmers of Newcastle, and registered in Leith. She ran aground during the night of 15 November 1921 near Red Head, Forfar between Arbroath and Montrose, while en route from Riga, Latvia to Dundee with a cargo of flax and timber. The crew remained on the vessel until daybreak. When the Arbroath and Montrose lifeboats arrived on the scene, the crew had already landed, with difficulty, on the rocky shore. The bottom of the hull of the *Fountains Abbey* was badly damaged, and later that morning she slipped off the rocks and sank. It was hoped that a considerable portion of her cargo could be salved before the wreck was broken up by tidal action.

HERRINGTON

Wreck No: 257
Latitude: 56 37 12 N
GPS Lat: 5637.092 N
Location: ¾ mile E of Red Head
Type: Steamship
Length: 230.5 ft   Beam: 36 ft
How Sunk: Mined

Date Sunk: 4 May 1917
Longitude: 02 27 36 W
GPS Long: 0227.843 W
Area: Arbroath
Tonnage: 1258 grt
Draught: 14.9 ft
Depth: 20 metres

The steamship *Herrington* was built in 1905 by S.P. Austin of Sunderland. While carrying a cargo of coal from Methil, she was mined on 4 May 1917. The wreck has been found in 30 metres of water, lying on a rocky bottom at 573712N, 022736W, three quarters of a mile east of Red Head. Least depth to the wreck is 20 metres. The wreck is complete, but not intact. The forward section, from the bow to the boilers is upside down, while the after section from the engines to the stern is lying over on its port side. There is one boiler and a three-cylinder engine. The bell was recovered in 1975, and cutlery found bears the inscription *Herrington*.

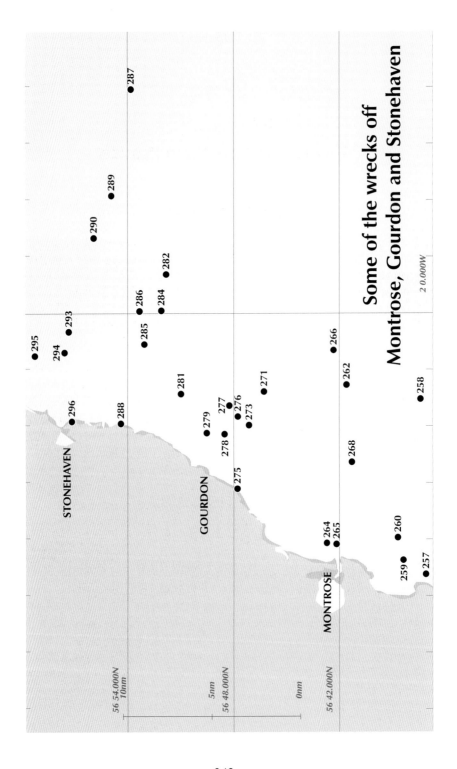

Some of the wrecks off Montrose, Gourdon and Stonehaven

9

Montrose,
Gourdon and Stonehaven

BLACKMOREVALE

Wreck No: 258
Latitude: 56 37 24 N
GPS Lat: 5637.401 N   **WGS84**
Location: 10½ miles SE of Scurdie Ness
Type: Minesweeper
Length: 232.3 ft   Beam: 28.1 ft
How Sunk: Mined

Date Sunk: 1 May 1918
Longitude: 02 09 06 W
GPS Long: 0209.150 W
Area: Montrose
Tonnage: 750 grt
Draught: 7 ft
Depth: 55–60 metres

The minesweeper *Blackmorevale* was built by Ardrossan Shipbuilders in 1917 (Yard No.279). She sank after striking a mine off Montrose on 1 May 1918. The wreck found in 1969 at 563724N, 020906W might be the *Blackmorevale*. The wreck lies N/S and is apparently about 200 feet long, and standing up 15 feet from the sandy seabed, 55 metres in 60 metres depth. An alternative reading of the position is 5637.392N, 0209.196W – WGS84.

PHINEAS BEARD

Wreck No: 259
Latitude: 56 38 24 N
GPS Lat: 5638.847 N   **WGS84**
Location: Lunan Bay, 4 miles S of Montrose
Type: Trawler
Length: 125.5 ft   Beam: 23.5 ft
How Sunk: By aircraft

Date Sunk: 8 December 1941
Longitude: 02 26 18 W
GPS Long: 0226.091 W
Area: Montrose
Tonnage: 278 grt
Draught: 12.7 ft
Depth: 28–30 metres

The Castle-class Admiralty trawler *Phineas Beard* was built in 1918 by Cook, Welton & Gemmell of Hull (Yard No. 383). She was requisitioned for use as a minesweeper in August 1939. At 1715 hours on 8 December 1941 the minesweepers *Milford Earl* and *Phineas Beard* of M/S Group 41 were steaming into Lunan Bay, one and a half miles north-east of Red Head, to anchor for the night, when they were attacked by German

A Castle-class trawler similar to Phineas Beard *(Author's collection)*

HE111 bombers. The enemy aircraft made four separate attacks, and all eleven aboard the *Phineas Beard* were lost. Two other minesweeper trawlers were undamaged apart from bullet holes. In total, three officers and 14 ratings were killed, and five wounded. *Phineas Beard* was reported to have sunk while under tow at 563824N 022622W.

She lies on a flat sandy seabed with a 30° list to port. Apart from bomb damage amidships, the wreck is almost completely intact, with a gun still mounted near the bow. Shell cases dated 1940 have been found in her. From June to September the wreck is usually buoyed. The entire wreck is covered in a dense growth of plumose anemones. Descending the shot line, the wreck first comes into view as a white cloud caused by the huge amount of plumose anemones growing on the wreck. From the gun on the bow it is normally possible to see the whole length of the wreck all the way to the stern. There is a big hole in the starboard side of the steel hull, caused by the bomb explosion, and the midship section is damaged, allowing access inside the wreck, but there are many snags to avoid, and silt can stir up very easily reducing visibility to zero. There is some net on the wreck, but most of it is flattened and not floating around above the wreck. Arched trawl gallows stand 10 feet high on both port and starboard sides. At the stern of the wreck, three of the four propeller blades are visible. The least recorded depth to the highest point of the wreck is 18 metres, but 24 metres is more usual. Depth to the sandy seabed is 30 metres.

MILFORD EARL

Wreck No: 260		Date Sunk: 8 December 1941
Latitude: 56 38 42 N		Longitude: 02 23 48 W
GPS Lat: 5638.741 N	**WGS84**	GPS Long: 0223.451 W
Location: 3 miles E of Lunan Bay		Area: Montrose
Type: Trawler		Tonnage: 290 grt

Length: 125.5 ft   Beam: 23.5 ft   Draught: 12.7 ft
How Sunk: By aircraft   Depth: 32 metres

The trawler *Milford Earl* (ex-*Duncan McRae*, ex-*Callancroft*, ex-*Andrew Apsley*) was built in 1919 by Cook, Welton & Gemmell of Beverley (Yard No. 414), engine by Amos & Smith of Hull. She was requisitioned for use as a minesweeper in August 1939. Six of the crew were killed and five wounded when she was sunk three miles SE of Usan by HE111 aircraft of KG26 from Stavanger. The *Milford Earl* is completely intact, and lies with a 20° list to port. A gun is still mounted on her bow and depth charges are still on her stern. Shells dated 1918 have been found.

In 1987 divers from Arbroath recovered an anti-aircraft gun from the wreck, which is charted at 563842N, 022348W. (The position has also been recorded as 5638.692N, 0223.844W – WGS84.) Depth to the top of the wreck is 32 metres, and 38 metres to the sandy seabed. *Milford Earl* has a curved stern and a four-bladed propeller.

NOIC Dundee, Captain H. Hurt recommended that Lieutenant Francis Roger Derek Corbett RNVR, First Lieutenant in *Milford Earl*, should receive a decoration. According to Hurt, Corbett "… assumed command when his commanding officer was killed at the beginning of the action. Although suffering from considerable facial injuries, he worked indefatigably to save his ship and to keep all available armament in action … he took all possible steps for the succour of the wounded and the safety of his crew."

Corbett was awarded a DSC. Hurt also recommended Leading Telegraphist Leonard Edward Welch RNVR who was on watch in the wireless cabin of *Milford Earl* when she suffered a direct hit. He salvaged a Lewis gun from the wreckage, improvised a mounting and "although he had not handled this weapon before, opened an accurate fire on the aircraft, thus helping to prevent the accurate aiming of a second salvo of bombs." Welch received a DSM.

Thomas Boudige – *a Castle-class trawler similar to* Milford Earl *(Author's collection)*

The Admiralty Board of Enquiry found that "These ships were not in the required state of readiness to meet attack by enemy aircraft, but they did eventually put up a strong, if not very effective, resistance to the determined attacks of the enemy aircraft, of which there may have been more than one." Lieutenant W. M. Morrison, the senior officer of the group, and one of those killed in *Milford Earl*, was blamed for the lack of preparedness, and Captain Hurt was instructed to improve the gunnery of all minesweepers operating from Dundee.

ST BRIAC

Wreck No: 261		Date Sunk: 12 March 1942
Latitude: 56 33 03 N		Longitude: 01 33 41 W
GPS Lat: 5633.046 N	**WGS84**	GPS Long: 0133.690 W
Location: 34 miles E of Arbroath		Area: Montrose
Type: Steamship		Tonnage: 2312 grt
Length: 316 ft	Beam: 41 ft	Draught: 14 ft
How Sunk: Mined		Depth: 62 metres

The twin-screw cross-channel ferry *St Briac* was built in 1924 by W. Denny Bros., Dumbarton for the Southern Railway Co., which used her for cruises and passenger services to the Channel Islands and St Malo in Brittany. She assisted in the evacuations from Dunkirk in June 1940, and was hired by the Admiralty on 7 June 1941. At the time of her loss on 12 March 1942, she was described as a Fleet Air Arm target vessel attached to HMS *Condor* at Arbroath. HMS *St Briac* had sailed from Dundee that morning, but shortly before 1500 hours Captain Lubbock sent distress signals to say that she had broken down in a strong south-easterly gale, and was drifting into the British minefield 20 miles east of Arbroath. She was reported to have struck a mine at 564030N, 012600W, and six of her Southern Railways crew were killed. The surviving crew members abandoned ship. Four armed trawl-

Southern Railways ferry St Briac *(Author's collection)*

ers, Arbroath Lifeboat *John and William Mudie* and Montrose Lifeboat *The Good Hope* were despatched. At 1832 hours the Free French rescue tug *Abielle IV* sailed from Aberdeen to assist. One of *St Briac*'s lifeboats was picked up by the tug *Empire Larch*. Another lifeboat drifted north and capsized before being driven ashore at Collieston, north of Aberdeen, at 0952 hours the following morning. Thirteen of the 17 occupants were drowned. A total of 47 lives were lost.

An oil patch appeared on the surface when the trawler *Bon Accord* fouled her gear on an obstruction near 564030N, 012600W PA on 22 April 1942. It was assumed that her gear had fouled the wreck of the *St Briac*.

In September 2008, 66 years later, the wreck was found and dived 7½ miles SSW of that position and identified by the bell. The dive was carried out from Eyemouth (44 miles away) but the wreck is actually nearer to Aberdeen (38 miles)!

St Briac *bell*
(Courtesy of Jeremy Cameron)

UNKNOWN – GRIMSBY ?

Wreck No: 262		Date Sunk: Pre-1929
Latitude: 56 41 39 N		Longitude: 02 07 30 W
GPS Lat: 5641.642 N	**WGS84**	GPS Long: 0207.596 W
Location: 10 miles E of Scurdy Ness Light		Area: Montrose
Type: Trawler		Tonnage:
Length:	Beam:	Draught:
How Sunk:		Depth: 60–66 metres

First reported in 1929 and charted as Wk 60 metres. Leith trawler *Grimsby* (LH 308) – foundered 10 March 1926 – or possibly the *Plethos* (1918). Another position recorded for the sinking of the *Nova* in 1917 was 10 nm ESE of Todhead. This wreck, which is 11½ nm ESE of Todhead, might even be the *Nova*.

PLETHOS

Wreck No: 263		Date Sunk: 23 April 1918
Latitude: 56 42 00 N PA		Longitude: 02 05 00 W PA
GPS Lat: 5642.000 N		GPS Long: 0205.000 W
Location: Off Montrose		Area: Montrose
Type: Trawler		Tonnage: 210 grt
Length: 115 ft	Beam: 22.6 ft	Draught: 12.1 ft
How Sunk: Mined		Depth: 45 metres

The steel steam trawler *Plethos* was built in 1913 by A. Hall of Aberdeen, engine by W.V.V. Ligerwood of Glasgow. She was requisitioned for use as a minesweeper, and was mined off Montrose on 23 April 1918.

CLINT

Wreck No: 264		Date Sunk: 15 March 1927
Latitude: 56 42 12 N		Longitude: 02 24 36 W
GPS Lat: 5642.191 N	**WGS84**	GPS Long: 0224.594 W
Location: 1 mile E of Scurdy Ness Lighthouse		Area: Montrose
Type: Steamship		Tonnage: 197 grt
Length: 125 ft	Beam: 20 ft	Draught: 9 ft
How Sunk: Foundered		Depth: 18–24 metres

The steel steamship *Clint* was built in 1896 by J. Fullerton of Paisley. She was overwhelmed by heavy weather and foundered off Montrose on 15 March 1927, while en route from Montrose to Weymouth with a cargo of potatoes and other vegetables. The wreck lies on its side. Underwater visibility here can be pretty poor.

BEATHWOOD

Wreck No: 265		Date Sunk: 11 September 1940
Latitude: 56 42 36 N		Longitude: 02 24 24 W
GPS Lat: 5642.591 N	**WGS84**	GPS Long: 0224.394 W
Location: 1 mile E of Montrose CG Lookout		Area: Montrose
Type: Trawler		Tonnage: 209 grt
Length: 115.5 ft	Beam: 22.5 ft	Draught: 12.4 ft
How Sunk: Bombed		Depth: 16 metres

The steam trawler *Beathwood* (ex-*Osborne Stroud*) was built in 1912 by A. Hall & Co., Aberdeen. While at anchor one mile off Montrose she was bombed and sunk by German aircraft at 2230 hours on 11 September 1940. Seven of the crew of nine were lost. The two survivors were rescued by the examination trawler *Viola*. Charted wreck one mile east of Scurdy Ness in 17.8 metres. When dived, this was found to be the after section of a steel trawler, from the stern to the boiler. It is lying with a 45° list to port on a muddy seabed.

NORDHAV II

Wreck No: 266		Date Sunk: 10 March 1945
Latitude: 56 42 17 N		Longitude: 02 03 48 W
GPS Lat: 5642.274 N	**WGS84**	GPS Long: 0203.896 W
Location: 12 miles E of Montrose		Area: Montrose

The steam trawler Beathwood *as* Osborne Stroud *(Courtesy of W. E. Butland collection)*

Type: Trawler   Tonnage: 425 grt
Length: 150 ft   Beam: 25.1 ft   Draught: 13.5 ft
How Sunk: Torpedoed by *U-714*   Depth: 51 metres

The Norwegian naval steam trawler *Nordhav II* (ex-*Sweeper*) was built in 1913 by Cook, Welton & Gemmel of Beverley, as a minesweeping trawler for the Royal Navy. She was sold in 1919, and converted to a fishing trawler. In 1936 she was sold again, this time to a Norwegian fishing company, and renamed *Nordhav II*. On 7 October 1939 the trawler was hired by the Royal Norwegian Navy and fitted out as a guard vessel at Harstad until 17 October, then left for Ramsund to be armed with one 76-mm gun (L/40 HK Armstrong, numbered 8916). *Nordhav II* belonged to the Finnmark Division (Capt. Lt. B. Bjerkelund). She was ordered to patrol the coast from Tanafjord to Kirkenes, stationed in Vardø, but also later in Honningsvåg and Hammerfest. After the German invasion of Norway in April 1940, she escorted small convoys from 9 April to 8 June, when orders to leave for the UK were received. The vessel escaped to the UK via Thorshavn in the Faroes, and arrived at Rosyth on 18 June. (Her 160 tons of bunker coal gave her a range of 3645 nm at 7 knots.) She was again requisitioned and converted once more in May 1942 to a minesweeping trawler with an additional 20-mm gun and four Hotchkiss machine guns.

Nordhav II served with the 71st Minesweeping Group based at Dundee. While escorting convoy FS 1753 off Dundee, she was torpedoed by the *U-714* (OL Hans-Joachim Schwebke), "off Dundee", two miles north of buoy No. 25 on 10 March 1945. She was torpedoed at 12.02 a.m. and lost with six men,[1] including the CO, Lt. A. Olsen, who

---

1   Five Norwegians and one British stoker who was using the name Harry Cook. His real name was John (Jack) Purcell. He came from Liverpool, and had joined the merchant navy while under age at the begining of WWII, by buying a seamans book and going to sea under this name.

The Norwegian minesweeper Nordhav II *(Author's collection)*

was on his first voyage with her after being transferred from more dangerous duty on MTBs. The Norwegian minesweeper *Syrian* rescued the 17 survivors, five of whom were wounded, and took them to Dundee.

The Hydrographic Department gave the position of sinking as 564230N, 020530W PA. The small wreck at 564217N, 020348W was the nearest charted wreck position, and this might be the *Nordhav II*, but as that position is 12 miles east of Montrose, and 25 miles north of the mouth of the Tay, it would be much more appropriate to describe that position in relation to Montrose, rather than Dundee. I do not know where buoy No. 25 was in March 1945, but the description "off Dundee", did seem to suggest the sinking position may have been further south, nearer Dundee.

UNKNOWN – PLETHOS ?

Wreck No: 267	Date Sunk:
Latitude: 56 42 18 N	Longitude: 02 07 30 W
GPS Lat: 5642.300 N	GPS Long: 0207.500 W
Location: 12 miles E of Scurdy Ness Light	Area: Montrose
Type:	Tonnage:
Length: Beam:	Draught:
How Sunk:	Depth: 51 metres

Charted as Wk 51 metres. Possibly the *Plethos*?

MARGARET

Wreck No: 268	Date Sunk: 28 October 1921
Latitude: 56 43 30 N PA	Longitude: 02 19 15 PA
GPS Lat: 5643.500 N	GPS Long: 0219.250 W
Location: 4 miles ExN of Montrose	Area: Montrose
Type: Steamship	Tonnage: 118 grt

Length: 89.1 ft   Beam: 19.8 ft   Draught:
How Sunk: Foundered   Depth: 35 metres

The iron steamship *Margaret* foundered in Montrose Bay, four miles E by N of Montrose on 28 October 1921. The vessel was built in 1886. There is a report of the sinking in the *Aberdeen Daily Journal* of 29 October 1921. The wreck site is within sight of Scurdyness Lighthouse. This PA is said to be within one mile of the true position, but the *Margaret* might be the wreck at 5641.283N, 0215.763W, 5¾ miles east of Scurdy Ness.

BUCCANEER

Wreck No: 269   Date Sunk: 9 November 1941
Latitude: 56 45 18 N PA   Longitude: 02 25 00 W PA
GPS Lat: 5645.300 N   GPS Long: 0225.000 W
Location: Mouth of River Esk, Montrose   Area: Montrose
Type: Tug   Tonnage: 1190 grt
Length: 175 ft   Beam: 34 ft   Draught: 17 ft
How Sunk: Ran aground/Refloated   Depth:

HM tug *Buccaneer* (pennant number W49) was a Brigand-class naval tug, built in 1938 by Fleming & Ferguson of Paisley. She had a bollard pull of 30 tons, and a maximum speed of 15 kts. Tugs of this class were employed to tow gunnery targets. and while towing a battle practice target in Lunan Bay, *Buccaneer* was attacked by He-111s of the Luftwaffe off Scurdy Ness at 1815 hours on 9 November 1941. She was driven ashore in very severe weather the following day, at the mouth of the River Esk, near Montrose. The crew of 43 were eventually rescued by breeches buoy, and the Johnshaven life-saving brigade was awarded the shield for the bravest rescue of the year. She was refloated to sail again, however, and was finally sunk by a shell while on target service with the Home Fleet on 25 August 1946, in Lyme Bay, Dorset.

The Board of Trade Shield (plaque) awarded to Johnshaven
life-saving brigade for the bravest rescue of 1941

HMT Buccaneer *with target (Author's collection)*

The photograph shows *Buccaneer* alongside the target she would normally tow some distance astern. The wreck in Lyme Bay, Dorset, lies completely over on its port side in general depths of 47 metres although the starboard rail is at 38 metres. There are many portholes – all still well attached! The ships 'Walker Trident Electric Log' has been re-covered along with a complete sextant. The brass helm is reported to still be in the lower bridge and crockery strewn around the galley.

PANSY

Wreck No: 270		Date Sunk: 11 December 1896
Latitude: 56 46 40 N PA		Longitude: 02 21 40 W PA
GPS Lat: 5646.670 N		GPS Long: 0221.670 W
Location: Eastness, Burnmouth, St.Cyrus		Area: Gourdon
Type: Trawler		Tonnage: 112 grt
Length: 95.7 ft	Beam: 19.8 ft	Draught:
How Sunk: Ran aground		Depth:

The South Shields iron-hulled steam trawler *Pansy* ran aground on the Eastness, Burnmouth, between St.Cyrus and Johnshaven on 11 December 1896.

QUEENSBURY

Wreck No: 271	Date Sunk: 6 June 1941
Latitude: 56 46 12 N	Longitude: 02 08 19 W

The steamship Queensbury *(Author's collection)*

GPS Lat: 5646.201 N	**WGS84**	GPS Long: 0208.309 W
Location: 6 miles SE by E of Gourdon		Area: Gourdon
Type: Steamship		Tonnage: 3911 grt
Length: 372.6 ft	Beam: 52.3 ft	Draught: 24.4 ft
How Sunk: Bombed		Depth: 50–56 metres

The steamship *Queensbury* was built in 1931 by Burntisland S.B. Co. for the Alexander Shipping Co. of London. She had three boilers and a triple expansion engine. En route from Buenos Aires to London with 7050 tons of grain and some general cargo, she was bombed and set on fire by German aircraft eight miles SE by E of Gourdon at 0146 hours on 6 June 1941. The ship was then at about 5650N, 0207W, and she was quickly ablaze from stem to stern. The Gourdon fishing boat *Elizabeth* (ME44) went to her assistance. (Her skipper George Milne, was also coxswain of the Gourdon Lifeboat *Margaret Dawson*.) The destroyer HMS *Sardonyx*, on passage from the Humber to Londonderry, diverted to the *Queensbury*, but was unable to get the fire under control. The tug *Abielle IV* reached her at 0815 hours but the *Queensbury* capsized at 0830 east of Inverbervie. It was obvious that there was no hope of saving the ship, and the M/S trawler *Sturton* sent her to the bottom with gunfire. Captain A. F. Cleary, nine of the *Queensbury*'s crew, and one gunner were killed, but the remainder of the crew transferred to the SS *Corrundum* and the Montrose Lifeboat *John Russell*.

UNKNOWN U-BOAT ?

Wreck No: 272		Date Sunk: Pre-1967
Latitude: 56 47 10 N		Longitude: 02 11 45 W
GPS Lat: 5647.158 N	**WGS84**	GPS Long: 0211.846 W
Location: 4½ miles E of Johnshaven		Area: Gourdon

253

Type:			Tonnage:
Length:		Beam:	Draught:
How Sunk:			Depth: 42 metres

This wreck was found by HMS *Blackwood* in 1966, and was considered to possibly be a U-boat. The wreck was standing up approximately 10 metres from the bottom. Least depth over the wreck was recorded to be about 43 metres in a total depth of 53 metres. In May 2001 divers reported that a scattered and flattened debris field was all that was found on the seabed at 65 metres. It was not possible to identify the wreck, nor even recognise if it was a submarine or something else. The rather large difference in the depths – 65 metres vs 53 metres – suggests that the 2001 dive might not have been on the same target as was recorded by the Royal Navy in 1966. The position has also been recorded as 564709.2N, 021141.3W, i.e. 5647.153N, 0211.688W (OSGB36).

The above position is very close to the *Baku Standard* – a substantial ship that could well have been standing up 10 metres from the seabed in 1966, although it only stands up 6 metres today. Position fixing in 1966 was done by Decca Navigator, which was less accurate than present-day GPS systems, and furthermore, did not give readings in latitude and longitude. HMS *Blackwood*'s Decca co-ordinates were red g 12.05, purple h 64.52 hi fix blue 776.13 brown 83.28. Perhaps the system's inaccuracies resulted in a slightly incorrect latitude/longitude? Maybe it was the *Baku Standard* that HMS *Blackwood* found?

BAKU STANDARD

Wreck No: 273			Date Sunk: 11 February 1918
Latitude: 56 47 10 N			Longitude: 02 11 45 W
GPS Lat: 5647.158 N		**WGS84**	GPS Long: 0211.846 W
Location: 4 miles SE ½E of Gourdon			Area: Gourdon
Type: Tanker			Tonnage: 3708 grt
Length: 331 ft		Beam: 43 ft	Draught: 32 ft
How Sunk: Torpedoed by *UC-58*			Depth: 52–58 metres

The 3708-grt tanker *Baku Standard* was built in 1893 by Armstrong Mitchell & Co. While en route from the Clyde to the Forth with a cargo of crude oil, she was torpedoed on 11 February 1918. *British Vessels Lost at Sea 1914–18* gives the position of the *Baku Standard* at the time of attack as 5 miles S by W ½W from Tod Head. *Lloyd's World War One Losses* says 7 miles off Gourdon.

Neil Masson provided the following description:

> The wreck of this tanker lies off Gourdon in 58 m with the deck at 52 m. The bridge superstructure has collapsed, and the bow is folded back and up as if she had run into something. There is a huge hole in the starboard side, where she was torpedoed. The stern section is intact, and boasts a most impressive gun. The decking has rotted

The tanker Baku Standard *(Author's collection)*

away in this area, allowing access to what appears to be accommodation cabins. Dropping over the stern, the top of the rudder is at 53 m, descending to the seabed at 58 m. The wreck is only rarely visited by local divers. It lies in a very exposed tidal area with only a very short period of slack water. Underwater visibility varies greatly – from less than 1 m to 20 m.

A headstone, erected by public subscription for three of the 24 members of her crew who were killed, can be seen in the cemetery at Gourdon.

HAWNBY

Wreck No: 274		Date Sunk: 10 September 1914
Latitude: 56 47 32 N		Longitude: 02 19 34 W
GPS Lat: 5647.530 N		GPS Long: 0219.570 W
Location: 150 yds E of Johnshaven harbour		Area: Gourdon
Type: Steamship		Tonnage: 2136 grt
Length: 280 ft	Beam: 40 ft	Draught: 15.6 ft
How Sunk: Ran aground		Depth: 8 metres

The steel steamship *Hawnby* was built in 1895 by R. Ropner & Son. En route from Hull to Archangel with a cargo of coal and crew of 21, she ran aground on 10 September 1914. No lives were lost. The position of stranding was originally reported as 150 yards north of Johnshaven, which is misleading, as that would put her inland, but her very smashed up remains lie immediately adjacent to the seaward side of a rock which dries at low water, 150 yards east of Johnshaven harbour.

BALMORAL

Wreck No: 275		Date Sunk: 9 September 1891
Latitude: 56 47 48 N PA		Longitude: 02 19 39 W PA
GPS Lat: 5647.793 N	**WGS84**	GPS Long: 0218.648 W
Location: Near Brotherton Castle		Area: Gourdon
Type: Sailing ship		Tonnage: 2045 grt
Length:	Beam:	Draught:
How Sunk: Ran aground		Depth: 8 metres

A wreck is charted approximately quarter of a mile offshore, one mile east of Johnshaven, in eight metres of water. This is just below Mains of Brotherton. The iron full-rigged sailing ship *Balmoral* was lost by stranding near Brotherton Castle on 9 September 1891, while en route from Chittagong to Dundee with a cargo of jute. Thirty members of the crew were lost. Shallow water extends for half a mile offshore in this area, before the depth exceeds 10 metres. As a result, any wreck near here is likely to be well broken up and scattered.

LOWDOCK

Wreck No: 276		Date Sunk: 19 March 1940
Latitude: 56 47 48 N		Longitude: 02 10 48 W
GPS Lat: 5647.824 N	**WGS84**	GPS Long: 0210.896 W
Location: 4 miles SE of Gourdon		Area: Gourdon
Type: Trawler		Tonnage: 276 grt
Length: 125.5 ft	Beam: 23.4 ft	Draught: 12.8 ft
How Sunk: Collision with *Lady Philomena*		Depth: 47–56 metres

This wreck was located in 1967, but its identity was not established until 2006. Two alternative WGS84 positions are 5647.816N, 0210.905W and 5647.810N, 0210.958W. The Fleetwood steam trawler *Lowdock* (ex-*Peter Lovett*) was built in 1917. During the night of 19 March 1940, while she was en route from Hull to Fleetwood, she was sunk off Todhead in a collision with the minesweeping trawler *Lady Philomena*. Skipper Frank Brunton and ten of the crew were killed. The only member of the crew to survive was the mate, who was on watch at the time. The *Lowdock* had survived a previous attack on 9 February 1940 when she was bombed and gunned by German aircraft two and a half miles east of Scarborough.

An anchor is still in place on top of the fo'c'sle at the tip of the bow. The foredeck has collapsed, but the rim of the hold is still visible. Just in front of where the wheelhouse once stood – only a few spars of its skeleton now remain – there is a large winch, with fishing cable still wound around the drum. Aft of the wheelhouse is the funnel hole – the funnel

Lowdock *(as* Peter Lovett*) (Courtesy of W. E. Butland collection)*

itself is long gone – and further aft again, the boiler and triple expansion steam engine are exposed. A small deckhouse still survives at the stern. The rudder and propeller are still in place, and there is no sign of any breach in the hull below the waterline. The *Lady Philomena* appears to have struck *Lowdock*'s stern, buckling a section of the deck up, folding it back on itself, and leaving the V-shape of the colliding vessel's stem embedded in the twisted metal. *Lady Philomena*'s bow then obviously rode up and over the stern, on to the deck of the *Lowdock*, pushing the stern under, and flooding it, causing the *Lowdock* to sink.

GREENAWN

Wreck No: 277	Date Sunk: 3 April 1941
Latitude: 56 48 10 N	Longitude: 02 09 30 W
GPS Lat: 5648.158 N	GPS Long: 0209.597 W
Location: 4½ miles ESE of Gourdon	Area: Gourdon
Type: Steamship	Tonnage: 784 grt
Length: 190.7 ft Beam: 29.1 ft	Draught: 11.9 ft
How Sunk: Bombed?	Depth: 60 metres

The steamship *Greenawn* was built in 1924 by A. Hall & Sons, Aberdeen (Yard No. 586). With a crew of twelve and two DEMS gunners, she had sailed from London on 25 March 1941 bound for Invergordon with a cargo of bagged cement. The ship was last seen off Montrose on 3 April 1941. Thereafter, she disappeared. The cause of her loss is unknown, but she is likely to have been bombed by German aircraft, as the 250-ton steamship *Cairnie* was bombed nearby on the same day, 6–8 miles S by W of Tod Head. Another description given

The steamship Greenawn *(Courtesy of Yorkshire Waterways Museum)*

for the position of the attack on the *Cairnie* is five miles east of Johnshaven. The *Cairnie* drifted ashore near Aberdeen on 13 April. The *Greenawn* was officially recorded as missing/ untraced on 28 May 1941, and a Joint Arbitration Committee considered her to have been a "War Loss" on 3 April 1941. The *Greenawn* was presumed to have sunk at about 5642N, 0205W, which might have been an estimate of the position in which she was last seen.

In 2006, however, the wreck of a single-screw steamship with two holds containing a cargo of bagged cement was found off Gourdon. The wreck lies on the Second World War coastal convoy route, and crockery found in the wreck has been dated to the years 1922–1948. Although the bows of the wreck point to the south, this does not necessarily indicate that her voyage was from the north to the south. She may have manoeuvred to avoid bombs, or perhaps her helm was affected by bombing? With no further information available to me at the time of writing, my assumption is that the wreck charted at 5648.158N, 0209.597W is possibly the *Greenawn*.

TAURUS

Wreck No: 278		Date Sunk: 6 June 1941
Latitude: 56 48 30 N		Longitude: 02 12 48 W
GPS Lat: 5648.466 N	**WGS84**	GPS Long: 0212.912 W
Location: 2½ miles SE of Gourdon		Area: Gourdon
Type: Motor ship		Tonnage: 4767 grt
Length: 408 ft	Beam: 55 ft	Draught: 25 ft
How Sunk: Bombed		Depth: 38–52 metres

The Norwegian motor ship *Taurus* was built by Akers of Oslo in 1935. While en route from Port Harcourt and Freetown, West Africa to Hull (via Oban) with 6922 tons of co-

Taurus *(Author's collection)*

coa, palm kernels and ground nuts, she was bombed off Montrose by a German aircraft at 0045 hours on 6 June 1941. Her engine was put out of action by two near misses. At 0145 hours she was attacked again by one enemy aircraft. Two bombs very close to her stern and the port quarter started leaks. Water gushed into the engine room and she started to sink by the stern, listing heavily to port. The leakage in the engine room caused the electric installations to be put out of action. The tunnel door was closed and orders given for the shackling in of the hand steering apparatus, but before this could be done the main motor had to be stopped because of the rising water. The emergency radio transmitter had also been rendered inoperable, but a message requesting tug assistance was sent by morse lamp to one of the other ships in the convoy.

Taurus *(Author's collection)*

259

At 0215 hours she was taken in tow by the A/S trawler HMS *Tarantella*, towards the sandy beach north of Montrose Bay. *Tarantella* had also made a request for tug assistance by wireless. The towing was interrupted for a while when another aircraft came in low and dropped three more bombs which exploded close to *Taurus*'s port bow, approximately 25 meters from the ship's side. Towing was resumed at 0300, but as the ship was now sinking faster, course was set for Johnshaven, while salvage assistance was asked for. The weather worsened, and by 0530 the after part was down to the deck in the water, so those of the crew who were not needed to continue with the towing were ordered into lifeboats and were soon afterwards picked up by the British trawler HMS *Chrysolite*. By 0615 the towing had to be given up and five minutes later the remaining men also abandoned ship. There were no casualties and her crew of 35 were picked up by the Montrose drifter *Eliza-beth* (ME44). *Taurus* reportedly sank at 0622 hours at 564700N, 021500W PA, in about 20 fathoms (36 metres) of water.

Another report gave the position of sinking as 564925N, 020925W PA. The wreck could not be found in that position in 1967, but in 1976 the Board of Trade War Risks Department advised that she had been found, but no position was given. The wreck of the *Taurus* has since been found, and is charted at 564830N, 021248W, two and a half miles SE of Gourdon. The position has also been given as 5648.491N, 0212.846W (WGS84). The wreck is mostly upright in 52 metres to the seabed. Depth to the bridge is 38 metres, and the engine room deckhouse is at 42 metres. Aft of the deckhouse the wreck is some-what broken up, but the stern section is still fairly intact, and lies on its port side. There is a strong tidal flow in the area, but there is a short period of slack water two hours after high water. Underwater visibility varies quite a lot, but in good visibility, this is said to be a very impressive wreck.

Taurus was in Sweden when the Germans invaded Norway on 9 April 1940, and was one of five Norwegian ships that broke out of Gothenburg on 23 January 1941. Operation Rubble was launched to provide them with air and sea cover across the North Sea, and involved cruisers, destroyers and aircraft. All of the ships reached Kirkwall safely at 0930 hours on 25 January.

NOVA ?

Wreck No: 279		Date Sunk: 27 March 1917
Latitude: 56 49 30 N		Longitude: 02 12 36 W
GPS Lat: 5649.491 N	**WGS84**	GPS Long: 0212.696 W
Location: 2½ miles E of Gourdon		Area: Gourdon
Type: Steamship		Tonnage: 1034 grt
Length: 207.2 ft	Beam: 32.3 ft	Draught: 15 ft
How Sunk: By *UC-77* – gunfire		Depth: 50 metres

A wreck standing up 6–8 fathoms (36–48 feet, or 11–15 metres) was found by HMS *Blackwood* in 1967 at 564930N, 021236W (5649.491N, 0212.696W – WGS84). This position is two and a half miles east of Gourdon. It is also a little over 18 miles south of Girdleness. The Norwegian steamship *Nova* was built in Bergen in 1915. She was sunk by gunfire from the German U-boat *UC-77* 18 miles south of Girdleness on 27 March 1917. The *Nova* had been bound from Blyth to Sarpsborg with a cargo of coal.

SOAR

Wreck No: 280		Date Sunk: 18 March 1940
Latitude: 56 49 10 N PA		Longitude: 02 17 20 W PA
GPS Lat: 5649.170 N		GPS Long: 0217.330 W
Location: 1 mile S of Gourdon		Area: Gourdon
Type: Trawler		Tonnage: 219 grt
Length: 117 ft	Beam:	Draught:
How Sunk: Ran aground		Depth: metres

The trawler *Soar* (A284) was returning to Aberdeen from a coaling trip to Methil on 18 March 1940 when she ran ashore during the night in a gale on the outlying reefs to the east of the Black Waugh Rocks, 200 yards offshore, one mile south of Gourdon. As it was wartime, there were no coastal lights to assist in navigation, and the strong southeasterly wind must have forced the vessel too far in. A villager discovered the first body washed ashore at daybreak. He rushed back to Gourdon and alerted the coastguards and other villagers. Just as the coastguards and fishermen reached the scene they saw the trawler's small boat drifting towards the shore. Coastguard John Penny and skipper John Stewart dashed into the water and with some difficulty managed to reach the boat. Sadly, it was empty. At the time there was no sign of the vessel itself, but at low water the ship's mast and boilers could be seen to the east of the Black Waughs. The bodies of all six crewmen were washed ashore and recovered during the day.

A more accurate position may be 564934N, 021720W (5649.567N, 0217.333W).

The steam trawler Soar *(Courtesy of W. E. Butland collection)*

REPRO

Wreck No: 281		Date Sunk: 26 April 1917
Latitude: 56 51 00 N PA		Longitude: 02 08 30 W PA
GPS Lat: 5651.000 N		GPS Long: 0208.500 W
Location: 4 miles E of Inverbervie		Area: Gourdon
Type: Trawler		Tonnage: 230 grt
Length: 117.3 ft	Beam: 22 ft	Draught: 11.7 ft
How Sunk: Mined		Depth:

The RN steel-hulled steam trawler *Repro* was built in 1910 by Cook, Welton & Gemmell, engine by C. D. Holmes. She was sunk by a mine on 23 April 1917, and is charted as a wreck with at least 28 metres over it in a general depth of 44 metres, three miles SE of Tod Head lighthouse. The mine she struck was laid by *UC-41*.

TANEVIK

Wreck No: 282		Date Sunk: 19 January 1945
Latitude: 56 51 48 N		Longitude: 01 55 42 W
GPS Lat: 5651.797 N	**WGS84**	GPS Long: 0155.880 W
Location: 12 miles E of Gourdon		Area: Gourdon
Type: Trawler		Tonnage:
Length:	Beam:	Draught:
How Sunk: Foundered in tow		Depth: 70–75 metres

Charted as Wk 70 metres, 11½ miles east of Inverbervie. The balloon barrage vessel *Tanevik* foundered in tow from Methil to Buckie on 19 January 1945. She was reported to have sunk two miles NE of No. 26 route buoy, or in 565230N, 015600W. The position has also been given as 5651.807N, 0155.799W (WGS84).

REINDEER

Wreck No: 283		Date Sunk: 19 November 1916
Latitude: 56 52 06 N		Longitude: 02 13 34 W
GPS Lat: 5652.095 N	**WGS84**	GPS Long: 0213.560 W
Location: Off Shieldhill, Kincardineshire		Area: Gourdon
Type: Steamship		Tonnage: 2412 grt
Length: 294 ft	Beam: 43.1 ft	Draught: 17.2 ft
How Sunk: Ran aground		Depth:

The steel-hulled steamship *Reindeer* was built in 1896 by J. Priestman of Sunderland, triple expansion steam engine by T. Richardson of Hepple. She left Dieppe on 14 November 1916, bound for Middlesbrough in ballast. After passing the Downs on the 15th, apparently neither she nor any of her 20 crew was seen or heard of again until wreckage was washed ashore at Todhead on the 19th. The *Reindeer* was reported at Lloyd's as missing, and was presumed to have foundered somewhere off Shieldhill, but the position was uncertain, and the wreck had not been found.

In 1919 the Senior Naval Officer at Granton gave the position for the sinking of the *Reindeer* as 564932N, 020900W, about four miles offshore, and a wreck is charted at 5649.524N, 0209.097W PA. Extremely close by another wreck position is charted at 5649.391N, 0209.581W PA. These are probably both intended to represent the *Reindeer*, but no wreck has been found in either of these positions. (I have not found any explanation as to why the *Reindeer* should have been anywhere near this area, when she was bound from Dieppe to Middlesbrough.)

Notwithstanding the position given by the SNO at Granton in 1919, for many years it was thought that the *Reindeer* had been lost by running aground off Shieldhill, Kincardineshire. Shieldhill is at Whistleberry Castle, one mile south of Todhead, at approximately 5652N, 0213W. (Todhead itself is at 5653N, 0213W.) A small amount of wreckage was found in the Shieldhill area, including a clock face and a 'brass sea serpent' – a brass bell bracket dolphin? – three brass brackets and a U-shaped piece of brass. No accurate location was given for these discoveries, nor could it be established which vessel they came from. After storms, various pieces of wreckage including brass bearings and other small items have frequently been found washed up in the small slot that dries out below the castle. Just off there, at a maximum depth of 8–12 metres, there are bits of brass driven into the rock face, and look as though they are part of the rock itself. As far as I am aware, no substantial pieces of ship wreckage were found nearby until 2001, when the ship's anchor and chain were found in the bay just below the ruined castle. Swimming northwards off the beach, many large pieces of wreckage were found, including copper and steel boiler plates, bollards, large winch drums, five-metre long shafts and many other pieces of angle iron, plate and general wreckage. All of this was located in a small area close to a large submerged boulder that projects up five

Reindeer *(Courtesy of World Ship Society)*

metres high from the bottom. It is surmised that this might be what the *Reindeer* struck. It would be interesting to search in the bay just north of the main wreckage site, as the ship may have been pushed further north from where the anchor and chain lie.

In 2006, however, the wreck of a steamship apparently matching the dimensions of the *Reindeer* was found in this area. Divers estimated the size of the wreck to be about 300 feet long by 40 feet beam – very close to the dimensions of the *Reindeer.*

It was tempting to assume that this recently-found steamship might be the *Reindeer*, particularly as no other vessel of this size is recorded as having been lost in this area. One problem, however, was that the recently-discovered steamship wreck has two holds containing a cargo of bagged cement, whereas the *Reindeer* was in ballast at the time of loss. Her holds should therefore be empty. While the *Reindeer* is the only ship lost in the area that matches the divers estimate of the size of the steamship wreck they found in 2006, they must have greatly over-estimated the size of the wreck, as there is only one candidate which matches the cargo of bagged cement – the *Greenawn.*

QUEEN ALEXANDRA

Wreck No: 284	Date Sunk: 13 June 1915
Latitude: 56 52 00 N PA	Longitude: 02 02 00 W PA
GPS Lat: 5652.000 N	GPS Long: 0202.000 W
Location: 8 miles E by S ½S from Tod Head	Area: Stonehaven
Type: Trawler	Tonnage: 208 grt
Length: 113.7 ft Beam: 21.6 ft	Draught: 12 ft
How Sunk: Mined	Depth:

Queen Alexandra *(Courtesy of W. E. Butland collection)*

According to *British Vessels Lost at Sea 1914–1918* the trawler *Queen Alexandra* was mined eight miles E by S ½S from Tod Head on 13 June 1915. *Lloyd's World War One Losses* gives the position as 5652N, 0202W, six miles ESE of Tod Head, and the date as 13 October 1915.

UNKNOWN – NOT THE LOWDOCK

Wreck No: 285		Date Sunk:
Latitude: 56 53 04 N		Longitude: 02 03 20 W
GPS Lat: 5653.060 N	**WGS84**	GPS Long: 0203.334 W
Location: 5 miles SE of Stonehaven		Area: Stonehaven
Type: Trawler		Tonnage:
Length:	Beam:	Draught:
How Sunk:		Depth: 47–56 metres

During the night of 19 March 1940, while the steam trawler *Lowdock* (ex-*Peter Lovett*) was en route from Hull to Fleetwood, she was reported to have been sunk in a collision with the minesweeping trawler *Lady Philomena* at 565304N, 020312W, 5¼ miles SE of Todhead lighthouse, or 4 miles E of Inverbervie. Skipper Frank Brunton and ten of the crew were killed. The only member of the crew to survive was the mate, who was on watch at the time.

A wreck located at 565306N, 020308W in 1967 was assumed to be the *Lowdock*, and the wreck is charted in 5653.090N, 0203.231W. The least depth was given as 47 metres in a total seabed depth of 51 metres, but the real depth is 60–65 metres.

This wreck was dived in 2006. The superstructure and decking had rotted away, and apart from noting that it was a small wreck of the expected size, sitting upright in about 60 metres depth, nothing was found to confirm its identity. Before any further investigative dives were carried out on this wreck, however, another wreck nearly seven miles to the south-west was dived and found to be the *Lowdock*. (See UNKNOWN ICELANDIC TRAWLER at 5653.300N, 0159.750W PA.)

UNKNOWN ICELANDIC TRAWLER

Wreck No: 286		Date Sunk: 1 October 1984
Latitude: 56 53 18 N PA		Longitude: 01 59 45 W PA
GPS Lat: 5653.300 N		GPS Long: 0159.750 W
Location: 9 miles E of Tod Head		Area: Stonehaven
Type: Trawler		Tonnage:
Length: 127.4 ft	Beam: 24.1 ft	Draught:
How Sunk: Foundered under tow		Depth: 40 metres

One of three Icelandic trawlers being towed to Grimsby for scrapping foundered while under tow by the Icelandic trawler *Solpakur* on 1 October 1984. The position was given as 565312N, 020018W in a general depth of 50 metres. The mast of the sunken trawler had already been removed, but the wreck was estimated to stand up about 10 metres from the seabed. The wreck was apparently marked by an unlit orange plastic buoy. The position of the buoy was given in Decca co-ordinates, and these plotted in 565318N, 015945W. The approximate position given for this wreck is less than two miles from the unidentified wreck, which was initially assumed to be the *Lowdock,* and the dimensions are almost identical.

BERYL

Wreck No: 287		Date Sunk: 9 August 1960
Latitude: 56 53 51 N		Longitude: 01 36 12 W
GPS Lat: 5653.845 N	**WGS84**	GPS Long: 0136.197 W
Location: 23 miles SE of Aberdeen		Area: Stonehaven
Type: Trawler		Tonnage:
Length:	Beam:	Draught:
How Sunk: Collision with *Eminence*		Depth: 115 metres

The wooden MFV *Beryl* left Aberdeen at 2245 hours on 8 August 1960, bound for the fishing grounds 55 miles to the south-east. At 1330 hours that same day, the 555-grt motor vessel *Eminence* had left Blyth, bound for Coleraine, Northern Ireland with a cargo of coal. At 0135 hours on the 9th, the *Beryl* smashed into the port side of the *Eminence* and sank. The crew took to a liferaft and were rescued by the *Eminence.*

GRANERO

Wreck No: 288		Date Sunk: 23 October 1933
Latitude: 56 54 30 N		Longitude: 02 11 36 W
GPS Lat: 5654.500 N		GPS Long: 0211.600 W
Location: South side of Crawton Ness		Area: Stonehaven
Type: Steamship		Tonnage: 1318 grt
Length: 242.9 ft	Beam: 37.3 ft	Draught: 16 ft
How Sunk: Ran aground		Depth: 16 metres

Granero aground at Crawton Ness (Courtesy of Aberdeen Art Gallery & Museums)

The spare iron propeller from the Granero *(Courtesy of Gavin Barnett)*

The Norwegian steamship *Granero*, built in Stavanger in 1913, ran aground close to the shore at the south side of Crawton Ness, about three miles south of Stonehaven on 23 October 1933. The position has also been given as 565428N, 021118W. While en route from Hango, Finland to Alloa with a cargo of pit props, she went on to the north side of the largest of the rocky fingers which stick out into Crawton Bay. This rocky promontory was used to mount the tripod for the breeches buoy during the rescue of the crew. The wreck is now very broken up, with plates and girders strewn over a wide area. Maximum depth is 14–16 metres, but some of the plates have been moved into 3–6 metres, the wave action moving them like scythes, cutting down the kelp forest. The largest mass found so far is the chain locker and chain. In 1970 part of the brass propeller, weighing 1 ton 7 hundredweight, was recovered about half a mile east of Crawton Ness, in 12 metres of water. Her spare iron propeller was recovered intact.

DESABLA

Wreck No: 289		Date Sunk: 12 June 1915
Latitude: 56 54 54 N		Longitude: 01 47 18 W
GPS Lat: 5654.907 N	**WGS84**	GPS Long: 0147.418 W
Location: 13½ miles ESE of Stonehaven		Area: Stonehaven
Type: Tanker		Tonnage: 6047 grt
Length: 420.3 ft	Beam: 54.6 ft	Draught: 32.4 ft
How Sunk: Torpedoed by *U-17*		Depth: 73 metres

Charted as a foul in about 73 metres. The tanker *Desabla* was built by Hawthorn Leslie in 1913 for the Bank Line of Glasgow. She was torpedoed 12 miles east of Tod Head on 12 June 1915 by the *U-17*. The Hydrographic Department has recorded her position as 565300N, 014520W PA, 15 miles east of Tod Head. She had been en route from Port Arthur, Texas, to the UK with a cargo of oil.

SANDVIK

Wreck No: 290		Date Sunk: 26 March 1917
Latitude: 56 56 00 N PA		Longitude: 01 52 00 W PA
GPS Lat: 5656.000 N	**WGS84**	GPS Long: 0152.000 W
Location: 11 miles E of Stonehaven		Area: Stonehaven
Type: Steamship		Tonnage: 584grt
Length: 164.5 ft	Beam: 29.1 ft	Draught: 12.3 ft
How Sunk: By *UC-77* – gunfire		Depth: 50 metres

The Norwegian steamship *Sandvik* (ex-*Elfsborg*) was built by Akers MV of Christiania in 1910. While en route from London to Christiania with a cargo of coke, she was sunk by gunfire from the *UC-77* seven miles off Todhead on 26 March 1917. The position recorded by the Hydrographic Department was 565600N, 015200W PA, but the wreck was not found within a two mile radius of that position during a search in 1966. As that position is almost 12 miles from Todhead, however, it seems to be several miles too far off the coast.

A bad obstruction or fisherman's fastener, considered to be a wreck, was recorded in the *Kingfisher Book of Tows, Vol. 1* at 5656.523N, 0201.465W (WGS84). (Position derived from Decca.)

PER SKOGLAND

Wreck No: 291		Date Sunk: 23 March 1928
Latitude: 56 57 18 N PA		Longitude: 02 11 45 W PA
GPS Lat: 5657.300 N		GPS Long: 5657.300 N
Location: Strathlethan Bay, Stonehaven		Area: Stonehaven
Type: Steamship		Tonnage: 500 grt
Length: 172.2 ft	Beam: 24.8 ft	Draught: 11.4 ft
How Sunk: Ran aground		Depth:

The Norwegian steamship Per Skogland *(as* Echo*) (Courtesy of Jahn Breiviks Samling)*

On 23 March 1928 the Norwegian steamship *Per Skogland* (ex-*Jern*, ex-*Stamford*, ex-*Echo*) was built at Stavanger in 1884. In 1895 she ran aground in Iceland, but the wreck was recovered and taken to Holland, where she was repaired and sold to Huding & Veder of Rotterdam in 1896. The new owners renamed the ship *Echo*. She changed hands several more times over the following 34 years until, in February 1928, she came into the owner-ship of the Skogland Line of Haugesund, Norway, who renamed her *Per Skogland*. Only a month later, while en route from Haugesund to Methil in ballast, she ran ashore in fog at Strathlethan Bay, just to the south of Stonehaven, and became a total loss.

ISFIORD

Wreck No: 292		Date Sunk: 19 September 1916	
Latitude: 56 57 18 N PA		Longitude: 02 11 45 W PA	
GPS Lat: 5657.300 N		GPS Long: 0211.750 W	
Location: Strathlethan Bay, Stonehaven		Area: Stonehaven	
Type: Schooner		Tonnage: 276 grt	
Length: 118.7 ft	Beam: 25.1 ft	Draught: 13.5 ft	
How Sunk: Ran aground		Depth:	

Wreckage from the Norwegian wooden auxiliary schooner *Isfiord* (ex-*Belgica*, ex-*Patria*) of Christiania, was washed ashore at Strathlethan Bay, one mile south of Stonehaven on 19 September 1916. The vessel seems to have been a pleasure yacht at some time.

GOWRIE

Wreck No: 293		Date Sunk: 9 January 1940	
Latitude: 56 57 24 N		Longitude: 02 01 42 W	
GPS Lat: 5657.360 N	**WGS84**	GPS Long: 0201.879 W	
Location: 5½ miles E of Stonehaven		Area: Stonehaven	
Type: Steamship		Tonnage: 689 grt	
Length: 178 ft	Beam: 30 ft	Draught: 12.3 ft	
How Sunk: Bombed		Depth: 58 metres	

The steamship *Gowrie* (ex-*Haller*) was built by Cochranes of Selby in 1909 for G. R. Haller Ltd. of Hull. Her name was changed to *Gowrie* in 1919 when she was sold to the Dundee Perth and London Shipping Company. She was bombed and sunk four miles east of Stone-haven while en route from Hull to Aberdeen on 9 January 1940. Her crew of 12 were all saved.. The Aberdeen lifeboat *Emma Constance* found only wreckage and a nameboard from the *Gowrie*. All 12 of the *Gowrie*'s crew were landed at Methil by Danish vessels on 11 Janu-ary. Although charted at 54 metres, the wreck lies on its port side in 58 metres depth.

The position has also been given as 5657.390N, 0201.798W. Apart from her stern hav-ing been blown off by a German bomb, the wreck is otherwise intact. There is lots of life on and around the wreck. It is possible to enter the wreck at the broken stern area, and swim through the engine room, past intact skylights, and exit via the funnel.

FERNSIDE

Wreck No: 294		Date Sunk: 27 February 1942
Latitude: 56 57 38 N		Longitude: 02 04 00 W
GPS Lat: 5657.607 N	**WGS84**	GPS Long: 0204.181 W
Location: 4 miles E of Stonehaven		Area: Stonehaven
Type: Steamship		Tonnage: 269 grt
Length: 117.1 ft	Beam: 27.6 ft	Draught: 9.1 ft
How Sunk: Bombed?		Depth: 46–58 metres

The wreck charted at 565738N, 020400W, and given as 5657.640N, 0204.098W (WGS84), was for many years assumed to be the steamship *Cushendall*, which was bombed and sunk off Stonehaven on 29 June 1941. In September 2007, however, the wreck was dived by Deeside divers Neil Masson and Jeremy Cameron, who recovered the bell, which identified the wreck as the *Fernside*. The bell was lying on the seabed immediately beside the wreck. Least depth had been recorded as 46 metres in 53 metres, but the true depth is 58 metres.

The 269-grt British steamship *Fernside* was built in 1921 by R. B. Harrison of Newcastle. On 26 February 1942 she left Hartlepool bound for Wick with a cargo of coal, but neither the ship, nor any of her eight crew and two gunners was ever seen again. She was presumed to have been sunk by aircraft off Banff on 27 February. Almost 60 years after the event, a brother of one of the crew, who lives in Peterhead, said he had the notion that the *Fernside* had been blown up off the Bullers of Buchan, 4 or 5 miles south of Peterhead, but he was unable to say why he had this impression. It was never known where the *Fernside* sank. All that was known was that she disappeared somewhere on her way to Wick. There were no reported sightings of her after she departed Hartlepool.

The wreck of this armed collier lies on her port side and is fairly intact, apart from the bridge area, which is a little more broken up, and the stern is even more damaged. The hold is full of coal. The discovery that this wreck is the *Fernside* leaves the question: where is the *Cushendall?*

Fernside *at the time of her launch in 1921 (Courtesy of Ron Mapplebeck)*

MATADOR

Wreck No: 295		Date Sunk: 9 OCtober 1924	
Latitude: 56 59 24 N		Longitude: 02 04 22 W	
GPS Lat: 5659.371 N	**WGS84**	GPS Long: 0204.565 W	
Location: 4½ miles E of Stonehaven		Area: Stonehaven	
Type: Yacht		Tonnage: 157 grt	
Length: 132 ft	Beam: 19.8 ft	Draught:	
How Sunk:		Depth: 45 metres	

The yacht *Matador* was built in 1879 by J. & G. Thomson of Clydebank (Yard No. 174). She sank after being abandoned 3–4 miles off Stonehaven on 9 October 1924. The wreck charted in 45 metres, 4½ miles east of Stonehaven may be the *Matador* or possibly the *Cushendall*.

BELLONA II

Wreck No: 296		Date Sunk: 8 October 1940	
Latitude: 56 58 00 N PA		Longitude: 02 12 00 W PA	
GPS Lat: 5658.000 N		GPS Long: 0212.000 W	
Location: Strathlethan Bay		Area: Stonehaven	
Type: Steamship		Tonnage: 840 grt	
Length: 231.9 ft	Beam: 34 ft	Draught: 13.6 ft	
How Sunk: Bombed		Depth: 46 metres	

The SS *Bellona* was built for DFDS Copenhagen by Deutsche Werke A. G. Keil (Yard No. 172). She was launched on 3 November 1923 and completed on 7 January 1924. She arrived in Glasgow on 4 April 1940, was requisitioned by the Ministry of Shipping and placed under the management of Ellerman Wilson Line Ltd. of Hull. She was renamed *Bellona II* on 17 May 1940.

The Danish steamship Bellona *(Courtesy of Billy McGee)*

En route from Hull to Reykjavik with 300 tons of ice, she was attacked by German aircraft 4½ miles east of Gourdon at 2000 hours on 8 October 1940, and was reported on fire 190° Catterline four miles. The Gourdon Lifeboat *Margaret Dawson* was launched at 2015 hours and on reaching the blazing ship 35 minutes later, rescued ten from the ship and collected another eight members of *Bellona*'s crew from a Dutch vessel that had picked them up from a small boat. One of the survivors had been injured and was taken to Montrose Infirmary. George Milne, the coxswain of Gourdon Lifeboat, was awarded a medal for his bravery in this rescue. Another survivor was picked up by a trawler and landed at Fraserburgh. Eight of the *Bellona II*'s crew were missing or killed, including the Master, Thyge Nielsen, and the Chief Officer, Johannes Alfred Peter Bergen. The auxiliary patrol vessel *Tervani* from Dundee, and the trawler *Strathderry* stood by the *Bellona II*, but she went ashore, still burning, in Strathlethen Bay "abreast of Dunottar Castle", Stonehaven on the 9th. She was declared a total wreck by the Salvage Officer from Aberdeen. Her Holman Projector and machine guns were salvaged.

The Hydrographic Department gives the position of the wreck as 5657.290N, 0212.097W, but this plots ashore. The description "ashore in Strathlethan Bay" suggests a position of about 5657.250N, 0211.700W. On the other hand, the description "abreast of Dunottar Castle" tends to suggest the wreck might be in Castle Haven – the bay between Dunottar Castle and Bowdun Head, at about 5657.000N, 0211.750W.

CUSHENDALL

Wreck No: 297		Date Sunk: 29 June 1941
Latitude: 56 57 00 N PA		Longitude: 02 03 00 W PA
GPS Lat: 5657.000 N	**WGS84**	GPS Long: 0203.000 W
Location: Off Stonehaven		Area: Stonehaven
Type: Steamship		Tonnage: 644 grt
Length: 186.1 ft	Beam: 27.7 ft	Draught: 10.8 ft
How Sunk: Bombed		Depth:

The Emperor *of 1904 was renamed* Cushendall *in 1929 (Courtesy of Jeremy Cameron)*

The steamship *The Emperor* was built in 1904 by Ailsa S.B. Co.,Troon, for J. Hay of Glasgow. Her machinery was by Muir & Houston of Glasgow. *The Emperor* was 644 grt, and measured 186.1 x 27.7 x 10.8 ft. In 1929 she was sold to J.Kelly, who renamed her *Cushendall*. The *Cushendall* was bombed close off Stonehaven on 29 June 1941 at 5657N, 0203W, while en route from Lossiemouth to Methil in ballast. Two of the crew were lost, but 14 were saved.

The wreck charted at 565738N, 020400W, and given as 5657.640N, 0204.098W (WGS84), was for many years assumed to be the *Cushendall*. In September 2007, however, the bell was recovered, proving that the wreck there is actually the *Fernside*. This leaves the question: where is the *Cushendall*?

The nearest wreck is the one said to be the *Gowrie*. It may well be the *Gowrie*, but I am not aware of any conclusive evidence having been recovered to prove its identity. Looking at the photograph of the *Cushendall*, and comparing the description given by one diver of entering the (*Gowrie?*) wreck at the broken stern area, and swimming through the engine room, past intact skylights, and exiting via the funnel, it strikes me that this might easily apply to the wreck of the *Cushendall*. It is frustrating that the diver who gave that description, apparently did not mention any details about the rest of the wreck, which might have been helpful in either suggesting that the wreck was indeed the *Gowrie*, or possibly the *Cushendall*.

UNKNOWN

Wreck No: 298		Date Sunk:
Latitude: 56 57 11 N		Longitude: 02 11 06 W
GPS Lat: 5657.190 N		GPS Long: 0211.097 W
Location: ¼ mile E of Bowdun Head		Area: Stonehaven
Type:		Tonnage:
Length:	Beam:	Draught:
How Sunk:		Depth: 18 metres

An unknown wreck lies quarter of a mile east of the rock known as Dunnicaer, at Bowdun Head, south of Stonehaven, in 5657.190N, 0211.097W. Another unknown wreck lies less than a quarter of a mile to the north at 5657.373N, 0211.097W. Both of these wrecks are in 18 metres depth. Are they two separate wrecks, or could they be two pieces of the same wreck?

UNKNOWN

Wreck No: 299		Date Sunk:
Latitude: 56 58 50 N		Longitude: 02 10 24 W
GPS Lat: 5658.830 N		GPS Long: 0210.400 W
Location: Garron Point, Stonehaven		Area: Stonehaven
Type: Steamship		Tonnage:
Length:	Beam:	Draught:
How Sunk: Ran aground		Depth:

The wreck of a wooden vessel, totally smashed up, lies immediately off Garron Point, to the north of Stonehaven. There is lots of brass amongst the debris. About 150 yards off the point, in 27 metres, lies the broken up remains of a steel vessel. The bow section is about 35 feet long, and the stern section lies about 30–40 metres from the bow section. There are two boilers in between the bow and stern, but the centre section of the wreck seems to be smashed up and buried in the seabed.

Bibliography

The following is a list of the principal sources and publications that were used for reference.

The Admiralty Hydrographic Department.

D C Thompson & Co., *The Scots Magazine*.

Everitt, D. (1999) *The K-boats: Steam-powered Submarines in World War I* (The Crowood Press).

Jeffrey, A. *Western Approaches* (Unpublished thesis).

Kemp, P. (1997) *U-boats Destroyed* (Arms & Armour Press).

Larn, R. & Larn, B. (1998) *Shipwreck Index of the British Isles, Volume 4: Scotland* (Lloyd's Register of Shipping).

Lloyd's of London. (1990) *Lloyd's War Losses – The First World War: Casualties to Shipping through Enemy Causes 1914–1918* (Lloyd's of London Press).

Lloyd's of London. (1990) *Lloyd's War Losses –The Second World War: British, Allied and Neutral Merchant Vessels Sunk or Destroyed by War Causes* (Lloyd's of London Press).

Lloyd's Register of Shipping.

Ritchie, G.F. (1991) *The Real Price of Fish* (Hutton Press).

Rohwer, J. (1983) *Axis Submarine Successes 1939–1945* (Patrick Stephens).

Rohwer, J. (1999) *Axis Submarine Successes of World War Two* (Greenhill Books).

Tennent, A.J. (1990) *British Merchant Ships sunk by U-boats in the 1914–1918 War*.

Whittaker, I.G. (1998) *Off Scotland* (C-ANNE Publishing).

Various newspapers have been consulted, as have numerous websites, and Admiralty documents held in the PRO/TNA, Kew.

Vessel Index

Name	Latitude	Longitude	Area	Wreck	Page
Harley	5618.900 N	0209.200 W	Fife Ness	222	207
Hawnby	5647.530 N	0219.570 W	Gourdon	274	255
Herrington	5637.092 N	0227.843 W	Arbroath	257	241
Hoche	5630.248 N	0236.591 W	Arbroath	250	237
Hoosac	5610.500 N	0233.500 W	May	175	162
Integrity	5602.270 N	0311.800 W	Inchkeith	120	114
Iona	5601.400 N	0306.800 W	Inchkeith	108	106
Iris	5604.000 N	0304.000 W PA	Inchkeith	104	102
Isfiord	5657.300 N	0211.750 W PA	Stonehaven	292	269
Island	5611.030 N	0232.870 W	May	181	166
Islandmagee	5617.500 N	0232.300 W	Fife Ness	217	202
Ivanhoe	5559.500 N	0310.000 W	Leith	100	97
Jane Ross	5616.130 N	0235.600 W	Fife Ness	204	195
Jasper	5611.200 N	0233.050 W PA	May	182	168
Jehu	5601.500 N	0307.500 W PA	Inchkeith	114	110
Jonkoping II	5625.084 N	0214.489 W	Arbroath	234	220
Ju-88 aircraft?	5617.857 N	0224.167 W	Fife Ness	216	201
Jupiter	5611.000 N	0258.500 W PA	Elie	154	144
K-4	5615.453 N	0211.507 W	May	197	185
K-17	5615.528 N	0211.494 W	May	196	178
Karen	5611.070 N	0258.750 W	Methil	136	134
Kate Thompson	5617.830 N	0237.400 W	Fife Ness	220	203
King Jaja	5557.750 N	0223.000 W PA	Dunbar	38	44
Kinloch	5607.500 N	0253.000 W PA	Elie	134	133
Kitty	5611.650 N	0145.000 W	Dunbar	70	71
Knot	5617.000 N	0234.500 W	Fife Ness	212	198
LCA 672? or LCA 811?	5602.970 N	0300.250 W	Aberlady	78	80
LCA 845	5605.450 N	0253.200 W	Aberlady	88	88
Leonard	5626.470 N	0238.720 W	Tay	241	230
Lettie	5555.000 N	0200.000 W PA	St Abbs	53	60
Lingbank	5615.170 N	0232.830 W PA	Fife Ness	208	196
Livlig	5554.000 N	0206.500 W PA	Dunbar	40	45
Lord Beaconsfield	5636.370 N	0229.500 W	Arbroath	255	240
Lowdock	5647.824 N	0210.896 W	Gourdon	278	256
Ludlow	5603.920 N	0245.970 W	N Berwick	82	82
LY120	5603.700 N	0310.700 W	Inchkeith	118	112
Magicienne	5556.100 N	0219.750 W	St Abbs	29	37
Magne	5552.469 N	0156.850 W	Eyemouth	7	13
Malabar	5559.700 N	0226.170 W PA	Dunbar	45	47
Mallard	5611.820 N	0235.420 W	May	189	174
Mare Vivimus	5608.000 N	0251.000 W	Elie	140	137
Margaret	5643.500 N	0219.250 W	Montrose	268	250
Maritana	5552.730 N	0205.000 W	Eyemouth	14	24
Mars	5611.580 N	0233.870 W	May	188	173
Matador	5659.371 N	0204.565 W	Stonehaven	295	271
Medusa	5603.330 N	0301.070 W	Inchkeith	101	99
Merlin	5609.000 N	0242.000 W PA	May	143	138
Metanol	5604.000 N	0246.000 W PA	N Berwick	97	96
Milford Earl	5638.658 N	0223.767 W	Montrose	260	244
Moresby?	5606.020 N	0231.120 W	Dunbar	61	64
Munchen	5607.300 N	0246.370 W	N Berwick	95	93
Musketier	5617.200 N	0234.500 W	Fife Ness	214	199
Nailsea River	5635.922 N	0209.370 W	Arbroath	254	239

Location Index

Latitude	Longitude	Name	Area	Wreck	Page
5616.130 N	0235.600 W	Jane Ross	Fife Ness	204	195
5616.200 N	0235.500 W	Pladda	Fife Ness	202	192
5616.750 N	0235.000 W	Vildfugl	Fife Ness	210	197
5616.830 N	0235.000 W	Spey	Fife Ness	207	196
5616.983 N	0235.208 W PA	Downiehills	Fife Ness	211	197
5617.000 N	0234.500 W	Knot	Fife Ness	212	198
5617.200 N	0234.500 W	Bjornhaug	Fife Ness	213	198
5617.200 N	0234.500 W	Musketier	Fife Ness	214	199
5617.500 N	0218.000 W PA	Einar Jarl	Fife Ness	215	200
5617.500 N	0232.300 W	Islandmagee	Fife Ness	217	202
5617.587 N	0219.584 W	Unknown	Fife Ness	218	203
5617.750 N	0234.500 W	Festing Grindall	Fife Ness	219	203
5617.830 N	0237.400 W	Kate Thompson	Fife Ness	220	203
5617.857 N	0224.167 W	Ju 88 aircraft?	Fife Ness	216	201
5618.000 N	0237.600 W	Success	Fife Ness	221	204
5618.900 N	0209.200 W	Harley	Fife Ness	222	207
5618.953 N	0217.297 W	Unknown – Einar Jarl?	Fife Ness	223	207
5619.600 N	0213.800 W	Unknown	Fife Ness	228	215
5620.000 N	0230.000 W PA	Blackwhale	Fife Ness	224	208
5620.399 N	0204.217 W	Unknown	Arbroath	230	217
5621.467 N	0154.403 W	Unknown – Aberdon?	Fife Ness	225	208
5621.783 N	0212.217 W	Unknown	Arbroath	229	217
5622.966 N	0216.763 W	Fylgia	Arbroath	231	218
5622.980 N	0227.670 W	Ugie?	Tay	232	219
5623.500 N	0235.750 W	Sophron	Tay	233	219
5625.084 N	0214.489 W	Jonkoping II?	Arbroath	234	220
5625.740 N	0236.460 W	UC-41	Tay	235	220
5625.870 N	0244.370 W	Unknown – Dalhousie?	Tay	236	224
5626.000 N	0223.500 W	Argyll	Arbroath	237	226
5626.000 N	0223.000 W	Quixotic	Arbroath	238	228
5626.170 N	0239.300 W	Fertile Vale	Tay	239	229
5626.470 N	0238.720 W	Clan Shaw	Tay	240	229
5626.470 N	0238.720 W	Leonard	Tay	241	230
5626.727 N	0236.978 W	Anu	Tay	242	230
5626.848 N	0235.725 W	Unknown Armed Trawler	Tay	243	232
5627.420 N	0241.570 W	Protector	Tay	244	232
5628.150 N	0219.200 W	Bay Fisher	Arbroath	246	233
5628.554 N	0138.466 W	Exmouth	Arbroath	249	236
5628.900 N	0204.400 W	Grenmar	Arbroath	247	234
5629.000 N	0057.000 W PA	Rockingham	Arbroath	248	234
5630.248 N	0236.591 W	Hoche	Arbroath	250	237
5630.996 N	0133.935 W	Burnstone	Arbroath	245	232
5631.780 N	0224.902 W	Primrose? or Dayspring?	Arbroath	251	238
5633.046 N	0133.690 W	St Briac	Montrose	261	246
5635.280 N	0221.527 W	Canganian	Arbroath	252	238
5635.000 N	0210.000 W	Braconburn	Arbroath	253	238
5635.922 N	0209.370 W	Nailsea River	Arbroath	254	239
5636.370 N	0229.500 W	Lord Beaconsfield	Arbroath	255	240
5637.000 N	0238.000 W PA	Fountains Abbey	Arbroath	256	241
5637.092 N	0227.843 W	Herrington	Arbroath	257	241
5637.401 N	0209.150 W	Blackmorevale	Montrose	258	243
5638.392 N	0226.444 W	Phineas Beard	Montrose	259	243
5638.658 N	0223.767 W	Milford Earl	Montrose	260	244